Sounds
Canadian

Sounds Canadian

Languages and Cultures in Multi~Ethnic Society

edited by Paul M. Migus

Peter Martin Associates

Canadian Shared Cataloguing in Publication Data

Migus, Paul.

Sounds Canadian : languages and cultures in multi-ethnic society/ edited by Paul Migus.

261 pp. (Canadian Ethnic Studies Association series; v. 4)

Selection of papers delivered at a symposium held 21-23 May 1971 at the University of Ottawa by the Canadian Ethnic Studies Association.

1. Minorities — Canada. 2. Canada — Languages. 3. Canada — Intellectual life. I. Title. II. Series: Canadian Ethnic Studies Association. Series — Canadian Ethnic Studies Association; v. 4.

F5028.M5   301.45'1'0971
F1035.A1
ISBN 0-88778-108-X

Peter Martin Associates Limited
35 Britain Street, Toronto, Canada M5A 1R7

United Kingdom: 17 Cockspur Street, London SW1 Y 5BP, England
United States: 35 East 67th Street, New York, N.Y. 10021

Contents

3   Ethnic Identity

4   European Multiculturalism

5 Conference Organization

PREFACE

The Canadian Ethnic Studies Association came into existence on 23 May 1971 when the Inter-University Committee on Canadian Slavs, formed in 1965, was renamed and reconstituted. The original object of the Inter-University Committee on Canadian Slavs had been chiefly to make arrangements to initiate studies on the Slavic ethno-cultural groups in Canada, and to create a forum for scholars and experts in the humanities and the social sciences to exchange ideas on the various aspects of Slavic Canadian studies.

The concept of a Conference on Canadian Slavs originated during the fall of 1964 in the Inter-Departmental Committee on Slavonic and Soviet Studies of the University of Alberta. After ascertaining by means of a questionnaire that there was sufficient need and interest in a conference, the University's Inter-Departmental Committee established an ad hoc five-man Conference Committee to make the necessary arrangements in conjunction with the University's Department of Extension. Professor B. R. Bociurkiw was chosen as Conference Convenor, while Professors Y. Slavutych, R. C. Eldwood, G. H. Wright and A. Malycky served respectively as Program Chairman, Financial Administrator, Publicity and Local Coordinator, and Calgary Representative.

The first National Conference on Canadian Slavs was held 9-12 June 1965 at the Banff Centre for Continuing Education. Over one hundred persons heard eighteen inter-disciplinary papers presented by scholars and civic leaders from across Canada. The consensus of the participants was that future conferences should be held every two years.

To organize this second conference and to realize the objectives of the conference resolutions, the Banff participants authorized the establishment of the Inter-University Committee on Canadian Slavs to be composed of elected representatives from interested Canadian universities. Professor Robert B. Bociurkiw, former Conference Convenor, was elected the first Chairman of the newly created body.

The Second Conference of Slavs in Canada was held at the University of Ottawa from 9-11 June 1967. The conference was well attended and covered such topics as: Immigration, Adaptation, Integration, Education and Socio-Cultural Surveys. The new President-elect for the upcoming two-year term was Professor J. A. Wojciechowski of the University of Ottawa.

The third bi-annual conference, at which twenty-four papers were presented, was held at York University in Toronto from 14-17 June 1969. The new executive under the presidency of Professor Constance Bida of the University of Ottawa began preparations to expand the framework of the committee to include studies on all Canadian ethno-cultural groups.

To this end the IUCCS sponsored a unique International Symposium devoted to "Languages and Cultures in Multi-Ethnic Society".

In addition to the successful realization of the Symposium, held 21-23 May 1971 at the University of Ottawa, the acceptance of a new constitution established the Canadian Ethnic Studies Association. The planned activities of the newly incepted Canadian Ethnic Studies Association, under its first president, Professor Cornelius J. Jaenen of the University of Ottawa, will include the continuing advancement of research into ethnic groups, the promotion of the establishment of centres for Canadian ethnic studies, and the publication of books and periodicals within this field of scholarship.

Parallel to the three-volume series of *Slavs In Canada* published bi-annually, the proceedings of the bi-annual symposiums of the Canadian Ethnic Studies Association will be published under the titles of those meetings. The papers in this first volume emanate from the first symposium— "Languages and Cultures in Multi-Ethnic Society". They reflect the high scholarly level of research and analysis of the various linguistic, cultural, historical and social problems of minority ethno-cultural groups in Canada.

No single symposium or volume can hope to cover all the topics of multiculturalism. These proceedings prove no exception. In the editing of these papers, some of the key aspects of Canadian multiculturalism seemed to emerge— language, education, religion, and ethnic identity. I have arranged the material into these sections, along with a very interesting section on comparative analysis of small minority groups in European multinational states. This subdivision appeared most compact and most serviceable. As to that the reader may decide.

The obligation remains to add some words of thanks to those who helped in this task. Apart from a fundamental debt of gratitude to the contributors of this volume there are those who have assisted with information and advice of some substance and deserve acknowledgement: Cornelius J. Jaenen, C.E.S.A. President and Professor of History at the University of Ottawa, who initially invited me to the task at hand when Professor A. Campbell took ill; Senator Paul Yuzyk who provided constant advice in all aspects of editing and publication; Professor Robert Karpiak of Queens University was very helpful, as also were Howard Palmer of the Department of the Secretary of State and Marcel Thérien of the Manuscript Division, Public Archives of Canada. Finally, I extend my warmest appreciation to my wife Oksana for her multicultural analyses and her assistance during the many evenings and weekends that I worked on the manuscript.

Paul M. Migus
Public Archives of Canada
Ottawa
April 1973

1 Multilingualism

A SOCIOLOGICAL ANALYSIS OF MULTILINGUALISM

Walter B. Simon
College of Social Sciences
University of Guelph

Where national pride is involved it is often difficult to be coolly rational in making decisions.
                    R. B. Le Page, The National Language Question

Language is not primarily a means of communication but a means of communion.
                    R. B. Le Page

All tensions and conflicts within societies result from antagonistic economic interests or from antagonism generated by cultural differences, or from combinations of diverse cultural and economic factors. Among causes of economic antagonism, conflicts between classes have long been the principle agents in civil strife and political tensions. Among the cultural factors that generate conflicts and tensions, differences in languages and religion stand out.

We are here concerned with the issues that arise from the necessity to accommodate different language groups within a society. We shall look at the social institutions and the political forces involved, and we shall pay special attention to the ways in which language conflicts emerge and have been resolved. Special attention will also be given to the role of the social sciences in efforts to resolve language conflicts.

Historical Perspective

Man differs from animals, among other things, by his capacity to communicate through symbols, that is, through language. Men differ from one another in the languages through which they communicate. Effective communication is only possible between people who speak the same language. It should be noted that language differences have become a source of serious conflict only recently as a side effect of changes (usually considered as "progress") that enhance the importance of spoken and written language for large numbers of people.

Among those who cannot read and write differences in language do not of and by themselves lead to serious conflict. Linguistic assimilation among illiterates seems to proceed smoothly and without much friction. This is probably due to their relatively limited vocabulary, and the fact that illiterate people usually earn their livelihood by working with their hands. Language differences, therefore, do not impede cooperation and may be overcome gradually as the people work and live together. In times of conflict the pronunciation of shibboleths may serve to identify friend and foe, but in preliterate or in predominantly illiterate societies linguistic differences do not cause conflict.

Language differences become a source of conflict only in the wake of progress. Urbanization and industrialization advance systems of universal education that prepare students for entry into government and other forms of public service where competent use of language in speech and writing are of the essence. In pre-industrial, rural, and predominantly illiterate societies diverse language groups may exist side by side peacefully while the members of a small educated élite perform the functions of government in a shared *lingua franca*. Thus language was not a source of tension in a predominantly rural and mostly illiterate multilingual Europe ruled by an élite that communicated in Latin and later in French. Similarly, language conflicts do not appear among post-colonial new nations as long as predominantly illiterate tribal groups follow their élites, who have been educated in the languages of their one-time colonial powers. The colonial language serves nearly all new nations as the official language.

In the days before literacy was wide-spread, identification with language groups was of secondary importance. This is illustrated by the fact that today both Poles and Germans claim the great astronomer Copernicus as their own. Actually, all we know about Copernicus is

> . . . that he came from the proverbially mixed stock of the border provinces . . . . that the language he wrote was Latin, the vernacular of his childhood was German, while his political sympathies were on the side of the Polish King against the Teutonic Order, and on the side of his German chapter against the Polish King; lastly, that his cultural background and heritage were neither German nor Polish, but Latin and Greek.[1]

It is obvious that Copernicus did not have to declare himself one way or another.

It is similarly significant that the protests against the Quebec Act by Anglo-Saxon settlers were not directed against the concessions to the official use of French, but only against the concessions made to the Roman Catholic Church. In the last third of the eighteenth century, the Protestant English-speaking settlers of North America were concerned primarily with religion and not with language. The educated knew French, and the interests of the farmers and craftsmen who formed the overwhelming majority of the population were in no way affected by language policies.

Similarly, identification with one's language group of the kind that is inspired by sentiments of nationalism

> . . . does not seem to have meant much to the ordinary man in Europe before the late 18th century, and in South Jutland not much before 1830. If one had asked a local farmer before that time whether he was Danish or German, he would certainly have assured that he was Schleswigian.[2]

In pre-industrial society, therefore, multilingualism is of little political consequence. Language policies that regulate the use of languages in offices and schools meant little to people engaged in agriculture who could neither read nor write and who formed well over ninety percent of the population. Most of the non-agrarian population was also illiterate and therefore not concerned with language policies. Practitioners of skilled crafts, whether literate or not, were likewise unaffected by language policies. They were able to move from country to country freely because their services could be contracted with a minimum of linguistic communication.

In pre-industrial societies language policies affect only the members of a small stratum of governing élites and their administrative aides who promulgate and document all acts of state craft, laws, injunctions and decisions. Since the ruling élites in pre-industrial societies employ a *lingua franca* they characteristically show little interest in the languages spoken by the masses of their fellow countrymen. This explains why ". . . prenationalist (i.e., pre-industrial and pre-urbanized) empires pursued no language policies among their subjects . . ." [3]

The philosophical origins of various types of nationalism cover a wide spectrum. The resulting political forces were stimulated by economic developments. It is probably a correct historical postulate that nationalism became a factor only with the development of extensive trade and the ensuing industrialization. The intellectual history of ideas may trace the roots of nationalism to various philosophical, religious, and literary sources but in its expression on the political scene it has invariably been closely tied to language, and has been most consequential when associated with language conflicts. Only since the emergence of universal education and the development of railroads have nationalism and concern with language policies become noteworthy. And only since then (the beginning of the nineteenth century) do we find governments that endeavor to impose linguistic uniformities upon their multilingual domains.

Social Strata and Multilingualism

Those engaged in agriculture are least concerned with policies regarding uses of language. Agriculturists want their language taught at school and used by the authorities and at court, but in disputes concerning language policies they tend to be conciliatory — unless they follow leaders who belong and appeal to a monolingual intelligentsia in a multilingual society. It is difficult to find dramatic illustrations for undramatic moderation but indications of this tendency abound. We find that agrarian parties in multilingual countries are always prone to form alliances across linguistic lines in order to advance their quest for favourable tariffs, subsidies, and other matters of agrarian concern.

Industrial workers, artisans and craftsmen are also conciliatory in language conflicts. Working class political parties in multilingual countries concentrate on economic issues that rally support across linguistic lines.

Workers and craftsmen are frequently most deeply concerned about the career chances of their children. This may induce them to advance language policies that favour their own language group. Very frequently, however, workers and craftsmen may encourage their children to become competent in the dominant language in order to improve their career chances, even at the cost of neglecting their mother tongue. This is often the case with working people who migrate to foreign countries. Of special interest here are the Italian migrants to the St. Leonard District of Montreal who battled to secure for their children an education in English rather than in French in order to maximize their career chances in North America. Occasionally, workers and craftsmen may rally behind intellectual leaders who are intransigent on the language question. When led by men from their own ranks they will become militant on language issues only when hard pressed, when, for instance, their rights of language are abrogated in their native land by dominating foreigners.

Those engaged in trade and commerce are most prone to accept compromise solutions in language questions. They have no choice but to accommodate the linguistic preferences of their clientele. Trade and tourism are therefore probably the most effective agents of accommodation and compromise in contacts between language groups.

Most deeply involved in issues concerning language policies and most profoundly affected by them are those whose work revolves around the use of words, written or spoken. Administrators, jurists, teachers, clerks, writers and others whose careers depend upon their linguistic competence are by necessity involved in politics that affect language policies in mixed language areas. It is therefore not surprising that universities and students play a crucial role in language politics. Their careers are affected profoundly by provisions that govern the use of languages in educational, administrative, legal and industrial institutions. Also, students are in a position to live more or less for politics and may exert considerable political pressure. They are able to disturb the public peace, and may easily rally support from other segments of the population. Disciplined paramilitary and militant cohorts of students are well equipped to advance political causes by violent action or by parading their strength peacefully. They may also provide political campaigns with a great deal of momentum as agitators or propagandists. Finally, from their ranks come the future leaders, teachers, spokesmen and administrators of society so that ideologies current among today's students often profoundly affect the direction of societies in the future.

Political-Pedagogic Aspects

It seems that educators who teach foreign languages focus exclusively upon questions of pedagogy to the exclusion of political aspects. This was appropriate as long as formal education was limited to the training of small clerical and administrative élites of pre-industrial societies. The institutionalization of universal education has made instruction in foreign languages a matter of policies that are subject to political controversy. This is even the case with second and third languages taught in schools in monolingual societies, since such instruction affects and reflects foreign relations.

In multilingual societies, decisions regarding languages to be used and taught in educational institutions are bound to evolve from political controversies. Language conflicts in multilingual societies usually break out over issues regarding the use of languages of instruction and the teaching of second and third languages in public schools and universities. Characteristically, we find dominant language groups defending the privileged position of their language against the challenge from subordinate language groups. It is quite possible that in the wake of such controversies those compelled to study the "other" language may suffer from psychological blocks that impede learning. We obviously need extensive exploration of this matter in order to cope with such destructive defense mechanisms pedagogically.

Here the role of universities is crucial. Universities that turn out graduates who speak the languages of their fellow citizens contribute considerably to the civic peace of their multilingual societies. Universities that turn out monolingual graduates in multilingual societies are bound to become hotbeds of agitation to disrupt efforts of accommodation and compromise.

Mobility and the Composition of Language Groups

Language conflict is related to proximity. Language groups that are territorially separated may be served by monolingual institutions. On this count, language has been less of a source of conflict than religion, since men have not gone on crusades to spread their language. We find serious conflict over languages only among neighbours. Technological progress is, however, shortening distances. Travel with the speed of sound, and communications with the speed of light, are kneading the whole globe into one multilingual society.

Industrialization and urbanization in the wake of technological progress also brings diverse cultural groups into immediate physical proximity. When these people have to adjust to one another at work and in urban settlements they invariably form different antagonistic social classes.

The tensions and conflicts generated by cultural differences and antagonistic economic interests are affected decisively by the composition of the various conflict groups. To the extent to which cultural cleavages coincide with one another and with economic conflict groups the resulting tensions will be exacerbated. The more such divisional boundaries cut across one another, the more tensions will be lessened.

For example, the comparatively benign nature of tensions over language issues in Switzerland (with the exception of the Jura) has been attributed to the tendency of linguistic divisions to cut across class differences and religion.[4] In Belgium, conversely, linguistic tensions have been aggravated by a high degree of coincidence of language groups with economic class and religion.[5]

Industrialization and urbanization tend to create such coincidences, because industry very often recruits those who perform similar functions from specific cultural groups. This phenomenon of selective recruitment has been found wherever people are brought together to live and work in cities. We observe in many places that people who work together in industrial cities cluster together in homogenous neighbourhoods as well, so that they form groups that are completely homogenous in language, religion, and social class. Democratic politics and democratic institutions that have evolved in western "developed" countries have been successful in accommodating religious and economic differences, including the antagonism of social classes, but they have not been very successful in resolving language conflicts.

In industrial urban societies status and prestige are based upon achievement rather than upon ascription. The achievement of status depends upon education, and here advancement is tied closely to competence in the officially recognized language. While those who work with their hands are not affected directly by language policies, the career prospects of their children depend upon them. The aspirations of working people for their children may therefore motivate compliance or defiance: they may wish to have their children acquire competence in the official language even at the price of neglecting their parental language; or they may militantly challenge the political order that accords another language precedence over one's own.

Political Implications of Language Situations

Tensions between language groups are of little political consequence in the absence of conflicting claims for official recognition that affect the use of languages in educational, administrative and legal institutions. Such conflicting claims are absent in monolingual societies, in predominantly rural societies, and in societies where clear-cut territorial separation makes it possible for monolingual institutions to provide educational services and exercise governmental authority.

In the absence of conflicting claims for official recognition multilingual immigrant groups may be absorbed without serious conflict in countries with but one official language. In North America, Latin America and Australia we find tensions between various immigrant groups and between them and the native born citizens that are often compounded by coinciding differences in religion and social class. Yet these tensions are accommodated in the context of democratic politics because here the immigrant groups readily accept the language situation as they find it. Such acceptance often involves a great deal of stress for the immigrants who must accept the alienation of their children from their native language. Their assimilation strengthens at the same time the political system that absorbs them and confirms the dominant position of the official language.

Multilingualism does not become a source of conflict when the educated members of the various language groups know the other languages. This is most readily achieved when the languages in question are languages of comparable world-wide importance. Switzerland comes to mind here. It should, however, be stressed that the Swiss case is *sui generis* and thus hardly serves as a model for other multilingual societies. Traditions cannot be transplanted or generated by acts of will. There is no "Swiss" language, and the three major languages used in Switzerland are, at the same time, world languages of some consequence.

Multilingualism does not become a source of conflict when the pressures upon members of diverse language groups to learn one another's languages are evenly balanced. This will be the case when the more important language at home is the less important language abroad. For example, in the Danish province of North-Slesvig Danish is the more important language at home and German the more important language in the world at large. Educational standards are high, and the overwhelming majority of the border population is so fluent in both languages that special criteria are needed to identify persons as belonging to one language group or the other.[6]

Similarly, the language situation among South African whites has been resolved, in part, because pressures to learn Afrikaans, the dominant language at home, are well balanced with pressures to learn the world language, English. Census figures indicate that bilingual command of English and Afrikaans has increased from 42.1 per cent in 1918 to 72.9 per cent in 1951 among whites seven years old or older.[7] Here the racial situation undoubtedly motivates the outnumbered whites to make every effort to resolve their language problems peacefully, but the relative balance in pressures to learn the two languages also appears as a probable factor. Further inquiry will, of course, be needed to check the extent to which this observation is valid. The general hypothesis seems, however, quite plausible.

Conversely, multilingualism becomes a source of conflict when the members of diverse language groups are under unequal pressures to learn one another's language. That will be the case when the most important language at home is also the most important abroad. Then the members of the dominant group will not be easily motivated to learn the other languages of their fellow citizens. We find such unbalanced pressures in Belgium and also in Canada.

The pressures upon members of language groups in multilingual societies to learn the languages of the others are also out of balance when the direction and/or the intensity of pressures to learn languages are changing. This may occur when the importance of one of the languages is decreasing at home or abroad. The direction and the intensity of pressures to learn languages may also change when a previously subordinate language group becomes more assertive. Such increased assertiveness may spring from changes in economic relations that focus the attention of a subordinate group on language policies for the first time. Thus a previously agrarian language group will be impelled by urbanization and industrialization to take language policies into account that had previously been of little consequence. Changes in assertiveness may also result from increases in political and economic strength, or by pressures from across the border.

It is usually extremely difficult to work out compromises between the demands of heretofore subordinate language groups and the dominant group. Members of the subordinate group are usually fluent in the dominant language while members of the dominant group are usually monolingual. Thus all measures that equalize the status of the languages in question actually favour the previously subordinate group. All concessions will limit the career chances of the dominant group members and enhance those of the frequently bilingual subordinate group. This explains why members of dominant language groups often offer extremely bitter and stubborn resistence to concessions that will limit the privileged position of their language.

The Extensive Latency of Language Conflicts

All conflicts have manifest and latent phases. Many of the conditions that give rise to language conflicts tend to keep them under cover in ways that render them all the more unmanageable and explosive when they finally come to the surface.

Conflicts and tensions regarding language policies tend to build up in the wake of industrialization, urbanization, and mass migrations. Initially, all energies are focused upon improvising, solidifying and expanding the needed educational, administrative, managerial, judiciary and governmental institutions. For a long time language issues are obscured under the weight of more urgent and pressing problems. The allocation of scarce material and human resources, the coordination of diverse activities, the planning for the future, efforts to anticipate consequences of decisions and their frequently inchoate implications leave no time for concern about incipient tensions over language. These tensions also tend to remain unnoticed in their early phases because those affected by language policies are themselves preoccupied with efforts to orient themselves in the hectic pace of a rapidly changing society. Thus we find that recently urbanized, uprooted rural migrants are at first hardly affected by language policies. Usually, language policies will affect them only when they send their children to school, the point at which they must choose between assimilation or efforts to preserve their own language. Among those poorly educated, whose ties to their culture are not very strong, or among the outnumbered, initial compliance with the dominant policies may be expected. This may or may not endure. Such vacillations on the part of linguistic minorities may keep tensions dormant longer yet.

When finally tensions begin to manifest themselves in demands for conflicting language policies in schools, offices, courts, and other institutions, decision makers tend to step up their activities in other areas because they sense that efforts to resolve language issues are not very promising. Such deliberate avoidance of evolving problems leads to vacillations and stopgap measures that compound tensions. As tensions mount, leadership positions fall into the hands of the most uncompromising language chauvinists. As soon as one language group presses its demands with militant intransigence the other groups respond in kind. Thus the prolonged period of latency leads to subsequent polarization which accounts for some of the resistence of language conflicts to rational and peaceful solutions.

The protracted latency of language conflicts may also result from unpredictable drift in language situations. A subordinate language group might meekly accept the dominance of another language only to come forward later with demands for official recognition. Similarly, groups who speak what are considered mere dialects may actually demand for them recognition as fully-fledged languages. Thus we find that language developments have been in two opposite directions: many local dialects and patois have been discarded, but on the other hand intellectual effort combined with political assertion has resulted in the number of recognized languages in Europe increasing from sixteen in 1800 to thirty in 1900 to fifty-three in 1937.[8]

In all monolingual societies diversity of dialects initially reflects primarily diversity in regions. However, selective migrations often combine with differentiations in occupations and urban settlement to associate dialects with social class.

Differences in dialects are not a source of language conflict even where they constitute class barriers as long as those who speak unofficial dialects accept the position of their idiom as deviant. In that case, they acknowledge the official language with its sanctioned rules of grammar and norms of pronunciation just as immigrants or migrants accept the privileged monopoly position of the language of their host country. Both speakers of lower class dialects such as London Cockney and working class immigrants encourage their children, whose advancement they desire, to acquire competence in the officially sanctioned mode of written or spoken language. They do this even though it means the neglect or even the abandonment of the idiom or language used at home. Consequently, language policies do not become political issues as long as those who speak dialects or other languages do not challenge them. Such acquiescent acceptance may, however, change. Language policies that compelled people to choose between assimilation and marginality have on occasion been challenged.

The criteria that differentiate fully-fledged languages from dialects are complex and need not be discussed here. It suffices for our purposes that language conflicts ensue when speakers of dialects claim language status for their idiom. The case of modern Norwegian suggests that such questions arise where universal schooling and with it universal literacy are achieved under alien rule.

In Norway as in most of Europe universal schooling and literacy evolved during the nineteenth century. The officially sanctioned Norwegian idiom was the "Rigsmol", the language of the Danish and Norwegian empire used by the upper class of Norway and closely affiliated with the court in Copenhagen. Napoleon's victors punished Denmark by transferring sovereignty over Norway to the King of Sweden. With the spread of literacy the dialect spoken by the common people asserted itself in the form of "Landsmol". The Swedish crown kept out of the ensuing dispute, and since the emergence of Norway as a sovereign country in 1905 its educational system and its public institutions have had to officially accommodate two idiomatic versions of Norwegian that are fairly similar but far from identical. Efforts to conceive a unified Norwegian language have so far failed while social and geographic mobility have intermingled the users of the two versions of Norwegian inextricably. The Norwegian school system can cope with the two versions of Norwegian only with great difficulty.[9]

The Norwegian case with its problems, tensions, and efforts to achieve accommodation is of special interest since we may expect the emergence of similar situations in developing countries among language groups whose members are now becoming literate in the absence of accepted codified grammars, rules of spelling, and standards of pronunciation.

The Irreconcilable Claims

Modern societies have been rather successful in containing strife between antagonistic economic and religious interests. Religious pluralism, on the whole, makes for assimilation and accommodation rather than conflict. Economic conflicts are usually characterized by a high degree of rationality that facilitates arbitration. Linguistic pluralism, however, generates nearly everywhere the formation of hostile camps that are intolerant not only of one another but of efforts to achieve workable compromise solutions.

Compromise in economic disputes is facilitated by the infinite divisibility of economic values. With language conflicts this is not the case. Language requirements are either-or propositions that are not divisible into infinitesimally small units. Also, conflicts involving the status of one's mother tongue and the career chances of one's children have strong emotional overtones. The spokesmen of parties engaged in economic disputes, furthermore, are usually rational men well versed in cost accounting. The spokesmen of parties engaged in language disputes often are marginal men who become politicians because of their lack of aptitude for more conventional careers. Their most outstanding ability is usually their skill in expressing the self-centred and narrow-minded fears of their own group. They also know how to intimidate effectively those members of their group willing to accept compromise solutions.

Finally, compromise solutions in language conflicts do not merely equalize the status of the conflicting groups but actually reverse the order of dominance. This very often rules out the possibility of genuine compromise solutions.

In economic disputes, compromise solutions result from a give-and-take of the parties upon the basis of their readily ascertainable strength to bargain. In conflicts between religious or racial groups compromise solutions are apt to modify but will never reverse established orders of dominance. Only in language conflicts may apparent compromise solutions actually reverse an existing order of dominance.

Compromises in language disputes frequently reverse the order of dominance because language conflicts often erupt after a subordinate language group has accumulated the strength to challenge the *status quo* its members had at one time accepted. During the period of subservient acceptance the ambitious and capable members of such a subordinate group acquire competence in the dominant language and soon compete successfully with members of the dominant group for élite positions that are open to the well educated. Many of them may in this process completely assimilate with the dominant group but some of them also cultivate their own cultural heritage. These are, of course, the most intelligent and most disciplined, capable of sustained high level intellectual effort. They usually succeed in careers in the dominant language, acquire competence in further foreign languages, and, at the same time, provide leadership for their own subordinate language group.

Once a subordinate language group has succeeded in developing a good educational system, qualified leadership, and a solid economic and social basis for showing political strength, its members will challenge the mono- poly position of the heretofore dominant language group. Unless the members of this group are, on their part, familiar with the formerly subor- dinate language, all compromises in matters of language use in schools, courts and offices will be extremely costly for them. Measures of equaliza- tion that make previously monolingual positions bilingual necessarily favour members of the previously subordinate language group who have become bilingual. This explains the bitter resistance of many members of the privileged language group to any form of linguistic equalization. When the members of the dominant group are monolingual and those of the previously subordinate group are bilingual any equalization of the status of the two languages literally reverses the order of dominance so that the last become the first.

Monolingual members of a group whose language loses its monopoly position find the study of the "other" language difficult for two reasons. They have to overcome not only the difficulties involved in the intellectual effort of learning a new language but also their emotional resistence to learning a language they have been accustomed to considering subordinate to their own. The resulting synthesis of rational economic interests with emotional aspects stimulates irrational claims based upon unrealistic per- spectives. The irreconcilability of such unrealistic claims have frequently exacerbated language conflicts to the tremendous cost and sorrow of all parties involved.

The polarization in language conflicts takes place even though most members of the contesting language groups prefer peace and compromise to disruption and civil war. Most results of elections in multilingual coun- tries indicate that the moderates prevail among the voters. The intransigent extremists succeed nevertheless in their efforts to escalate the conflict. This is the case because the extremist chauvinists predominate where they are in a position to sabotage compromise solutions effectively and disturb the public peace: in the mixed-language areas and in the colleges and uni- versities.

Compromise solutions require for their effectiveness the cooperation of those who are closest to the conflicts to be resolved. In the case of lang- uage conflicts these are the inhabitants of mixed-language areas and the academicians because these are the people most affected by language regulations. In almost all language conflicts we find that rioting students on both sides impede compromise solutions by causing intermittent unrest even where the great majorities of both language groups and the govern- ment sponsor compromise solutions. In the course of such unrest we find rational, pragmatic, bread-and-butter issues often overshadowed by emo- tional considerations of prestige and by utopian aspirations.

The study of language conflicts also provides insights regarding other aspects of conflict situations in general. Such studies confirm findings to the effect that group conflicts are usually provoked and escalated by marginal group members or by leaders whose positions are threatened and who promote conflicts in order to confirm their authority over their groups. Especially in language conflicts extremist leaders emerge who otherwise would merely subsist on the margin of civic society.

Language conflicts also reflect with exceptional clarity upon the complex relations between pacifist-minded moderates and militant extremists. We find that the pacifism of the moderates often leaves the initiative to the extremists, compelling the moderates to follow their lead in spite of themselves, because at crucial junctures they are exposed primarily to extremist pressures. Especially in language conflicts we often find peace-loving majorities reduced to puppets of developments they might have stopped earlier by a firm stand against the extremists in their own camp. It is, however, very easy to propagate extremist demands and much more difficult to argue against them within the fold of an interest group — especially when language policies are involved. Consequently, small numbers of fanatics suffice to thwart compromise solutions desired by silent majorities and they may even commit the moderates to battle despite their desire for peace. Thus the pacifism of moderate majorities may paradoxically facilitate the designs of extremists bent upon staking all in battles for the imposition of final solutions.

Final Solutions and Ideologies

Political solutions of all social conflicts may be either democratic, authoritarian or totalitarian. Democratic solutions result when the conflicting parties fight it out within an arena provided by democratic institutions according to rules mutually agreed upon. Authoritarian solutions are imposed on the basis of compulsory arbitration by authorities who may acknowledge the legitimacy of the various conflicting parties and their claims but who presume or assume the authority of adjudication. We consider as totalitarian all efforts to impose "final solutions" in accordance with the ideology of one side with no consideration for contesting claims.

The history of language conflicts seems to favour final solutions through forced assimilation, mass expulsions, or mass murder in the spirit of totalitarian ideologies. Campaigns for such final solutions, incidentally, invoke democratic principles of majority rule when this fits their purpose. Past triumphs of programs for final solutions of language conflicts and current tendencies in that direction lend substance to doubts, expressed by George Orwell, Aldous Huxley and others, about man's capacity to cope with his own history.

Several countries have already disintegrated because they were unable to cope with language conflicts within their borders. Several western countries and a large number of developing countries are at present confronting perilous language problems.

The empire of the Habsburgs as well as its successor states in the Danube basin foundered on questions of language policies in schools and the public services. The government of Imperial Austria in Vienna before 1914 and the republican government of Czechoslovakia in Prague between 1919 and 1934 strove to achieve workable compromises in the language question. It is noteworthy that in both countries election results showed that the moderates who were prepared to accept compromise solutions outnumbered the extremists in all language groups by wide margins. Yet the uncompromising extremists had the last word.

It is especially noteworthy that the political movements committed to a policy of moderation failed in Imperial Austria as well as in the Czechoslovakian Republic because of their inability to commit their followers in the mixed-language areas to their policies of compromise. Both the international socialist party, supported mainly by industrial labour, and the pro-clerical conservative party that was tied to the supranational Roman Catholic Church and supported mainly by farmers and craftsmen, favoured compromise solutions in the language question. Yet we find that both parties were split into autonomous sections on the basis of language. Furthermore, both parties invariably found themselves hard-pressed in their efforts to maintain their following in the mixed-language areas whenever they proposed compromise measures regarding language policies.

Efforts to achieve workable compromises by the governments and by the major political parties were obstructed effectively by the students and the intelligentsia of all language groups led by the extremists who were able to rally support in the mixed-language areas. The irrationality of the conflicting claims in language conflicts appears most clearly in matters of minor importance. Thus it occurred in mixed-language areas of Imperial Austria that public buildings remained without signs because no agreement could be reached on whose language should appear first or on top. The railway station of G. in Imperial Austria (from 1918 till 1945 Italian and since then Yugoslav) remained for long periods without signs because agreement could not be reached upon the sequence of the German *Goerz*, the Italian *Goricia* and the Slovenian *Gorice*. Problems of greater complexity and consequence, such as the use of languages in schools and courts, were of course even more difficult to resolve.[10]

Contemporary language conflicts are similarly characterized by a high degree of irrationality. The language conflict in canton Berne in Switzerland is a case in point. Here the "Rassemblement Jurassien" or R.J. wants the predominantly French-speaking Jura to secede from the predominantly German-speaking canton Berne to form a canton of its own. The R.J. is obstructing the possibility of peaceful solutions by making it clear that no adverse verdict of a plebiscite would be accepted. In order to assure victory at the polls the R.J. present as one of its requests that German-speaking migrants to the Jura from other parts of the canton be excluded from the polls while French-speaking Jurassians who have migrated away from Jura be allowed to vote in the plebiscite.[11]

It is not likely that the language problem in the Jura will ever threaten the integrity of Switzerland where

. . . the principle of equality of all national languages is studiously respected because it is recognized as a cornerstone of the national ideology.[12]

The uncompromising stance of the Jurassian extremists represents the kind of utopian irrationality that renders language questions frequently so hopelessly explosive. The difficulties encountered in the efforts to resolve the comparatively minor language problems in the miniscule Swiss Jura does not serve as a favourable omen for the major language problems that trouble countries such as Belgium[13] or Canada[14] which are not to be discussed here.

The difficulties western developed countries experience with their language problems do not portend favourably regarding prospects for solving language problems in developing countries, especially in former colonies. The situation does not appear hopeful in Africa[15] and even less so in India. There conflicts over the use of languages have already led to a great deal of violence and more is probably to be expected. Thus we find in India in all major cities fierce competition for institutional accommodation of the demands of language groups whose claims compete with English and Hindi.[16] The competing claims are legitimated on the basis of non-negotiable, axiomatic principles and values not subject to rational argument, such as the rights of the local population to preferential recognition of the language of the countryside that surrounds a particular city, the rights of Indians to settle with full recognition of their cultural needs in any part of the country, and demands for local autonomy regarding languages employed in schools as languages of instruction, or as subjects to be taught. These basic rights are in conflict with one another yet they are presented as absolute. Groups that constitute "majorities" in cities or parts of cities demand "democratic solutions" upon the basis of gerrymandering arrangements that maximize the weight of their numbers. Spokesmen of the various language groups are quite inconsistent in their recourse to "basic values" and "principles" which they adjust to specific local situations.[17] Irreconcilable demands regarding language policies are advanced with great fervour since

. . . the problem of multilingualism of the Indian cities is not only, or even primarily a problem of organizational efforts and financial outlays, it is a problem of communication and social relationships complicated by regional prejudices, economic rivalry, and rivalry for a share in the centres of power . . .[18]

As a consequence:

. . . today, there is an absence of policy [in India] and it is left to the individual leaders to define those limits and to press their claims according to political convenience.[19]

Systematic study of language conflicts should also help to clarify the complex relationships between perceived interests, conflicts, and ideologies. The record of language conflicts suggests that it is hardly ever sound sociology to explain the motives underlying social conflicts as generated by ideological commitments. In the case of class conflicts as in the case of language conflicts the nature of the interests involved inspire the ideologies that are appropriate to the positions of the antagonists. This proposition is confirmed by the observation, cited above, that the international socialists as well as the pro-clerical protagonists of the supranational Roman Catholic Church failed in their efforts to rally their followers in the mixed-language areas of Imperial Austria behind their conciliatory positions in language questions. This, in turn, casts doubts upon the position of sociolinguists to the effect that

> Divisiveness [in languages] is an ideologized position and it can magnify minor differences; indeed it can manufacture differences in languages as in other matters almost as easily as it can capitalize on more obvious differences. Similarly, unification is also an ideologized position, and it can minimize seemingly major differences or ignore them entirely, whether they be in the realm of religion, culture, race, or any other basis of differentiation.[20]

According to this statement, conflicts and harmony may result from good will or ill will generated by ideologies that are subject to deliberate manipulation. Is it really true that ideologies and philosophies are generated by deliberate acts of volition? All evidence accumulated in the light of the findings of sociology of knowledge indicate the opposite, to wit, that philosophies and ideologies arise in response to perceived situations in accordance with the interests of the parties concerned.

Historical studies confirm the thesis that language conflicts generate ideologies rather than result from them. Thus the language conflicts between Czechs and Germans did not result from divisive ideologies but generated them. On the Czech side, extremist chauvinism contributed considerably to the appeal of pan-Slavism that enjoyed for decades greater popularity among the Czechs than among other Slavic nations. Similarly, the German-speaking Bohemians and Moravians, now known as Sudeten-Germans, did not take an uncompromising position in the language question because of a chauvinistic ideology. Instead, their position on the language question motivated them to defect from the internationalist socialist party and from the supranational pro-clerical party to the extreme German-nationalist camp which had spawned the ideology of Hitler's party long before Hitler had ever been heard from. As early as 1907 we find in the Sudetenland a "German National-Socialist Workers' Party" that accepted ideological positions that were to become characteristic of Hitler's party and that were to guide the policies of his regime. Hitlerite anticapitalism, anticlericalism, condemnation of international socialism, and racial antisemitism all assume logical consistency against the background of language conflict, for all of these positions followed from condemnations of positions in favour of compromise on the language issue. One may insert here that outside of the Sudetenland the appeal of racial antisemitism was very limited. Only in the Sudetenland, in other mixed-language areas, and at the universities did racial antisemitism find a favourable response. This appears to have been due entirely to the tendency of assimilated Jews, including Jewish converts to Christianity, to take conciliatory positions on the language question. It is also noteworthy that Hitler's party enjoyed a far greater following in the Sudetenland than in any other German-speaking part of Germany or Austria.[21]

In short, all evidence suggests that the observation recorded by Jacques Brazeau regarding the language conflict between the Walloons and the Flemish in Belgium is, as a matter of fact, universally applicable:

> Movements that plan on changing arrangements and those that work for their maintenance have recourse to ideologies and political philosophies . . .[22]

Social Sciences and Solutions

Neither liberal-minded scholarly statesmen like the American President Woodrow Wilson nor revolutionary theoreticians like Lenin have yet succeeded in their efforts to conceive of theories or programs that contributed in any way to resolving language problems. During the First World War the concept of "self-determination of nations" was elevated by President Wilson's endorsement to a principle that was to guide peacemakers. Lenin also endorsed a variation of this principle.

The principle of self-determination of nations actually aggravated tensions because it legitimized conflicting claims at the expense of accommodation and compromise in its implication of majority right to the detriment of the minority. In all territories where language groups collided the principle of self-determination of nations could be invoked on the basis of claims for revisions of boundaries that would shift the composition of majorities one way or another. It has by now become clear that disputes between language groups may be accommodated effectively only within the context of joint acquiescence in which little weight is placed upon incidental "majority decisions". Democratic decision-making is only legitimate within the context of a shared value system and this cannot be provided by any simple formula, be it autocratic or democratic.[23]

Of special interest are the Belgian efforts to contain and accommodate language conflicts by institutionalizing monolingualism for its traditionally monolingual provinces and limiting official bilingualism to the capital district of Brussels. This approach appears to be overly static since no accommodations are made for migrants across the language line. Also, concentrating all language disputes upon the capital may simply focus all concern with language upon the most important part of the country. Also, the monolingual character of the surroundings of Brussels might also confine Belgium's capital city unduly since neither language group is likely to welcome any encroachment of bilingualism upon its monolingual domain.[24]

Sociologists who have studied language conflicts in the context of sociolinguistics have brought together a great deal of useful material that may serve as a source of understanding and insight. Their approach, however, in trying to encompass too many diverse aspects of the various

problems of interhuman communication, has been too broad and unsyste-
matic. They also tend to underrate the seriousness and complexity of
language conflicts and have given them comparatively little space in their
work.[25] Some sociologists also try their hands at formulating guidelines
for solving language problems. These guidelines are well meant but they
fail to take into account the needs, perceptions, and sentiments of the conflicting parties. In this vein we find sociolinguists who presently counsel
developing nations to adopt as official languages "European languages", for

> . . . building up a [new developing nation] . . . because they admit
> of no relationship to regional positions and traditional antagonisms,
> and they favor or disadvantage all groups of citizens equally.[26]

Such well meant advice fails to take into account that the adoption of a
European language as official language would exclude from élite positions
all those who do not know these languages well, and they are usually in
the overwhelming majority. We may expect that the great masses of people
in developing countries are about to become literate while a much smaller
number is likely to become very articulate and competent in English or
French. We find in many developing countries tribes with millions of members who undoubtedly will consider themselves strong enough to build a
society in which their native tongue, the language of their fathers, enjoys
preferred status, and even — wherever possible — a monopoly in schools,
offices and courts. In this context one also has to keep in mind the wide-
spread and extreme poverty in many developing countries, the lack of
career opportunities for those able to read and write and the often quite
unrealistic expectations of the recently urbanized.

A study of the language situation in India shows clearly that matters are
far too complex for simple prescriptions. This is reflected by the fact that

> The provisions of the Indian constitution regarding language explic-
> itly avoided the notion of common or national language . . . The
> official report of the Committee on Emotional Integration refers to
> all the fourteen languages listed in the original Eighth Schedule of
> the Constitution as having the "status of national languages" although
> the report of the Official Language Commission refers to those lang-
> uages [excepting Sanskrit] as "regional languages".[27]

Uncertainty regarding the place of English, Hindi, and the various regional languages in India is so pervasive that the meanings of the various
terms differ according to those who use them:

> . . . the limited range and depth of the acceptance of English in
> India made it a language of élite communication rather than a
> medium of mass communication . . .[28]

This means that the use of English as an official language limits access to
the office of government to a small educated élite excluding the broad
masses of the people in all regions of India. With the spread of literacy we
may expect increasing resistance to the official use of English from members of language groups strong enough to gain official status for their own

language. English-speaking social scientists who counsel developing nations to adopt English (or French) as *lingua franca* undoubtedly mean well but they should not expect literate members of sizeable language groups to defer to such counsel which would considerably limit their opportunities for advancement.

When dealing with language problems social scientists are well advised to take to heart Max Weber's injunctions against entering upon the basically political role of offering counsel under the aura of objective scholarship. This is especially true for counsel promulgated in a language not understood by those to whom it is meant to appeal. Social scientists who try their hand at formulating guidelines for resolving language problems are also well advised to take into account the needs, perception, and sentiments of the conflicting parties as well as their potential for action. Social scientists are, of course, free to enter conflicts as mediators or as partisans, and they may and should enhance their effectiveness in such roles through their insights and knowledge gained as social scientists. The roles of inquiring social scientists, impartial mediators, and participating partisans should, however, be kept scrupulously apart. Under no circumstances should social scientists ever promote partisan solutions while they strike a pose of peacemaking mediators guided by scientific insights.

The author of this paper considers it the primary task of social scientists to provide conceptual schemes that facilitate the formulation of testable theories which, in turn, provide a basis for diagnosing the state of problematic situations such as language conflicts. In medical practice applications of therapeutic or curative measures without diagnosis constitute quackery. Social scientists who proceed without competent diagnosis also reveal themselves as mere quacks. Social problems are, however, more complex than medical problems in that humanist values provide clear guide lines only for the latter but not for the former. In medical practice generally accepted humanist values clearly favour the prevention of disease and death and the preservation of life and health. In the case of social problems the claims advanced by the conflicting parties cannot be dismissed out of hand on the basis of *a priori* formulations of any kind. Sociological diagnosis of conflict situations should, as a matter of fact, encompass the essential features and aspects of the conflicting positions and their crucial implications.

It appears therefore, that the most urgent task for the social sciences is to design methods for early diagnosis of latent language conflicts. Social scientists, at least, should not be taken by surprise when conflicting claims for language recognition make their appearance. They should develop instruments that will enable them to anticipate their emergence well ahead of time. In this context psychologists and pedagogues have the urgent task to conceive of methods which would enable people with modest linguistic capacity to acquire competence in foreign languages. In the process of such efforts they might also gain generally valid insights regarding the learning capacity of various age groups with diverse educational background, and to design appropriate teaching methods for them. Such insights should also serve the vocational training and general education in this period of rapidly changing educational prerequisites for participation in the world of work and for effective citizenship.

Multilinguism also has economic aspects of great consequence because of the latent and manifest costs that arise where multilingual personnel has to serve multilingual clients.

Technological progress is about to transform all of mankind into one single multilingual society. Unless the political aspects of multilingualism are coped with effectively the whole edifice of human progress may well turn into a Tower of Babel.

NOTES

[1] Arthur Koestler, The Sleepwalkers, *A History of Man's Changing Vision of the Universe* (London: Pelican Books, 1968), p. 132.

[2] Kaare Svalastoga and Preben Wolf, "A Town in Danish Borderland", *Studies in Multilingualism,* ed. N. Anderson (Leiden, The Netherlands: E. J. Brill, 1969), p. 29.

[3] Konstantin Symmons-Symonowicz, *Nationalist Movements: A Comparative View* (Meadville, Pa.,: Maple Woods Press, 1970), p. 66.

[4] K. D. McRae, "The Constitutional Protection of Linguistic Rights in Bilingual and Multilingual States", *Human Rights, Federalism, and Minorities,* ed. Allan Gottlieb et al. (Ottawa: Canadian Institute of International Affairs, 1969), pp. 219-220.

[5] *Ibid.*

[6] Svalastoga and Wold, *op. cit.,* p. 37.

[7] McRae, *op. cit.,* pp. 223-224.

[8] Karl W. Deutsch, "The Trend of European Nationalism – The Language Aspects", *Readings in Sociology of Language,* ed. Joshua Fishman (The Hague–Paris: Mouton, 1968), p. 606. See also Ronald F. Inglehart and Margaret Woodward, "Language Conflict and Political Community", *Comparative Studies in Society and History,* Vol. X, No. 1 (October 1967).

[9] Einar Haugen, *Language Conflict and Language Planning: the Case of Modern Norwegian* (Cambridge, Mass.: Harvard University Press, 1966).

[10] Walter B. Simon, "Multilingualism, A Comparative Study", *Studies in Multilingualism,* ed. N. Anderson, *op. cit.,* pp. 11-25.

[11] Kurt B. Mayer, "The Jura Problem: Ethnic Conflict in Switzerland", *Social Research,* 1968, pp. 707-741.

[12] *Ibid.,* p. 720.

[13] A standard work on the language situation in Belgium is the opus by Jacques Brazeau, *Essai sur la Question Linguistique en Belge: Rapport final préparé par la Commission Royale d'Enquête sur la Bilinguisme et le Biculturisme* (Ottawa, 1966). For a concise summary of the language conflict in Belgium see Val R. Lorwin, "Cultural Pluralism and Political Tension in Modern Belgium", paper presented at the meetings of the Canadian Historical Association in Toronto in June 1969.

[14] Among the wealth of material on the Canadian language situation the author has selected for interested students in the United States and in Europe the following sources: A. Davidson Dunton, André Laurandeau, *et al., A Preliminary Report of the Royal Commission on Bilingualism and Biculturism* (Ottawa: Queens Printers, 1966); E. C. Hughes, *French Canada in Transition* (Chicago: University of Chicago Press,

1943); Nathan Keyfitz, "Canadians and Canadians", *Queens Quarterly,* Vol. 70 (Summer 1963). pp. 163-182, Stanley Lieberson, "Bilingualism in Montreal: A Demographic Analysis", *American Journal of Sociology,* Vol. 71 (July 1965). pp. 10-25. This list could, of course, be continued indefinitely.

[15]Pierre L. van den Berghe, "Africa's Language Problems − Too Many, Too Late!" *Trans-Action* (November 1968), pp. 48-53.

[16]Among the material on the language situation in India the author has selected as sources: Jyotirindra Das Gupta, *Language Conflict and National Development − Group Politics and National Language Policy in India* (Berkeley: University of California Press, 1970); M. S. Gore, "Language in Metropolitan Life", *Economic and Political Weekly,* Vol. IV, No. 28-20 (July 1969, Special Issue); K. Ishwaran, "Multilingualism in India", *Studies in Multilingualism,* ed. N. Anderson, *op. cit.,* pp. 122-150.

[17]M. S. Gore, *op. cit.*

[18]*Ibid.,* p. 1.

[19]*Ibid.,* p. 6.

[20]Joshua A. Fishman, "Nationality-Nationalism and Nation-Nationism", in *Language Problems of Developing Nations,* ed. Joshua Fishman et al. (New York: John Wiley & Sons, 1968), p. 45.

[21]Walter B. Simon, *op. cit.,* p. 16.

[22]Jacques Brazeau, *op. cit.,* Vol. I, II-B, p. 18.

[23]Walter B. Simon, *op. cit.* pp. 17-18.

[24]Jacques Brazeau, *op. cit.,* Vol. II, Part B, pp. 11-12.

[25]The tendency of sociologists to underestimate the importance of language conflicts is also reflected by the following reader: *Readings in the Sociology of Language,* ed. Joshua A. Fishman − the Hague-Paris: Mouton, 1968). Among the seven sections with forty-four contributions we find only two sections that contain contributions that deal with problems of multilingualism: Section V under the title "Multilingualism", and Section VI under the title "Language Maintenance and Language Shift". In the extensive subject matter index of this reader we do not find a single reference to language conflict. Joyce O. Hertzler, *A Sociology of Language* (New York: Random House, 1965), likewise contains no reference to "language conflict" or "conflict" in its subject matter index. The whole problem area of conflict between language groups is dealt with by a reference to "linguistic intolerance", pp. 257-258.

[26]See Dieter Froehlich, "Multilingualismus und der Aufbau der Nation", in *Aspekte der Entwicklungssoziologie,* ed. Rene Koenig, Sonderheft 13 of the *Koelner Zeitschrift fuer Soziologie and Sozialpsychologie* (Koeln-Opladen: Westdeutscher Verlag, 1969), p. 482. It is significant that in this volume of 816 pages on the sociology of developing countries we find only the eighteen-page article cited above on the problem of multilingualism. The reader *Language Problems of Developing Nations,* ed. Joshua A. Fishman, cited in footnote 20 above, gives a great deal of space to problems of multilingualism but discounts the importance of conflicts over languages as quoted in the text of this paper. Here, too, we find no reference to language conflict or conflict in the subject-matter index.

[27]Jytirindra Das Gupta, *op. cit.,* pp. 38-39.

[28]*Ibid.,* p. 45.

LANGUAGE MAINTENANCE IN CANADA: RESEARCH PROBLEMS

L. G. Kelly
Department of Linguistics and Modern Languages
University of Ottawa

The question of maintaining a living language is often seen by an ethnic group as crucial to survival as a separate entity. With the exception of the work of the Royal Commission on Bilingualism and Biculturalism, very little truly scientific research has been done in the study of language maintenance in Canada. In the United States Joshua Fishman's *Language Loyalty in the United States* appeared in published form in 1966 and gave a fairly complete picture of the health of a number of language groups in the United States. The work of the Royal Commission on Bilingualism and Biculturalism, due to the limitations imposed by its mandate, concentrated on the French-English question in Canada.

Language maintenance is a complicated area. First we need to know how widespread a language is in the total population of a country or political unit. This has to be correlated with geographical factors, such as place of residence, density of population and ease of communication with populations which do not speak the language under consideration. This data in turn has to be correlated with social factors such as religion, work, education, mass media and relations with government at all levels. The age-range of the population is a ready index to the health of the language, as is the vitality of literature produced in that language. A language that is the property of the old is a dying language, as is one in which there is little oral or written literature.

On the linguistic side, a small language group having access of communication with other groups that speak the same language is more likely to hold on to its language. From this flows the question: Has the development of a minority language been affected by the language spoken around it? Has it, in Heinz Kloss's phrase, become dialectalized? Has it undergone borrowings and other types of mixture from the majority language? Have its dialects become levelled to one standard? Languages develop continuously, and we can hardly speak of language maintenance, if outside influences have blocked the natural avenues of language development for the population.

The starting point for many maintenance studies has been census data. As Lieberson and Macrae pointed out at the International Seminar on the Description and Measurement of Bilingualism held at Moncton in 1967, census data has its limitations. In Canada there are three questions related to language: the respondent's ethnic origin, his mother tongue, and his knowledge of the two official languages. The first problem in using the data is that all the variables mentioned above are not covered by census data, nor can they be, for the census cannot cover all the factors involved in maintenance. Secondly, many of the cross-tabulations that would be useful in maintenance studies, such as tabulating language against work, are irrelevant to the census and are not done. The third problem lies in the definition of mother tongue. One is asked to declare the language first learnt and still understood as one's mother tongue, thus ignoring facts like change in language dominance, quality of language spoken and dialectal changes where various dialects are included under one language, as is the case with Italian. The problem with this data, like any self-administered mass questionnaire, is that the data is biased by the vagaries inherent in self-reporting, so that the basic material is not rigorous enough for the rather delicate question of maintenance. What we do get by comparison of data from various censuses is an index of acculturation and of total language gain or loss; there is no way of gauging from this the factors involved, or the weaknesses, other than demographic, in the situation of the language group under study.

Some work has been done on the French and English groups. We have a fair picture of the various French groups in the country in the research files of the Royal Commission on Bilingualism and Biculturalism, and some of the research studies done for the Commission cover ethnic groups, particularly those in Montreal and Toronto. Some of the briefs for the Commission, especially from the Ukrainians, provide data that can be sifted to get some sort of maintenance picture; but if a study of the same standard as that of Fishman and his associates is to be produced in Canada, we are still at the very beginning of work on groups other than French and English.

Outside the French and English population Canadian ethnic groups are predominantly bilingual. This means that unless the languages are specialized to certain domains, the survival of the minority language cannot be assured. For a language to survive it must be of some independent use, otherwise, in a bilingual situation the language with more prestige will crowd the other out. Work by Gumperz and Cooper on ethnic communities in the United States has isolated a certain number of "domains" of language use: home, neighbourhood, church, work, school. As a first step in the intensive study of language maintenance among particular ethnic groups, these have to be validated for each group, and other domains created where necessary to cover changing social conditions. I am assuming that the effect of each of these domains will be different, not only for each ethnic group, but also for individuals according to their geographical position and place in the hierarchy of their local societies. In short I am speaking about Charles Ferguson's concept of *diglossia*. It has been assumed, especially by nationalist members of linguistic groups, that bilingualism means acculturation to the majority and results in a slow loss of the language and traditions of the group. If bilingualism is undifferentiated across domain boundaries, this is a fairly accurate assumption. If however, the use of languages in a contact situation is compartmentalized, the risk of loss is lessened.

Let us assume that the five areas isolated as domains by the Fishman team are valid, and discuss each one of them in turn. The character of the home will vary according to the extent of the family group. In a nuclear family, as compared to the family unit which has the tribal characteristics of older societies, a minority language will have less chance of maintenance. Contact with the more conservative elders of a society will keep old values, one of which is the language, alive. Much depends on how the family group is made up linguistically. If the group is largely endogamous, there will be no pressure towards language shift rising from the nature of the marriage relationship, so that the language being common, it will be in a stronger position than otherwise. However, the impulse to marry outside the group, especially in urbanized populations, increases with each new generation and its greater distance from the mother country. Thus we find the Italians and Mennonites, for instance, tending to equate the retention of traditional values with the cohesion of their group. Therefore one of the most important factors in cohesion is marriage within the group and keeping the family ties over several generations.

Other factors that can be treated with family activity are the use of mass-media. These are normally utilized at home or within the family. There are two steps here: the existence of mass-media and their use. Figures on the existence of mass-media are relatively easy to obtain from trade sources. These should be supplemented by use figures, and by judgements on the quality of the language used by the media.

If the home provides a nucleus for language retention, this is reinforced by ethnic neighbourhoods. It is the experience in North American cities that certain districts tend to be identified with certain ethnic groups: in Ottawa, for instance, the area around Preston Street is predominantly Italian, to the extent that there is an Italian parish. This type of situation is reproduced in rural districts — in the Prairies Ukrainian communities are spread over considerable areas of country. Such areas will be served by ethnic shops and other services which allow the language to be used in ordinary life. They will provide recreational facilities which allow the group to mix within itself and exclude strangers; such facilities will often include, as they do among Ottawa Italians, films in the language of the group, which, I am told, play to large houses.

John Gumperz has done work in this area in the Puerto-Rican communities of New York. His main concern was the pattern of language use. Armed with a tape recorder, he lived in the Spanish communities of Jersey City; and once he had been accepted as a harmless stranger, if slightly mad, he was able to fade into the woodwork and observe what was going on in the matter of diglossic strategies and language interaction. Among the incidental results of his work was a good picture of language maintenance. To my knowledge, nothing of this nature has ever been attempted in Canada.

In Canada it has been traditional to say that "la foi est gardienne de la langue et la langue, gardienne de la foi". This has been true of the French, the Ukrainians and the Mennonites, among others. The value of religion is not so much in the language of worship — traditionally these groups have not worshipped in their normal languages — but in the social cohesion that develops around a parish. It would seem that in Canada language and religion are separating. In Ottawa, for instance, many French Catholics go to the nearest church, whether it be French or English, or even alternate their attendance: in good weather they take the extra trouble to go to the French church, in bad, they go to the English if it is nearer. However, even though the theology of the churches is the same, there is a difference between French and English Catholicism which is expressed in the type of parish organization and the services given parishioners outside the purely religious. The value of religion to language maintenance is the fact that it acts as a separative factor in the population, and to a very large extent underwrites the other factors of family and social group.

The effect of work is ambiguous. If one can work in one's own language, that language is strengthened, but it is the experience of most of the ethnic work force that work is not available in one's own language, unless one is in a service industry catering to the ethnic group. In any case, the language of work often causes hybridization of languages by reason of the technical terms that have to be used, and relationships with administrators. Many of the tensions associated with language maintenance are related to work: very often the sole road to advancement is through the majority language, or legally, the majority languages are the only vehicles of communication legally accepted. For a full discussion of this I would refer you to Professor Simon's paper. The difference between the legal aspect of language use in Canada and the situation caused by the existence of other languages still needs full investigation. In French and English it was exhaustively looked into by the Royal Commission on Bilingualism and Biculturalism.

Schooling is an important factor, not only for the existence of the languages, but also for their integrity. This is well shown by the varying standard of French across the country, from Quebec, where schooling in French is assured, to British Columbia and the Prairies where, until recently, it was not. From the point of view of research we need to look at the pattern of ethnic schooling. The Ukrainians, for instance, have a vigorous system of unofficial schools, and Ukrainian is a subject in school. Together with the question of availability of schooling we should look into the question of training of teachers, availability of textbooks and other details of an educational system.

What the research outlined here would give us would be the sociological factors which allow the minority languages to be used, or, in other words, an index to the rules of diglossia which the various language communities obey.

Other research techniques on diglossia have been described many times by Fishman, Gumperz, Ferguson and Cooper, so there is no need to repeat them here.

This work on diglossia should be linked to statistical surveys of the type referred to by Macrae at Moncton (*Description and Measurement of Bilingualism,* Toronto University Press, 1969, p. 320). The first step is a more rigorous listing of languages, especially in regard to the Indian and Eskimo group. The second is defining the "mother tongue" in such a fashion as to reveal language dominance. This could be achieved by distinguishing between "home language" and "work language". I would agree with Macrae's idea that it is possible for a person to have a double mother tongue, where two languages have been learnt in the same environment from childhood. The French population of parts of Ontario would surely contain individuals of this type. Diachronic shift could be checked by noting the languages of parents and children and comparing extent of language use in both generations.

Some work of this type was done by the Royal Commission on Bilingualism and Biculturalism. The French population was fairly well covered, as was the Italian population in Montreal and Edmonton. However, in the raw data collected by the Commission and used for its purposes, there is a considerable amount of information on language maintenance that was irrelevant to the main concerns of the Commission, and hence was not mined to the fullest extent possible. There are, also, several researchers in Canada working on minority languages: Dr. Bausenhart of the University of Ottawa on Ontario German, for instance. In addition there is data on publications in ethnic languages and readership figures that could be updated by reference to the ethnic press associations and ethnic publishers. Some collection of data was done by the B & B as raw material for their volume on ethnic groups. This was not fully utilized and could be supplemented. There is some interest in Canadian literature in languages other than English and French, as indicated by a publication of translations from "the unofficial languages of Canada" which is soon to appear from the Department of Creative Writing of the University of British Columbia.

There are external manifestations of language maintenance, and valuable as they are, they should be supplemented by studies of the languages themselves. There have been extensive studies of Canadian French and of its borrowings from English and Indian. Similar work is being done on the Indian and Inuit languages; and some interest is being shown in Canadian English dialectology. Something similar is needed in other ethnic languages. Again studies have been made in the United States on Spanish, French and Italian, much of the work proceeding from that of Uriel Weinreich. Even a brief look at the periodical *American Speech* will show the extent of the work being done in the U.S. I am not aware of similar dialect studies in Canada. What is needed is a rigorous description of the languages spoken in Canada, both from the point of view of synchronic description and of contact studies; indeed, a description at all levels of these languages as they are spoken here. They will, naturally, have varied from the source varieties of these languages even without contact features. The isolation of contact features is a separate issue. What we need to establish is whether the evolution has been parallel with that in the United States, the effect of the various waves of migration on retarding the development of separate varieties, and the balance between the conserving effects of diglossia and the innovative effects of isolation from the metropolis and of contact with English.

To sum up, then, the problem of language maintenance should be looked at from two points of view. By closer cross-tabulation of census data we can gain a better idea of who speaks what languages; and this can be cross-checked with data from ethnic organizations. On-the-spot investigation of each community in turn can show us whether languages are specialized as to domain, and the transmission patterns of languages within the family and other social groups. The important thing here is validating the idea of domain for each group. Parallel with this will be studies of the languages themselves. Whether this implies new research, or merely co-ordination of the old, I am not qualified to say. In general, a language worth preserving will be preserved. A language does not fall out of use until it is felt to be useless either by reason of its irrelevance in the community, or of its weakening by absorption of contact features beyond the point of recognizability. It is also important to know whether a language is being fed by immigration: this involves a study both of the number of native speakers arriving in the country and the extent to which they are absorbed into the community. The rejection of outsiders, for example, has been one of the weaknesses of the French community in Canada.

I cannot say whether the ethnic languages in Canada are holding their own. This question still waits investigation with the rigour that such questions have been investigated elsewhere.

Bibliography

Fishman, J. A. *et al. Language Loyalty in the United States; The Maintenance and Perpetutation of Non-English Mother Tongues by American Ethnic and Religious Groups,* The Hague: Mouton, 1966.

Jacobovits, L. *Foreign Language Learning: a Psycholinguistic Statement of the Issues.* Rowley, Mass.: Newbury House, 1970.

Kloss, H. *The Bilingual Tradition in the United States.* Rowley, Mass.: Newbury House, 1970.

Kelly, L. G. (ed.), *The Description and Measurement of Bilingualism; An International Seminar.* Toronto: Toronto University Press, 1969.

Lepage, R. B. *The National Language Question, Linguistic Problems of Newly Independent States.* London: Oxford University Press, 1964.

Royal Commission of Bilingualism and Biculturalism, *Final Report.* 1967-1970.

THE PROBLEM OF
"UNOFFICIAL" LANGUAGES IN CANADA

J. B. Rudnyckyj
Department of Slavic Studies
University of Manitoba

The two official languages of Canada — English and French — co-exist alongside several other languages used in this country in various spheres of private and community life. The official and "unofficial" languages form the Canadian linguistic reality which can be viewed from several aspects.

Legal Aspect

The first and the main aspect of the problem is the legal (constitutional) status of languages in Canada. As far as English and French are concerned they have the status of official (federal) languages with provisions included in the B.N.A. Act of 1867 and the Official Languages Act of 1969. As far as the languages of the other ethnic groups are concerned, they are, from the legal viewpoint, "unofficial" languages of Canada. Their existence is confirmed by Article 38 of the Official Languages Act.

Taking the above status of languages into consideration, the following types of bilingualism in Canada emerge:

1. Official bilingualism: English-French or French-English depending on which language is the mother tongue of the individual concerned. Therefore, there are two kinds of official bilingualism in Canada.

2. Semi-official bilingualism: knowledge and use of one of the official languages (English or French) along with an ethnic mother tongue. The main types of such bilingualism in Canada are as follows: English-German, English-Italian, English-Ukrainian, English-Polish, etc., and French-Polish, French-Ukrainian, French-German, French-Italian, etc.

3. "Unofficial" bilingualism: knowledge and use of languages other than English and French, e.g. Eskimo-Indian, Russian-German, Ukrainian-Icelandic, etc.

4. Extended or multiple bilingualism: a combination of all types of bilingualism — knowledge of both official languages in addition to other "unofficial" ones, e.g. English-French-German-Ukrainian, French-English-Polish-Russian, English-French-Italian-German-Hungarian, etc.

Concerning the degree of bilingualism of individuals there are the following types:

1. Perfect bilingualism: the highest bilingual achievement, viz. mastering another language in speaking and writing as a "second mother tongue".

2. Basic bilingualism: an adequate knowledge of one language and the basic (essential) understanding, reading, speaking, and writing knowledge of

the second language.

3. Passive bilingualism: an adequate knowledge of the mother tongue and a passive comprehension of another language in reading and hearing.

Historic Aspect

From the historic aspect the languages in Canada might be grouped into three main categories: (1) indigenous, (2) colonial, and (3) immigrant languages. The indigenous languages are those formerly or currently spoken by Eskimos and the various Indian tribes. According to 1961 statistics, there are 166,531 Eskimo-Indian speakers in Canada. The colonial languages are those initially spoken by seventeenth and eighteenth century European colonizers of areas that later became Canada. Out of those languages, English and French established themselves as official languages of the country. The immigrant languages (totalling about sixty) were brought to Canada by settlers predominantly from European countries in the nineteenth and twentieth centuries.

With regard to their *kinship* the immigrant languages in Canada belong to the following Indo-European families:

German (Teutonic):	German	563,713
	Dutch	170,177
	Yiddish	82,448
	Norwegian	40,054
	Swedish	32,632
	Danish	35,035
	Flemish	14,304
	Icelandic	8,993

Total Germanic languages: 947,356 speakers

Slavic:	Ukrainian	361,496
	Polish	161,720
	Russian	42,903
	Slovak	42,546
	Serb. Cr.	28,866
	Czech	21,454
	Slovene	4,281
	Bulg.-Macedonian	2,500
	Belorussian	768

Total Slavic languages: 666,533

Romance:	Italian	339,626
	Portuguese	60,000
	Spanish	10,000
	Rumanian	10,165

Total Romance languages: 419,791

The above presentation indicates that numerically German, Ukrainian, and Italian occupy the first place in their respective groups. I have ventured to designate them as "regional languages" of Canada. The remaining immigrant languages, accounting for some 407,000 speakers, belong to a wide variety of language families (Indo-European, Ugro-Finnish, Semitic, etc.).

Most of the ethnic immigrant tongues are influenced by English as one of the official languages of Canada and the dominant language on the North American continent. This influence is evident both in grammatical structure and in the vocabulary. On the other hand, English in Canada expands from year to year in official and unofficial use, and replaces more and more the mother tongues of various ethnic groups. Interference and transplacement of that kind is due to the following factors: (1) dominant official language status, (2) linguistic pressure of the U.S. and U.K., (3) structural and lexical peculiarities of English, (4) inert attitudes of Canadian society toward acquiring the knowledge of more than one language, (5) other factors, e.g. economic, political, technological, etc.

The impact of English is particularly great on languages which are akin to it (although other factors have also been at work) e.g.:

German:	ethnic origin (in thousands)	1,156
	German as mother tongue	564
	relative difference: 51.2%	
Dutch:	ethnic origin	430
	mother tongue	170
	relative difference: 60.4%	
Scandinavian:	ethnic origin	387
	mother tongue	117
	relative difference: 69.8%	

Among other immigrant languages the highest degree of language loss is as follows:

Polish:	ethnic origin (in thousands)	329
	mother tongue	162
	relative difference: 50%	
Hungarian:	ethnic origin	126
	mother tongue	86
	relative difference: 31.9%	

Finnish: ethnic origin 59
mother tongue 45
relative difference: 24.7%

Eskimo-Indian: ethnic origin 220
mother tongue 167
relative difference: 24.3%

The above languages and some other minor tongues show *sharp losses* among the claimants of the respective ethnic groups.

On the other hand, among these Canadians of Ukrainian ethnic origin, more than 100% have, at times, claimed Ukrainian as their mother tongue, viz.:

Census	Ethnic origin	Language retained or expanded	Percentage
1931	225,000	252,000	112.3%
1941	305,000	313,000	102.4%
1951	395,000	352,000	89.2%
1961	473,000	361,496	76.4%

Ukrainian is the only immigrant language in Canada to have produced this phenomenon. It is explainable by the linguistic kinship of Ukrainian and other Slavic languages; during the first quarter of the nineteenth century Polish, Slovak and Belorussian assimilated to Ukrainian as the leading Slavic tongue in the Prairie Provinces. This trend was interrupted after World War II with influx of new immigrants of Polish, Slovak, Belorussian, and other origins; thus Ukrainian decreased in its numerical strength.

Global Aspect

Considering the historical global expansion of the Indo-European languages, three main branches spread throughout the world in medieval and modern times:

1. *Teutonic* – Anglo-Saxon in Europe, North America, Australia and New Zealand; Dutch in Central and South America, Asia, etc.

2. *Romance* — French in North America and Africa; Spanish and Portuguese in Central and South America.

3. *Slavic* — Russian and Ukrainian in Eastern Europe, Northern Asia, and North America (until 1867 Colonial).

No other language groups, whether Indo-European or not, can claim such global status in their expansion.

In Canada, a parallel linguistic situation is to be found. English as an official and major language in the Teutonic group, and French in the Romance, co-exist in Canada along with the unofficial Slavic and other languages. As such, Canada is unique in reflecting in microcosm the repartition of languages throughout the world.

Conclusion:

In headlong pursuit of the twenty-first century Canadians of the twentieth century must not ignore these important problems. As no other country today, Canada has an obligation to do its best in language planning. She must meet not only her internal needs in this domain, but also, in recognizing the linguistic reality of the world, play her predestined role on the international level.

Appendix 1

In connection with the sudden cessation of the activities of the Royal Commission on Bilingualism and Biculturalism as of March 31, 1971, I submitted to the Government of Canada on March 16, 1971, the following:

SUPPLEMENTAL B & B RECOMMENDATIONS
regarding the legal and factual status of "the other ethnic languages":

RECOMMENDATIONS REGARDING AMENDMENTS TO THE *Official Languages Act*

RECOMMENDATION 1   (See Appendix 5)

RECOMMENDATION 2

Whereas the *Official Languages Act* in its Section 38 deals also with languages other than English and French, and

Whereas this Act as well as the Commissioner of Official Languages shall be concerned with all the languages of the country (official, regional, non-official, etc.), and

Whereas the present designation of the Act and the Commissioner might be interpreted as implying a discriminatory attitude towards the other ethnic languages by ignoring them by the very title of the Act and by the designation of the Commissioner,

I recommend

that both the *Official Languages Act* and the *Commissioner of Official Languages* be renamed to "Canadian Languages Act" and to "Commissioner for Language Protection and Linguistic Planning in Canada" respectively.

RECOMMENDATIONS REGARDING VOLUME IV OF THE *REPORT*

Whereas the recommendations of Volume IV of the *Report* are still waiting for their implementation, and

Whereas this delay causes a growing concern, criticisms and indignation among the "other ethnic groups" in Canada, and

Whereas those recommendations were unanimously endorsed by the *Manitoba Mosaic Congress* held in Winnipeg on October 12-17, 1970, and

Whereas the Government promptly acted upon the release of the previous volumes of the B & B *Report,*
I recommend
the acceleration of the whole process of the implementation of these recommendations, and
I further recommend
the immediate dissemination of news regarding plans and/or actions in this respect through the *Information Canada* in Ottawa.

Appendix 2

RECOMMENDATIONS OF BOOK IV OF THE REPORT OF THE ROYAL COMMISSION ON BILINGUALISM AND BICULTURALISM regarding "The Cultural Contribution of the Other Ethnic Groups

1. We recommend that any provinces that have not yet enacted fair employment practices, fair accommodation practices, or housing legislation prohibiting discrimination because of race, nationality, ancestry, or place of origin, do so; and that legislation be made binding upon the Crown and its agencies. We further recommend that all provinces make provision for full-time administrators of their human rights legislation.

2. We recommend that the same conditions for citizenship, the right to vote, and to stand for election to public office be accorded to all immigrants, with no regard to their country of origin.

3. We recommend that the teaching of languages other than English and French, and cultural subjects related to them, be incorporated as options in the public elementary school programme, where there is sufficient demand for such classes.

4. We recommend that special instruction in the appropriate official language be provided for children who enter the public school system with an inadequate knowledge of that language; that provincial authorities specify the terms and conditions of financial assistance for such special instruction; and that the federal authorities assist the provinces in mutually acceptable ways through grants for the additional costs incurred.

5. We recommend that more advanced instruction and a wider range of options in languages other than English and French, and in cultural subjects related to them, be provided in public high schools, where there is sufficient demand for such classes.

6. We recommend that Canadian universities broaden their practices in giving standing or credits for studies in modern languages other than French and English both for admission and for degrees.

7. We recommend that Canadian universities expand their studies in the fields of the humanities and the social sciences relating to particular areas other than those related to the English and French languages.

8. We recommend that CRTC remove restrictions on private broadcasting in languages other than English and French, except those restrictions necessary to meet the administrative and legal responsibilities of the licensees and those that also apply to English- and French-language programmes.

9. We recommend that the CBC recognize the place of languages other than English and French in Canadian life and that the CBC remove its proscription on the use of other languages in broadcasting.

10. We recommend that the CRTC undertake studies in the field of broadcasting in other languages to determine the best means by which radio and television can contribute to the maintenance of languages and cultures and that the CBC participate in these studies. We further recommend that these studies include pilot projects on either AM or FM radio in both Montreal and Toronto.

11. We recommend that research be undertaken through the CRTC concerning the effects of the portrayal of other cultural groups on both publicly- and privately-owned English- and French-language radio and television stations.

12. We recommend that the National Film Board undertake to publicize the fact that it produces prints of many of its films in languages other than English and French, particularly in regions where there are concentrations of persons who speak languages other than English and French. In addition, we recommend that the voluntary associations of cultural groups stimulate interest among their groups in the use of these films.

13. We recommend that the National Film Board continue and develop the production of films that inform Canadians about one another, including films about the contribution and problems of both individuals and groups of ethnic origin, other than British and French, and that the National Film Board receive the financial support it requires in order to produce such films.

14. We recommend that the appropriate federal, provincial, and municipal agencies receive the financial means they require to maintain and extend their support to cultural and research organizations whose objectives are to foster the arts and letters of cultural groups other than the British and French.

15. We recommend that the administrative costs of the Canadian Folk Arts Council or a similar body be provided for out of public funds through the Citizenship Branch of the Department of the Secretary of State.

16. We recommend that the National Museum of Man be given adequate space and facilities and provided with sufficient funds to carry out its

projects regarding the history, social organizations, and folk arts of cultural groups other than the British and French.

Appendix 3

RESOLUTIONS of the Manitoba Mosaic Congress
(Plenary Session, October 17, 1970.)

1. WHEREAS English and French are the official languages of Canada within the public agencies of the Federal Government,

   BE IT RESOLVED that the Manitoba Mosaic Congress recommends that the Government of Manitoba study ways and means of preserving the multilingual and multicultural reality of the Manitoba Mosaic.

2. WHEREAS the official Languages Act of 1969 does not determine the status of the languages other than English and French,

   BE IT RESOLVED that the Manitoba Mosaic Congress recommends that the question of legal status of languages, other than English and French be studied by Provincial and Federal governments for the purpose of determining if additional legislation on the subject should be enacted and that the languages used by ethnic communities in Canada should be regarded as Canadian languages and that they be deemed to be the other languages protected by Section 38 of the Official Languages Act.

3. WHEREAS at present a student is frequently denied the opportunity to study more than one second language,

   BE IT RESOLVED that the Manitoba Mosaic Congress recommends that steps be taken to find ways and means of making such language options available to all students in the Province wherever there are sufficient numbers interested and that such Federal grants now available for this purpose be so applied.

4. BE IT RESOLVED that for a class where a second language is taught, that class be entitled and encouraged to study that language in the context of the literature of that language.

5. WHEREAS the Government acknowledges the positive contributions of bilingual civil servants, and

   WHEREAS the Province of Manitoba has within its boundaries a vast linguistic diversity,

   BE IT RESOLVED that the Manitoba Mosaic Congress recommends that in employing civil servants, the Government of Manitoba take into consideration the qualifications of applicants who have fluency in more than one language.

6. BE IT RESOLVED that the Manitoba Mosaic Congress recommends to the Department of Education that it instruct the staffs of the curriculum development departments, audio-visual aids departments, teacher train-

ing departments to develop programs which would reflect the multi-cultural and multi-lingual reality of Manitoba.

7. BE IT RESOLVED that the Manitoba Mosaic Congress recommends the support of the development of ethnic archives in the Province of Manitoba, in association with the Provincial archives, the Museum of Man and Nature, and the existing ethnic archives, for use by historians and interested individuals for the purpose of research, displays, and education, and

   BE IT RESOLVED that this Congress support the establishment of a central union file for the Province of Manitoba, showing the location of existing material, and that this file be duplicated for deposit in the other Western Provinces, in the hope that these provinces and eventually the Federal Government, will produce a central union file of ethnic material for the whole of Canada.

8. BE IT RESOLVED that the Department of Education take under advisement the revision of existing texts to present a more comprehensive picture of the contribution of all the ethnic groups in Canada to the cultural, economic, social and political life of our province and country.

9. BE IT RESOLVED that the Manitoba Mosaic Congress recommends the publication of an anthology of creative ethnic literature in both the original language version and that competent translations in both English and French be financially supported by the Government.

10. WHEREAS the Royal Commission on Biculturalism and Bilingualism has made 16 recommendations in its fourth volume,

    BE IT RESOLVED THAT all levels of Government and their agencies begin implementing these recommendations.

11. BE IT RESOLVED that MMC recommends that an ethnic library be created within the new Winnipeg Public Library in cooperation with the various ethnic groups in the province — the facilities of such a library be made freely available to all the citizens of Manitoba through the present Regional Library System.

12. BE IT RESOLVED that the Manitoba Mosaic Congress recommends that a Cultural Council of Manitoba be established by the Provincial Government to serve the whole community, and that the 15-member steering committee of this Congress act on an interim basis until this Cultural Council be established with the purpose of pursuing the objectives of the Manitoba Mosaic Congress.

Appendix 4

MANITOBA BILL 113

An Act to Amend the Public Schools Act (2)

(Assented to in 1970)

HER MAJESTY, by and with the advice and consent of the Legislative Assembly of Manitoba, enacts as follows:

Sec. 258 rep. and sub.

1   Section 258 of The Public Schools Act, being Chapter P250 of the Revised Statutes of Manitoba, 1970, is repealed and the following section is substituted therefore:

English and French as languages of instruction.

258 (1)   Subject as otherwise provided in this section, English and French being the two languages to which reference is made in the British North America Act, 1867, are the languages of instruction in public schools.

Use of other languages.

258 (2)   When authorized by the board of a school district, school division or school area, a language other than English or French may be used in any school in the school district, school division or school area
   (a) during a period authorized for religious teaching;
   (b) during a period authorized by the minister for teaching a language other than English or French; and
   (c) before and after the regular school hours prescribed in the regulations and applicable to that school.

Establishment of English Language Advisory Committee.

258 (3)   The minister shall establish a committee (hereinafter in this section referred to as the "English Language Advisory Committee") composed of nine persons to which he may refer matters pertaining to the use of English as a language of instruction in public schools.

Membership of English Language Advisory Committee.

258 (4)   The members of the English Language Advisory Committee, of whom
   (a) two shall be appointed from not less than four persons nominated by the Manitoba Association of School Trustees;
   (b) two shall be appointed from not less than four persons nominated by the Manitoba Teachers Society;
   (c) one shall be appointed from not less than two persons nominated by the Faculty of Education of the University of Manitoba; and
   (d) one shall be appointed from not less than two persons nominated by the Faculty of Education of the University of Brandon;
shall be appointed by the Minister for such terms as he may determine.

Establishment of French Language Advisory Committee.

258 (5)   The minister shall establish a committee (hereinafter in this section referred to as the "French Language Advisory Committee") composed of nine persons to which he may refer matters pertaining to the use of French as a language of instruction in public schools.

Membership of French Language Advisory Committee.

258 (6)   The members of the French Language Advisory Committee, of whom
- (a) two shall be appointed from not less than four persons nominated by l'Association des commissaires d'école de langue française du Manitoba;
- (b) two shall be appointed from not less than four persons nominated by les educateurs franco manitobaines; and
- (c) two shall be appointed from not less than four persons nominated by Le College de Saint Boniface;

Languages of Instruction Advisory Council.

258 (7)   The English Language Advisory Committee and the French Language Advisory Committee together constitute a council to be known as: "Languages of Instruction Advisory Council", to which the minister may refer matters pertaining to the operation of this section.

Use of English or French as language of instruction.

258 (8)   Where there are in any school district, school division or school area
- (a) twenty-eight or more pupils in an elementary grade who may be grouped in a class for instruction; or
- (b) twenty-three or more pupils in a secondary grade who may be grouped in a class for instruction;

and whose parents desire them to be instructed in a class in which English or French, as the case may be, is used as the language of instruction, the board of the school district, school division or school area may, and upon petition of the parents of those pupils requesting the use of English or French, as the case may be, as the language of instruction in respect of those pupils, shall group those pupils in a class for instruction and provide for use of English or French, as the case may be, as the language of instruction in the class.

Minister's discretion for fewer pupils.

258 (9)   Where the number of pupils concerned is less than the numbers mentioned in subsection (8) as requirements for the application of that subsection, the minister, where he considers it practical and upon the advice of the English Language Advisory Committee or the French Language Advisory Committee, as the case may be, may require the board of a school district, school division or school area to make arrangements for the use of English or French as the language of instruction in any class.

Language of administration.

258 (10)   The administration and operation of a public school shall be carried out in the English language or the French language as the minister may, by regulation, provide.

English as subject of instruction.

158 (11)   Notwithstanding any other provision of this Act, English
  (a) may be a subject of instruction in any grade; and
  (b) shall be a subject of instruction in every class in Grades IV, V, VI,
       VII, VIII, IX, X, XI, or XII where French is used as the language of
       instruction.

Agreements by boards.

258 (12)   A board of a school district, school division or school area may
enter into an agreement with the board of another school district, school
division or school area for providing jointly, classes in which the language
used for instruction is English or French as the case may be, and the pupils
in those classes may be included in the numbers required to meet the requirements of any provision of this section or the regulations.

Regulations.

258 (13)   The Minister may make regulations for carrying this section
into effect.

Commencement of Act.

2   This Act comes into force on a day fixed by proclamation.

Appendix 5

RECOMMENDATIONS REGARDING AMENDMENTS TO THE *Official
Languages Act**

Whereas the *Official Languages Act* in its Section 38 provides for a very
general ("antilinguicidal") protection of the "other ethnic languages" of
Canada and as such does not offer any affirmative provisions for the legal
status of those languages, in particular of the major ones, as e.g. Ukrainian,
German, Eskimo-Indian, etc., and

Whereas after the extensive work of the Commission the awareness of
the Canadian society with regard to languages other than English and
French considerably increased, and

Whereas there is a general trend in the modern world to grant a legal
status to various minority languages in the respective countries,

I recommend

that the present Section 38 of the *Official Languages Act* be extended
by addition of two Subsections which would precede it as Subsection 38
(3), namely:

38(1) Notwithstanding anything in this Act, any language other than Eng-

*From the author's *Brief* presented to the Joint Committee on the Constitution,
Ottawa, June 17, 1971.

lish and French used by ten per cent or more of the population of any province or territory shall be declared a REGIONAL LANG-UAGE with such provisions as the governments concerned may specify and approve in response to public demand.

38(2) Whenever in any province or territory the population whose mother tongue is other than English and French reaches ten per cent or more in the appropriate administrative unit and this tongue has the status of a regional language in the respective or any other province or territory, this unit shall be constituted into a REGIONAL BILIN-GUAL DISTRICT with public services in one of the official languages and with admission of the given regional language as specified and approved by the governments concerned.

FRENCH AS AN ADOPTED LANGUAGE IN QUEBEC

Léon Dion
Départment de science politique
Université Laval

The language question in Quebec is a thorny one. To raise it is to set sail in dangerous waters and undertake, at the risk of foundering, to define a variety of coordinates of demographic, economic, socio-psychological, cultural, juridical and political bearing. Great are the risks of misunderstanding along the way. The problems to be resolved are more than likely to beget violent disputes, since they are visceral in quality and invite irrational reactions.

Canadians are rapidly becoming aware of the seriousness of this language question in Quebec itself. Two important commissions of enquiry have looked, or are looking, into it. The Commission on Bilingualism and Biculturalism largely concerned itself with the situation in Canada as a whole and, except in the third volume of its report, has made few recommendations relating directly to the francophone population of Quebec. However, its list of proposals constitute in the aggregate the framework of a possible action program applying to Quebec. The Commission of enquiry into the French language in Quebec (Gendron Commission) is concerned with matters relating to the quality of the language, its teaching, the use of second languages, and diverse aspects of the coexistence of two languages in the same environment.

Whatever benefits may ensue from these labours, the situation is such as to require immediate action. The passing of Bill 63 "to promote the French language in Quebec", and the need to pursue consideration of Bill 62 "concerning school organization on the Island of Montreal", are most urgent reasons in that regard.

On the other hand, it would be wrong to consider the matter exclusively in the light of problems resulting from these two laws. This is not the time for polemics. Although the situation prompts us to action, it also suggests broadening the range of our concerns in such a way as to cover the numerous aspects of this language problem. This first step should lead to the formulation of a balanced program likely to find concrete expression in projects both coherent in themselves and in relation to one another.

If the integration of immigrants and non-francophone ethnic groups has recently moved to the centre of discussions on the future of the French language in Quebec, this is perhaps chiefly due to the demographic situation. With the abrupt decline in the Quebec birth rate since 1965, the "revenge of the cradles" era has come to a close. In order to maintain their ratio of about 80% of the province's whole population, or even continue to exist as a separate language group, Quebec's francophones have only one recourse: to proceed as quickly as possible with the integration of non-francophones, especially those of non-British stock. Since their assimilative capacity with Quebec is weaker than ever at present, can the latter expect to improve it rapidly and, if so, how?

Besides, the problem of integrating the non-francophones cannot be considered separately from other aspects of the language question. Any careful analysis of this subject must take into account the constraints peculiar to this environment, as well as the means of modifying it. Consideration must, therefore, be given to such factors as the flow of immigrants, education levels, the professional aspirations of individuals, and the relative weights of French and English in the economic field both nationally and internationally.

I have no intention here of dealing with every aspect of this problem of integrating the non-francophone ethnic groups in Quebec. I shall merely attempt to clarify it somewhat and suggest some elements of a possible solution. My aim is rather to stimulate reflection, a process which will be long and difficult, I know. These questions are in fact complex and do not easily lend themselves to dogmatic or even satisfactory responses. My remarks will more often assume the conditional mood, occasionally the indicative, and seldom the imperative. After setting out certain premises basic to a study of the subject, I shall briefly outline the language situation in Quebec and suggest the goals that Quebec's language policy should pursue.

The Basic Premises

Let us begin with a painful but necessary confession. The human sciences on which we rightly depend to guide man in his uncertain attempts to gain more knowledge of himself and the world, have devoted very little effort to perfecting multi-disciplinary tools for examining the conditions of a bilingual environment and its influence on individual languages, persons, institutions, groups and the community as a whole. Certain general observations more or less substantiated have been advanced, for example that in order for a language to survive in a bilingual environment there must exist unilingual nuclei, that is, sufficiently numerous groups of persons who find it very inconvenient to use the other language. We now possess, thanks to the patient labours of the Commission on Bilingualism and Biculturalism, a great deal of information on the most diverse aspects of the language situation in Quebec. However, this information hardly goes beyond factual description. It might on occasion inspire caution, but it is not of much use for the development of working methods likely to produce more useful guides to action than those of instinct, goodwill, stubbornness, and suicidal or vindictive impulses. Is it possible in the present state of our disciplines to develop processes capable of achieving results of relatively uncontested worth? To answer such a question will require far more extensive research work than has been conducted until now.

Failing the aid of science, many look to natural law for guidance and justification. Nothing could be more hazardous. Is it not said of principles that if you lean on them long enough, they always give way? True, there are certain inalienable rights to life and the integrity of the person which cannot be legitimately infringed upon for any reason. But their guarantee is far from assured in practice. Moreover, the tests employed to determine their modes of application are often uncertain; and they are based on Christian and humanist concepts which are not always as clear as one would wish. Furthermore, the exercise of such rights is often governed by special conditions, as a result of which both individuals and groups remain subject to many external constraints in the most varied aspects of their lives.

Those who feel that there exists an inalienable right to education calling for positive action on the part of the state (building schools, staffing them with teachers, etc.) can point to an almost universal consensus on this subject in contemporary societies. But does there exist as obvious a right regarding the language of instruction? In unilingual countries, the problem does not arise. But the diversity of school systems found in bilingual countries, as well as the often deep antagonisms dividing these countries, suggest that the parents' right to have children educated in the language of their choice is everywhere relative at best, and often subject to severe restrictions rooted in history and in particular sociological conditions.

The same comment applies to collective rights. Group rights often result from the outcome of historic struggles. They usually benefit the victorious side to the detriment of the vanquished, which casts some doubt on their essential merit. Even undisputed, the exercise of a collective right involves limits of time and place imposed either by equity or the play of opposing forces.

Lastly, there is the question of acquired rights. Whatever its origin, an individual or collective right is so considered when a presumption of legitimacy is established in its favour, and it may be exercised with impunity under certain conditions. While an acquired right is not as soundly based as one considered inalienable, the conditions of its use are often much more precise. It is generally difficult to abolish an acquired right, even when the possibility to do so exists and circumstances require it: equity or decency stand in the way. There are thus some privileges it seems best not to grant for fear that the consequences might be such as to require their cancellation.

In the field of language, the law of might was applied implacably everywhere in Canada except Quebec. With a wealth of laws voted by democratic majorities, French was banished from schools and denied conditions of use likely to preserve its vitality. Subsequently, a disingenuous notion of justice was invoked for a long time in order to oppose bringing legislative remedy to a situation resulting from legislative action, which condemned French to a slow death: one had to be especially careful not to mix politics with language and culture!

The federal Government's current efforts to promote the use of French in all fields of activity under its jurisdiction and the creation of bilingual districts coordinated with the programs of some provincial governments, appear as tardy reparations for an ancient wrong. One should forgive the repentant sinner, and hope it may still be possible for him to repair the damage done. More importantly, one must avoid falling into the same error.

The francophones for their part have had plenty of time to realize that "between the mighty and the weak, it is liberty that oppresses and the law which liberates". Who could reasonably be offended by the desire of Quebec's francophone majority to rely on the government they control more immediately to remedy the necessary insufficiency of federal laws in the linguistic field, by adopting measures designed to ensure the supremacy of French in all fields of activity within Quebec, with due regard to circumstances and the legitimate rights of the anglophone minority? Any attempts to inhibit the francophone people of Quebec in their desire to establish a coherent language program for themselves are bound to fail. In my view, however, their action should not be based principally on a "collective right", since such a justification would only generate opposition in the name of "individual rights" and lead into a conflict of abstract ideas.

The decision to legislate in the language field, like any other group decision, is first of all a political question. It is up to the government and people of Quebec to decide on the merit of putting paid to an old policy of inaction in that respect. With equity safeguarded, any law concerning languages should then only be judged on its merits and foreseeable effects. The sole justification of a legislative measure on languages in Quebec is the individual and collective distress it echoes, and should aim to alleviate.

Like all other laws passed by the National Assembly of Quebec, this language legislation will be examined in relation to the country's constitutional framework. It will undoubtedly open a new dimension in federal-provincial relations and be an additional source of possible conflict. However, it is at this time of constitutional review that the main lines of a language program should be laid down in order to formulate in advance, in case they are required, the necessary constitutional provisions.

The demands addressed by the people to their political representatives on the question of language rights are without doubt contradictory; we do not yet know to what extent the political system may be able to entertain them, any more than we can foretell the effects of a language bill.

But we have no other option than to act. And in this obligatory search for an appropriate strategy, the government cannot go it alone: it must have the support of the entire community. Our common task consists, therefore, in developing under the government's auspices a coherent program of action embracing the main aspects of the language situation. We must conceive and put into effect measures designed to correct tendencies prejudicial to the French language, without interfering with the free circulation of goods, ideas and persons.

The Situation

Between the francophone and anglophone people of Quebec, there has developed a kind of division of labour: the anglophones dominated the economy while the francophones dominated politics. Now the latter are no longer content with that state of affairs, having finally realized that the economy is the determining force behind policy. It is hardly surprising that the economic organization of Quebec should not favour the interests of the majority, since it is not subject to any real political control. This "surrender" of economic control to the anglophones is not, of course, the only reason for the inferiority of francophones. The effects of an obsolete educational system, of a religion promising all too easy compensation for the hardships of this world, the paternalism of leaders — all these are inter-related factors which have contributed in one way or another to the pre-vailing status of inferiority in which the francophones find themselves.

In the third volume of its report, the Royal Commission on Bilingualism and Biculturalism undertook to review the facts. The situation it described is bad in many respects, almost desperate. In the matter of earnings, educa-tion and control of business, the francophones are far behind the anglo-phones and hardly better off than the Italians who have for the most part lived less than twenty-five years in Quebec. This largely explains the wretch-ed position of French as a working language, and it is clear that the necessary corrective steps go well beyond measures directly related only to languages. Also involved are problems of education, career options, indus-trial investment and control of business affairs.

There is one aspect of the problem, as it emerges in Quebec, that the commission of enquiry did not come to grips with. And that is the demo-graphic situation. Yet this question is one which raises the most serious doubts about the future of French in Quebec.

It is a fact that despite the predictions of alarmists, the percentage of francophones in Canada has been remarkably stable since 1881 (30% in 1881 and 30.4% in 1961, as regards ethnic origin). The proportion of francophones in Montreal today is higher than it was at the time of Confederation.

Fears are entertained, however, about the growing influence of urbani-zation and technology. The preservation of a traditional social framework has long served as a protective shield against contamination from the out-side. But now that Quebec has taken up the challenge of modernity, con-cern is felt about the possible survival of five million francophones on a continent peopled by 215 million anglophones, which is at the threshold, moreover, of the post-industrial era. Given a more favourable environment French would stand an excellent chance here, since the inferiority of the francophones is especially apparent by contrast with the superiority of their neighbours. On the world scene they rank among the best, but the absolute and solid superiority of the Anglo-Americans sets them down. Having been in contact, long before France, with the increasingly exciting progress of an English-speaking world, Quebec's francophones are con-demned, in order to avert assimilation, to be the eternal translators of a foreign mentality and vocabulary undergoing constant and incredibly rapid transformations. Hence the vital significance of the dictionary for the francophone Quebecer. He might well serve himself as a live dictionary for the entire francophone world. Dictionaries are, in a manner of speaking, the cemetery of language . . .

This accession then to the modern world is taking place at an awkward turn of the francophone demographic cycle. The birth rate, which had regularly been about thirty per thousand of population during the two previous decades, suddenly began to decline in 1965-66, dropping in 1968 to 16.3, one of the lowest indexes in North America. Furthermore, as a result of poor economic conditions, the net migration balance which had been favourable since 1954 began to swing downward, and it has been unfavourable for the past two years.

Demographic experts tend to be cautious about long-term predictions. Thus, in an article published in the November 4, 1969 issue of *Le Devoir*, which was the subject of much comment during the debate on Bill 63, Charbonneau, Henripin and Légaré formulated two sets of hypotheses, one favourable and the other unfavourable. According to the first, the percentage of francophones in the year 2000 would be virtually unchanged, whereas the second foresaw a considerable decline in the percentage of francophones in the province from 82.3% to 71.6%, and a drastic reduction of their numbers in Montreal from 66.4% to 52.7% which would at that time contain more than half the total population of Quebec.

How can one explain the anxiety felt in certain quarters about the demographic future of the francophone element in Quebec? It owes less to the actual situation or even to foreseeable trends than to the realization that the birth rate can no longer be counted on to safeguard the francophone position. Given the progressive aging of the population in the coming years, the natural growth of the francophone element will decline substantially unless the birth rate rises, and might even drop to nothing.

Thus the only long-term hope for the francophones lies in immigration. But even in Quebec the bulk of immigrants are integrated with the anglophones and, as a result of alterations in the employment structure as well as changes in the socio-economic character of immigrants, this trend has become stronger in recent years. The assimilating power of the francophones is so slight that the number of those among them who become anglicized in Quebec is greater than that of anglophones who adopt French (68,339 as against 53,383 according to the census of 1961, representing, however, only 1.6% of the total francophone population, as opposed to 9.4% of the anglophone population). To the extent that the demographic growth of francophone Quebecers depends on immigration, the future thus appears gloomy. Hence the pressure increasingly brought to bear upon governments for the adoption of measures designed to reverse current trends.

Apart from the problem of population, concern is also expressed about the quality of oral and written French. Some fear its "galloping bastardization"; others say that the language is improving thanks to the influence of better teaching and the electronic media; while yet others feel that the linguistic gap between the élite and the mass of the people is widening dramatically. Only scientific studies will enable us to establish these evolutionary trends, and the Gendron Commission is expected to shed light on this vitally important question.

It is admissible not to share these fears about the future of French in Quebec, yet it is impossible to prove that they are groundless. Demography, although a relatively exact science, helps to generate both alarmist and optimistic views. The truth is that we do not know if there exists a critical level below which a language cannot survive. Languages spoken by large numbers of people have nevertheless disappeared, while in other cases a few thousand individuals have managed to ensure the survival of some tongues. Besides, in the case of minor languages at least, the transition from a traditional to a modern society is always a period of crisis. There are important languages in Africa which industrialization and urbanization are threatening with extinction.

Now it is precisely at this critical moment of evolution that the fate of the French language in North America is being settled. A community long held back by its traditions is at last embracing modern ways — in an exceptionally favourable environment for all its plans. Yet a doubt persists: in the post-industrial society of tomorrow, are there any guarantees for the survival of French in Quebec? The answer to this question will require a collective decision, and it is up to the government to assume the burden as spokesman for the community.

The solution of the language problem in Quebec should be sought in final analysis at the economic and cultural levels. The prestige of a language is closely tied to the image of those who speak it, and in our own context that prestige is assessed according to economic criteria. Like the dollar, science and machines — it is said — speak English in North America. Insistence on the use of French by the business community in Quebec would, according to some, isolate it from the rest of a continent which does not know French, and ensure its debility. In replying to this criticism, one must distinguish between the knowledge of English and the use of it as a working language. Like it or not, the current international scientific and technological context favours the use of English. At a time when young Frenchmen, Germans, Italians and Japanese are learning English in order to improve their career prospects not only in the international field but in their respective countries as well, only an ignoramus or a fanatic would advise young Quebec francophones not to learn English. What seems abnormal, in my opinion, is that they should be told at the same time that they will have to earn their living in English in Quebec itself. While admitting the supremacy of English in the international business world and maintaining essential connections with this wide-ranging network of affairs, we should aim at establishing in the Quebec labour field a sufficiently broad francophone base so that French may be used as a language of work at every level. Francophone Quebecers may desire in addition to learn English in order to increase their mobility and pursue a more diversified career.

This is a legitimate ambition which must be differentiated nevertheless from the obligation of working in English in order to live a normal life in Quebec.

As long as Quebec's francophone element think of themselves as "beggars", they will have a beggar's mentality. And while one may take pity on beggars, few will extend sympathy to the point of becoming beggars themselves. One is not moved to integrate with a community or a people by a feeling of mercy, adopting its language as well as its style of thought and action. Nor can this be brought about by force. One has to be impelled by the conviction that this is a valid option materially and spiritually; that one is giving up one's nationality for an equal if not better way of life.

An investigation would no doubt substantiate in some measure the accuracy of impressions gained by observing the reaction towards "foreigners" and the "English": suspicion, aggressiveness, envy, feelings of inferiority, etc. But if this is true, what is the cause of such rather unflattering traits? Here we have to refer to history. Quebec's francophones must in one way or another settle their accounts with history. They must stop considering themselves a conquered people. There may be pity for the conquered party, but very few membership applications.

Quebec's francophones now accept the challenge of modern living but they cannot do so successfully by merely jettisoning the undisputed traditional values long associated with them. They must undertake the formidable task of transforming these characteristics, now outmoded and cumbersome, into new values better adapted to the times. They must fashion themselves a new soul. Should they reject this "conversion", they will become mere by-products of the fallout of American civilization, that is, human refuse. One may pity human scrap, but one is hardly inclined to join up with it.

The "denominational" character of public schools forms part of the traditional values that must be reassessed in the light of this orientation toward modern living. This question involves not only francophone Quebecers but also the children of immigrants who have to attend French public schools, and whose historical background contains quite different convictions about religious freedom and the schools question.

However, it would be a pity to waste time and energy on a new conflict over denominationalism. Efforts must be devoted instead to constructive tasks: improving the quality of teaching, creating a more meaningful popular culture and a liking for business, developing higher studies and the progress of scientific research in all fields. Folk cultures may be entertaining, but few are tempted to make them their own.

Nothing is more characteristic of the low prestige of French in Quebec than the eagerness of francophones to speak English at every opportunity. Persons of other tongues who want to speak French are almost unable to do so in Quebec unless they already know it well. Efforts designed to raise the value of French as a language of work will meet with apathy or, in some cases, with opposition from many francophones who are among the first to hold that the dollar "speaks" English in North America, and that this is quite all right. Those who suffer from cultural alienation may deserve sympathy, but they attract few imitators.

This long list of handicaps under which francophone Quebecers apparently labour may seem cruel, yet it corresponds sadly to reality. And it is not complete. We have here a community organized for its own "protection" and "preservation", but not for its "development". Having been trained to live curled up on itself, is it surprising that it should now be frightened by strange new developments? Or to be wondered at that it lacks absorptive capacity? An immigrant landing in Quebec or anywhere in America is first of all looking for security and freedom. He hopes to find here a promising future, a materially and spiritually enriching environment. He will inevitably gravitate toward those who best conform to the image he has of a free and prosperous people.

Objectives and Conditions

A coherent language program for Quebec has to comprise an option concerning the official status of languages, and calls for measures leading to the attainment of objectives having to do with the teaching language, the working language and the assimilative capacity of French.

1. *Official bilingualism*

The first question to settle is the choice between official bilingualism or French unilingualism within Quebec borders. One way or the other, this is apt to generate many acrimonious debates. This is certainly an important question because of the symbolic character it assumes, and of the moving force symbols of this nature are likely to engender.

It must be agreed, however, that whatever option is chosen the difference in practice might be very slight. Indeed, a declaration making French the only official language would have to be balanced with clauses defining English language rights, whereas the maintenance of bilingualism presupposes the adoption of measures aimed at making French the dominant language in Quebec. Whatever their own choice, if people are reasonable they will have to accept the constraints imposed by actual social conditions, which cannot be rejected with impunity.

The fact that Quebec is a part of Canada and that this country is increasingly strengthening its position as an officially bilingual entity not only at the federal level but in the two provinces containing the next largest numbers of francophones, New Brunswick and Ontario, should encourage Quebec to remain officially bilingual.

There is also a strategic aspect to this question. The official proclamation of French unilingualism is likely to create extreme concern among the anglophones, which would then have to be appeased by means of practical concessions that would not have to be offered if Quebec stayed officially bilingual.

2. *The language of instruction*

a) French should be the language of instruction for the children of all francophone parents. I am not aware that Quebec parents can invoke an inalienable right to the free choice of the language in which their children are educated. There are many bilingual countries where such freedom of choice does not exist, or else is subject to various restrictions. It does not appear, moreover, that any pressing demands have been made by the francophones to obtain a right not previously granted to them. This right was initiated, without sufficient study or caution, by Bill 63. Until then freedom of choice had been withheld on religious grounds which served also to safeguard the French language, since all francophone children were considered Catholic by law and in fact required to attend French schools.

To grant freedom of choice is to create an acquired right that could not subsequently be abolished, even if it had the most troublesome consequences, without grave prejudice to those who were accustomed to exercising it. If francophone parents are given the right to decide in which language their children will be educated, no one can foresee what choice the parents will finally make or what the situation will be five, ten or twenty years from now: the future of the French language on this continent is already too uncertain. It would be extremely dangerous to strike such a spark today and risk starting a blaze that could not later be controlled.

It may be objected that in the second volume of its report, the Commission on Bilingualism and Biculturalism recommended (Recommendation No. 9) "that parents have the right to choose for their children either the school of the majority or the school of the official language minority, if both exist in the locality".

The purpose of this principle is to promote bilingualism, not to create major problems for either one of the two official languages. It does not, in my view, take into account the true situation of the majority language in Quebec, particularly in Montreal. It seems to me, therefore, that it should not apply unilaterally in the case of the two official majorities. It should be judged legitimate and acceptable that, through laws enacted by the provincial assemblies and carrying the approval of a large majority of the public, this principle be balanced by restrictive clauses (New Brunswick might eventually have to do this as regards English) or even declared inoperative should the linguistic situation of the majority reasonably require it.

There are many restrictions of all kinds which citizens must accept for the good of all. The obligation for francophone parents to send their children to French schools should be looked upon as a constraint of that nature.

b) English should be the language of instruction for the children of all anglophone parents who so desire. The anglophones in Quebec have an acquired right to their own schools, which could not be abolished without serious injustice toward them and without exposing the entire community to a violent backlash. Furthermore, they have an excellent school system to the financing of which, given their high income, they contribute adequately. Following a recommendation of the Commission on Bilingualism and Biculturalism, the federal Government may grant a financial and technical compensation to the provinces to help them defray the additional costs of school systems for official minorities. Its educational autonomy being guaranteed, Quebec might take advantage of this aid.

There is also the fact that, since the English language is deeply anchored in North America and French is the language of the majority in Quebec, the children of anglophone parents should be given access to French schools.

Lastly, while the principle of English instruction for the children of anglophone parents seems to me indisputable, the organization of an appropriate school system for that purpose has sociological implications and raises problems of administrative efficiency.

c) An attempt should be made to ensure attendance at French schools by the greatest possible number of children from immigrant families whose mother tongue is not English. Various means of persuasion and dissuasion should be used to encourage the immigrants to opt for a French education. Perhaps a special tax might be levied on parents whose children attend English schools. Although our experience with bilingual schools in Canada has not been encouraging, such schools might be established and would probably be attended by the children of immigrants from countries where bilingualism is currently the rule. Should it turn out despite every effort to be impossible to attract a substantial number of these children to French schools, more radical measures of coercion would have to be resorted to. As a matter of principle, such attendance might be made obligatory, but this would be a hard rule to apply, at least while there are still English schools. Moreover, the existence of such a measure might well dissuade immigrants from settling in Quebec. A study of immigrant motivation should doubtless be conducted in order to assess the possible results of such a measure and, should the need arise, to facilitate the choice of means likely to prevent the undesirable effects foreseen.

d) The children of all anglophones and immigrants should acquire a working knowledge of French, and steps should be taken to bring this about. French could be taught in English schools from the earliest grades; summer camps could be established for the practical use of French, etc. Various penalties might also be imposed on those who have not acquired adequate knowledge of French after five years or more of residence in Quebec. They might, for example, be ineligible for graduation diplomas, in which case the impartiality of the tests and of the persons giving them would have to be guaranteed.

Once the knowledge of their mother tongue is assured, young franco-phones should be given every opportunity to learn English, since it will in all probability remain the principal working language of the continent on which the francophones will spend their lives. Its knowledge will, therefore, be required for the full and free exercise of most professions. Furthermore, as the language of technology and to a great extent of science and politics, English has become the foremost *lingua franca* in the world.

3. *The language of work*

Let us first set out the objectives which should guide our steps in this field. Bill No. 63 "for the promotion of the French language in Quebec" provides that "the French Language Board should under the direction of the Minister . . . *b)* advise the government on any legislative or administrative measure that might be adopted in order to make French the language of work in all public and private enterprises in Quebec; *c)* develop, in consultation with these enterprises, programs designed to ensure that French is the language of work, and to impart to their managers and employees a practical knowledge of that language; . . . *d)* establish a language research centre and coordinate throughout Quebec all research activity in this field." Also worthy of note is Recommendation No. 42 in volume III of the report of the Commission on Bilingualism and Biculturalism, regarding *The Work World,* which reads as follows:

> We recommend that in the private sector in Quebec, governments and industry adopt the objective that French become the principal language of work at all levels, and that in pursuit of this objective the following principles be accepted: *a)* that French be the principal language of work in the major institutions of the province; *b)* that, consequently, the majority of work units in such firms that until now have used English as the principal language of work in the middle and upper levels become French-language units; and that such firms designate all management and senior positions as posts that require bilingual incumbents; *c)* that the majority of smaller or specialized firms should use French as their language of work, but that there should be a place for firms where the language of work is English, as there should be a place anywhere in Canada for such firms where the language of work is French; and *d)* that the main language of work in activities related to operations outside the province remain the choice of the enterprise.

For its part, the counter-draft to the defunct "Bill 85", submitted by the Parti Québécois, stipulated that "French is the principal language of economic activity" (Section 1, sub-section 1).

Although the phrasing varies, these three recommendations all have the same purpose: promoting French as the language of work in Quebec in order to make it, in the words of Bill 63, the "language of current use" in any enterprise, or according to the more cautious wording of the Commission on Bilingualism and Biculturalism "the principal language of work at all levels", or again according to the Parti Québécois "the principal language of economic activity". There may be better ways of defining this objective, but this one has the merit of clarity. The aim is to ensure that French really becomes the language of work in Quebec.

The essential concern, therefore, bears on the means of establishing and developing this francophone work base in Quebec. This is a very complex question requiring for its solution an accurate knowledge that we do not yet possess of all the practical problems involved. We should, therefore, tackle it without delay, since 75% of Quebec's francophones are unilingual, and those who are bilingual find it seriously inconvenient for the most part to use English. This represents, of course, a guarantee for the survival of French in the province. When two languages are thus spoken in close contact, only the existence of substantial unilingual groups can ensure that neither one disappears. The advent of integral bilingualism in Quebec would mark the end of French in North America.

One must distinguish clearly, first of all, between the many possible fashions and levels of familiarity with a language, and then differentiate language requirements according to the types of enterprises and activities involved. The ultimate aim of this process of discrimination is to facilitate the adoption of French in firms that have heretofore operated in English. It also aims at discovering the circumstances required so that a firm may adopt French as its principal language of work, and what is meant by the expressions "language of work" and "predominantly francophone enterprise".

The degree of mastery one must have of a second language in order to use it as a language of work is often greatly exaggerated. The misconceptions held by anglophones on this subject, often as a result of views expressed by francophones, must be dispelled. To require that an anglophone have an advanced knowledge of French in order to be able to work in that language would be to invite failure for any program of reform. It is hardly by such radical means that the anglophones on this continent succeeded in converting to the use of English tens of thousands of persons of other languages and cultures. True, the social and economic context favoured the use of English, whereas it is prejudicial to French. That is the reason why, as regards the development of French, one cannot trust to the normal course of events. One must endeavour in some way to reproduce systematically in various enterprises conditions favouring the use of French, similar to those that the balance of affairs has so long maintained in favour of English.

That is why it should be easier to implant the use of French in business by opting for institutional rather than individual bilingualism. A firm could thus operate in French without all of its members being obliged to know French, or even to know it perfectly in order to use it as a language of work. The choice of institutional bilingualism would permit an optimal utilization of all degrees of linguistic ability. Between persons who understand and read the second language (passive bilingualism) and those who speak and write it easily (active bilingualism), or again between those who have a partial knowledge of the second language restricted to their work requirements (functional bilingualism) and others who know it perfectly (total bilingualism), there is a broad and fruitful range of language abilities which, properly employed, should facilitate the language conversion of any firm and reduce the stress on individuals. The institutional bilingualism option requires a definition of the linguistic capacity demanded for each job, and the assurance that all employees have the necessary language qualification to do their work satisfactorily: the elevator operator, the foreman, the engineer, the personnel director, the sales manager and the president of the firm are all concerned with different types of oral and

written communication. Each of these functions carries special language
requirements and a correlative vocabulary.

Besides, language conditions vary enormously according to the different
firms. There are firms that have been in operation since the establishment
of an anglophone community in Quebec, and must be regarded in a
special light: such are, for example, enterprises of a cultural character
(newspapers, radio or television) and the anglophone educational establish-
ments, or again small firms of all kinds located in an anglophone environment, whose staff and customers are anglophone. Head offices of firms
offer another case in point, and because of their importance to the enterprise as a whole, require special consideration. Here a distinction should be
made between headquarters' operations directed abroad, often the more
numerous and significant, and, in the case of firms that have branches in
Quebec, operations relating directly to their environment. Furthermore,
language requirements may differ considerably according to whether these
are manufacturing, financial, professional or service organizations. One
must also take into consideration the geographical location of the firm and
distinguish between different types of activities, since language demands
vary substantially according to whether plant, office, management or
collective agreement operations are involved. Finally, one must take into
account the orientation of communications, internal or external, vertical
or horizontal, addressed to special clients or the general public, and so on.

This question of the language of work is clearly a very complex one.
Discrimination of the different possible categories, and the placement of
firms and activities within these categories, is an operation requiring time
and expert knowledge. Unless one proceeds with caution, there is the risk
of becoming locked in sterile discussions, and of generating antagonisms
that would prevent reaching any valid solution. Such a task is beyond the
normal capacity of individual firms as it is of the regular public service. It
is unsound to divide responsibility for the promotion of French between
three different branches of the public service, as is presently the case in
Quebec. Nor is it appropriate for the Prime Minister either to engage in
personal dialogue with individual firms about the use of French, as he did
last autumn, or to announce along the way technical details concerning
the implementation of French programs by a particular firm. There is no
need for special legislation with respect to language of work requirements,
the present law for the promotion of French in Quebec being at least
adequate in that regard. It would be enough to amend the labour code in
such a way as to require that French be used in the collective bargaining
process, as the Quebec management council itself recommended in a recent
statement. However, in order to ensure the wider use of French throughout the labour field a broad, systematic and concerted effort will be
required.

That is why, as the Commission on Bilingualism and Biculturalism has
recommended, there must be appointed a special action group responsible
for defining the scope of the objective according to circumstances prevailing in each category of enterprise; for providing appropriate information and

technical assistance needed to reach the objective; for counselling advertising and publicity services about the use of French terms; for locating experts whom the firms might need to attain the objective, etc. This action group will also exercise such control as seems proper in order to ensure that the necessary measures are carried out efficiently and on time.

The action group will comprise representatives of business, unions, the universities and the government. It will be established by the government with the status of an independent and permanent board. It will submit an annual report to the National Assembly on the exercise of its mandate. Its members will be appointed for a period of five or seven years, and may not be dismissed except on evidence of incompetence or prejudice.

As an independent board, the action group will enjoy State support without interference by the government of the day, and will be protected from the hazards of political life. Moreover, it will have a freer hand by not being subject to the delays and hesitations of administrative services. It will have a higher degree of credibility among private firms. Lastly, it will be more exposed to public scrutiny and subject to control by public opinion.

The practical measures to be adopted will of course vary according to the different categories of firms and operations. The following seem to be among the more promising: the organization of special mobile teams charged with assisting and advising firms in the implementation of their French language programs, notably as regards the establishment of francophone units and the identification of strategic jobs from the linguistic standpoint; the preparation by experts employed by the language board, in consultation with the firms, of special French textbooks and vocabularies for management training programs; the listing of key words for different classes of employment, for publicity, labelling, posters, collective agreements, etc.

The federal Government itself has a special responsibility concerning the language of work in Quebec. It must ensure that French is the principal language used in federal undertakings and offices in Quebec; that the francophone population is served in French; and project a French image in Quebec as well as in francophone countries. Moreover, the federal Government might act as spokesman for Quebec with private enterprise in Ontario and abroad, especially the United States, drawing to their attention the fact that French is the basic language of economic activity in Quebec.

These and similar measures taken by business firms with the continuing assistance of the language board will reduce the psychological tension experienced by francophones who have to use English as a language of work, and enhance their career opportunities. However, were this reform movement to be limited to the linguistic field, it would accomplish only half the task required for a complete revaluation of French. Beyond language, there is in fact the problem of culture, and the dominant culture of any organization is that of its executives. This raises with particular emphasis the problem of big business control in Quebec. It is essential, through the increase of public and private investments and the improvement of manage-

ment ability, to extend the control by French-Canadians of private enterprise.

Efforts by Quebecers to make French the principal language of work in
business enterprises comes into conflict with the interests, prejudices and
fears of anglophone and even francophone businessmen. Avoiding needless
provocation, it would be wiser to try to convince these persons of the
legitimacy and realistic character of these efforts. The reforms to be
accomplished will require both money and time. On the technical plane
at least, the State will be called upon through its language board to assist
firms for a certain length of time. These firms, of course, have well-defined
responsibilities to the community in which they are established and prosper-
ing. And in the final analysis, it is the firms that will be the first to benefit
from the improved status of French as the language of work. Enabled at
last to contribute to the common undertaking in their mother tongue, the
francophone employees will indeed be off to a quicker and better start in
their careers, and will give a more efficient performance throughout their
life.

4. *The assimilative capacity*

All efforts to promote French as the language of instruction and work
would be more or less useless if one were to overlook a third point
directly concerned with French as a language of adoption. It is probably in
dealing with this third aspect that the root of the trouble may be uncovered
and acted upon.

The diagnosis is as follows: francophone Quebecers have no assimilative
capacity. One is surprised to note how superficial are the reasons advanced
until now to explain this phenomenon, and how inefficient the steps
proposed to remedy the situation. There is need to consider this question
without delay.

At first sight, the situation of the francophone Quebecers is paradoxical:
here is a community which has an overwhelming popular majority in the
province, yet must be protected in order to ensure, if not its survival, at
least its normal development. This dual phenomenon of an "overwhelming
majority" and of "a community in need of protection" gives weight to the
theories of "foreign occupation" of the territory, as of Anglo-American
"colonialism". In every situation of this kind, whether the case be that of
Eastern Europe under the iron rule of Germany and Russia, of "colonial"
Africa or of "exploited" South America, politics provide the solution. I
share the opinion of those who feel that Quebec has not known how to
use to best advantage all the possibilities inherent in Canada's political
framework, either at the federal or the provincial level. It nevertheless
remains to be demonstrated that the Quebec community could achieve
full development within the limits of a Canadian confederation. A functional approach to politics is probably the best that might be conceived in the
present circumstances. Yet it is essential to state the problems accurately,
to clearly define the objectives, and to take courageous action.

The root causes of the trouble must be dealt with first, if the promotion of French is to succeed and these are of a political, economic and

cultural character. Now the primary source of any corrective action — one is tempted to say redemptive — is the State. But the State alone would be powerless: it needs the support of all the major social institutions — especially industry, the labour unions, and the universities. It is not the worth of the individual Quebecer that is in question: he has demonstrated in the past that he is endowed with surprising physical and spiritual qualities. The shadow of doubt lies on the social cadres: groups, institutions and leaders in all fields.

The promotion of French in Quebec is thus indestructibly linked with the progress of society itself. When French becomes socially useful, non-francophones will need no urging to learn the language. A language policy must, of course, be formulated and applied, but the legislative safeguards will seem less odious and be more effective — some may even become superfluous — if their implementation is accompanied by a broad economic, social and cultural move toward the use of French.

Quebec would run a dangerous risk if the two main aspects of the problem — the linguistic and the socio-political — were to be dissociated. Legislation on languages alone, even applied with perseverence and courage, will not produce the anticipated results. Uncontrollable waves of mounting frustration will then appear. It is the failure of politics that is the true cause of direct action and violence. The challenge is a formidable one, but it must be met.

LANGUAGES IN CONTACT: POLISH AND ENGLISH

Yvonne Grabowski
Department of Foreign Literature
York University

Although there are well over 300,000 people of Polish descent in Canada, there have been no studies of Canadian Polish. The only works on Polish and English in contact discuss Polish as spoken by bilinguals in the United States.[1] The materials collected by these studies are applicable in Canada only to a certain extent. Conditions under which Polish immigration to Canada took place and the way English influenced the language of the Polish immigrants and their descendants, have not been similar in both countries. The main difference can be said to lie in the scope of linguistic interference which in Canada has not been so pronounced as in the United States. Also the integration of English loans into Polish has been less extensive and the English patterns have as a rule been less firmly established.

This is mainly due to the fact that English and Polish have been in contact in Canada for a considerably shorter period than in the United States. Polish immigration to Canada is more recent and the number of immigrants is much smaller. Canada has only a few large Polish amalgamations in cities. There are no such great Polish communities as in Chicago or Newark with their complex net of Polish schools, community centres, institutions and communications media.

As a result of this situation a number of loan words and constructions, quite common and established in American Polish, appear in Canada only sporadically or do not appear at all. Canadian Polish sounds less strange to the ear of a visitor from Poland than does American Polish. Another factor affecting the development of Canadian Polish in the last two decades is the more prominent role played by the new wave of post-war immigration which culturally, intellectually, and above all, linguistically, was superior to the old, which consisted mainly of individuals from the poor and un-educated strata of society.

Polish language as spoken in Canada is certainly too vast a subject to be covered in one paper. Therefore I shall have to limit myself to pointing out general tendencies of development and confine the illustration of these points to examples taken from the speech of Polish Canadians in Toronto, Hamilton, Kitchener and Ottawa. This paper is based on the data collected from about one hundred informants from these cities, as well as on materials collected from meetings, radio broadcasts, church announce-ments and similar sources.

The informants chosen from the Polish community could be roughly divided into two groups: 1) the actual immigrants, whose primary language system is Polish and 2) the first generation of Polish Canadians. The latter group includes not only people born in Canada, but also those who came here at an early age and whose primary language system is English.[2] Both groups might be further subdivided into the so-called old immigration, that is people who themselves, or whose parents, came here before the beginning of the Second World War. The frequency of lexical and grammatical interference is highest in this group since its members had little formal education and no special linguistic awareness. The so-called new immigration—people who have come to Canada since the War and their children—consists mainly of the intelligentsia. Members of this group make a conscious effort to keep the two language systems apart, though, quite naturally, they are not as successful as they would like to be.

The scope of this paper does not permit me to go any deeper into the various groups and factors affecting the speech of Polish Canadians. It should be remembered, however, that Polish as spoken in Canada varies from group to group and from individual to individual depending on the degree of education received, the profession of the speaker, the occasions on which Polish is spoken and the individual's length of stay in Canada.

The Sound System

Phonic interference is very limited in the speech of the bilingual immigrants. They tend to keep most of the features of their sound system intact, including even the peculiarities of their dialect. They tend to integrate the English loan words completely into the Polish sound system. Although attempts to reproduce correctly the English phonemes of a loan are made by many immigrants of the new immigration, these attempts are often not successful.

Among people with English as their primary system, instances of interference are extremely common. In some cases one set of phonemes is used for both languages—English and Polish. Many of the speakers of the first generation tend to introduce the English vowel system wholesale into Polish including diphthongs. However, a general tendency among the speakers of the first generation is to have a mixed set of phonemes. This mixture varies from individual to individual, but the general trend is to identify English phonemes with those of Polish that have a similar point of articulation and are thus felt to be "similar".[3]

As far as the Polish palatalized consonants are concerned the tendency is towards obliterating or lessening the distinction between the hard and soft consonants. This tendency is less pronounced in certain groups of phonemes. Most of the informants distinguished very well between the soft and hard nasals /m/ /m'/ /n/ /n'/. The distinction was less pronounced with the labial and labiodental stops and fricatives /p/ /p'/ /b/ /b'/ /v/ /v'/ /f/ /f'/. However, only a few informants made no difference at all between such pairs as /lub'i/ and /luby/. The velar and palatal stops /k/ /g/ become as a rule hardened (kedy) for (k'edy), (v'igylja). There is also a tendency to pronounce these stops with aspiration (kʰedy).

Alveolar and palatal fricatives and affricates of which Polish has twelve present the greatest difficulty. /s, s', š, z, z', ž, c, c', č, dz, dz', dž/ become reduced to the number of seven: /s, š, z, ž, dž, c, č. There is a tendency to over-palatalize the /s'/ /c'/ /z'/ and /dź/ sounds /dženkuje/ /yaš/ /čoča/.[4] Many speakers make an attempt to differentiate between phonemes like /š/ and /s'/. The result of such attempts are soft palatalized affricates and fricatives /š'/ /ž'/ /č'/ /Kaž'u/.[4] These are not special allophones of /š/ /ž/ and /č/ but separate phonemes, used by bilinguals of the first generation only in their Polish speech and never appearing in their English.

The lateral English /l/ often becomes substituted for both the Polish semivowel /w/ as in /ladny/ instead of /wadni/, and for the Polish /l/. As a rule such speakers use the English back allophone of /l/ as in the words *hall, ball* for the Polish /w/ phoneme, and the allophone of /l/ appearing in the words like *lot* for the Polish /l/. The English bilabial /w/ phoneme is very rarely identified with the Polish /w/ phoneme. This appears to be the influence of the written form of these words.

I would like to say here a few words about the phonic adaptation of the English loan words into Polish. Many substitutions for loan words are made on such a straightforward basis that they do not require a special discussion; as when /yard/ becomes /jart/. However, in other cases there seems to reign a great confusion. This is especially true with regard to the English mellow fricatives /Ø/ and /b/. These can be rendered in Polish as /t/ and /d/: /tik/ for *thick* and /brader/ for *brother*. They can also be transferred as /s/ and /z/: sri/ for *three*, /sotful/ for *thoughtful*, /viz/ for *with*. The third combination is the /c/ /dz/ rendition /cik/ for *thick* and /dzer/ for *there* (on je dzer). In a few cases it has been observed that the voiceless fricative /Ø/ was pronounced as /tx/ /batxurst/.

Some of the vowels present a similar difficulty. The English barred i /i/ can be rendered either as /i/ or /y/: /drynk/ /byznes/, but also /b'iznes/ /perm'it/ /f'iksovač/. The /ae/ as in *ham* can be rendered either by /a/ or /e/. The old immigration is inclined to use the /e/, the new has a preference for /a/. Thus we have multiple double forms /hem/ and /ham/, /stent/ and /stant/. Both the /ɔ/ and /o/ phonemes are reduced to the Polish /o/. The /u/ and /u'/ are reduced to the Polish /u/ /bučer/, /kuler/. There may be, however, an occasional quantitative change as in /su:sy/.

The greatest variegation can be observed in the /shwa/ phoneme which can be rendered by /e/, /a/, /o/, /u/ and /y/. The most common rendering is /o/ or /e/ especially among the old immigration: *fornes, fork, kontry, lonč, or fernas, gerlsa.* However other versions are also common especially among the new immigration: /lanč/ or even /lunč/, /trak/ or /truk/, /kostomer/ and /kustomer/. The forms are obviously influenced by the graphic shapes of the English words borrowed. The influence of the graphemic shape can also be seen in the rendering of the English bilabial /w/ by the Polish /v/ onevejka/[5] /viski/.

Morphology and Grammar Relations

The English morphemes transferred into Polish are as a rule of the un-bound type. The use of unbound English morphemes is fairly common even among those immigrants whose knowledge of English is limited to a few words. In daily use are: (oh tak) under the influence of *oh yes*, (šur), (no), (bay), (o:key). The transfer in (oh tak) includes quantitative changes in the Polish vowel and the English intonation pattern. (o:key) is trans-ferred with its English stress.

The English loans can be either adjusted to the Polish morpho-phonemic system or can be inserted as "quotes" unaffected by the Polish morphology. This latter trend is much in evidence among more educated speakers as well as recent arrivals when they wish to be particularly careful about their speech. However, even uneducated speakers may use English words as "quotation" forms. The situation results in an abundance of double forms such as *grocery, grosernia, byłem na shopping plaza, byłem na shopping plazie*, even in the speech of the same individual.

The most common loan words are nouns. There exists a considerable fluctuation in the gender of the adopted nouns except for animate nouns, where *the nurse* quite predictably becomes /nersa/ or /norsa/ and where forms like /bos/ or /forman/ stay masculine. With inanimate nouns the gender depends often on the English form of the loan. *Parking, bojler, bond, stop, stend* are masculine. For the same reason Toronto, Peter-borough, and bungalow are neuter (o ending).[6] Sometimes the neuter is also used when the word has not been integrated into the Polish system: /montovane šassis/. Loan words with the English suffixes *-tion, -sion* become feminine in Canadian Polish under the influence of the Polish suffixes *-cja, -zja*. Thus *egzaminacja, telewizja, donacja, transportacja. Plaza* is feminine because of its *a* ending. Other nouns may adopt the gender of the Polish word they are displacing. Thus *sztryta* and *lota* are feminine because *ulica* and *dzialka* or *parcela* are feminine. *Kara* has acquired its gender because of the North American habit of referring to the car as she.[7] Quite often two variants of the same word exists with two genders. Thus /šop/ and /šopa/, /lodž/, /lodža/ /inč/ and /inča/. Even when the original English ending of the loan word remains unchanged, the word may still have two genders: /ta klač/ and /ten klač/, /moja kotedž/ and /muy kotedž/.[8]

Among the noun suffixes the most productive for generating new words is the masculine ending *-ista*, the feminine *-na, -nia, -a, -ka: unia, onevejka, farmerka, plasterka, dystylarnia, groçernia, czipizna*, and the neuter suf-fixes *-nie* and *-stvo: bukmacherstwo, drajwowanie, serwowanie, plasterowanie.*

Diminutive suffixes are much less productive, but there are still in evidence: *darlinguś, ofisik.*

Some Polish nouns, regardless of their gender, may become un-declinable under the influence of English: *Proszę dzwonić do Leon Kucharski, Pani Zwolinski nie ma w domu.* This happens predominantly with first names and family names.

Many loans become transferred into Polish in their plural form, such as /šusy/, /stempsy/ or /stampsy/, /pičesy/, /krakersy/, /čipsy/. Some of those nouns are used in plural only, such as /taytsy/ or /nyusy/. With others, the English plural marker which has lost its meaning is kept even in the singular. The singular of /p'ilsy/ is /p'ilsa/. Similarly, we have /čips/, /krakers/, /p'ičes/, /čersa/. Still other forms drop their English plural marker in the singular: the singular of /boysy/ is /boy/, of /stepsy/ is /step/.[9]

The verbs are the second largest group borrowed from English. The only creative suffix appears to be *-ować: mufować, klinować, pejntować, rentować.*[10] The verbs become as a rule adapted to the Polish verbal system. Forms like *zaorderować, wysprejować, nasprejować, posprejovać, wyklinować, wypejntować* are quite common. Some verbs seem to be less integrated into the Polish system, as for instance *fiksować* or *mufować* and are used only in their imperfective form for both the perfective and imperfective aspect. Among the bilinguals whose primary language system is English, there is a general tendency to reduce the highly complex Polish verbal system to the imperfective aspect only.

The number of adjectival loans in Canadian Polish is limited, even more limited than in American Polish. However, many new adjectives are being constantly generated by subjecting English words to Polish derivation. Three adjectival suffixes appear to be most productive—*owy: jetowy, byznesowy; -ski* and *-cki: farmerski, torontoński, montrealski, kebecki;* and *-ny: rezydencyjny, komercjalny, profesjonalny, milenijny, misyjny.*[11] Sometimes nouns can be generated by derivation from English adjectives, for instance /čip'izna/ (cheap trashy goods), or adjectives may be coined from other parts of speech: *fed up, spedupiały*, even *fedupny*.

Transfers of other parts of speech have been noticed only sporadically: prepositions, some numerals.

English grammatical relations exercise a much greater influence on Canadian Polish than many bilinguals are aware of or would care to admit. Changes of modulation are common among speakers of the first generation. They are not so frequent among the immigrants. English contour patterns for questions of the type:

"When are you going home?"

are often used for Polish questions instead of using the Polish rising contour. A rising contour is frequently used for statements which demand a falling contour in Polish. With some speakers the shift of modulation is so complete that to a listener standing at a slight distance away they seem to be talking in English. With others the influence of English can be noticed mainly in the pitch of voice which sounds monotonous by not being subject to the more rapid changes of Polish.

The general tendency among bilinguals is to attempt to identify English grammatical categories with Polish ones. Once the identification has been made by a bilingual, he has the tendency to apply the Polish form in the grammatical functions derived from English. Thus sentences or phrases such as *Ja to mam zrobione; karty kredytowe akceptowane, or pieniądze trzymane w banku są chronione przed ogniem, pieniądze trzymane w domu nie są*, are the direct result of identification of the role of past participle in English and Polish.

Similarly phrases like: *przepis do gotowania, zawiadomienie do Polonii, pracuję z obiema rękami, jestem na telefonie, wcieraj Roxodium na miejsca bolące, zabieraj to precz*, result from the identification of English prepositions with what are felt to be their Polish equivalents: *for* and *do, with* and *z, on* and *na, away* and *precz*. There is a strong trend in Canadian Polish to use prepositional constructions in cases where such use is unwarranted in standard Polish. *Dał to do tatusia, skład z meblami.*

Possessive pronouns abound in the speech of Polish Canadians in sentences where they would sound superfluous in standard Polish *Wyjął książkę z jego kieszeni.*

The identification of grammatical functions causes an obliteration of distinctions which are obligatory in Polish, but not in English. The failure to distinguish cases is especially common among bilinguals of the first generation. The nominative may be used not only for accusative and genetive, but also for all other cases. The case markers may even become redistributed and attached to forms with which they would never appear in S.P. *koniów, nauczycielków, doma.* A similar confusion reigns in the domain of the verb, where frequentative and perfective aspects tend to be forgotten, and passive voice becomes extended to cases where Polish uses impersonal constructions.

Lexical Changes

The massive introduction of English loans and the transfer of new concepts and translation of English words and phrases are the most obvious changes that occurred in Canadian Polish. The greatest number of loans pass into Canadian Polish on a straightforward transfer basis, with their phonemic shape also imported or with a partial or complete substitution of Polish phonemes.[12] These words often become integrated into Canadian Polish by means of derivation or affixation. Whole phrases such as *rummage sale, take it easy*, are also being transferred.

The second important group consists of semantic loans where a new meaning of the word already existing in Polish is introduced under the influence of English. The number of semantic loans in Canadian Polish is quite considerable since Polish possesses numerous Latin and French loans with a strong phonetic resemblance to English terms.

English	Can. P.	Meaning in S.P.
rate	rata	installment
application	aplikacja	type of stitch
blanket	blankiet	form
actual	aktualny	topical
eventual	ewentualny	probable

The previous meaning of the word in Polish was in some cases close enough to facilitate the transfer:

English	Can. P.	Meaning in S.P.
lunatic	lunatyk	sleepwalker
licence	licencja	permit
argument	argument	argumentation
question	kwestionować	to put in doubt

In other cases the meaning of the term became extended:

English	Can. P.	Meaning in S.P.
division	dywizja	former meaning *army* division only
department	departament	formerly a department of ministry only
student	student	university student
matron	matrona	old matron
absolutely	absolutnie	used in the negative sense only

Loan translations are also fairly common in Canadian Polish especially in the speech of the first generation. Loan translations may be either single words such as *podłoga* for *floor*, or whole phrases and expressions (syntactic substitution):

Bliźniaczy brat,—twin brother
stacja gazolinowa—gasoline station
płytki podłogowe—floor tiles
osobiste konto czekowe—personal checking account
salon piękności—beauty parlour
kobieta trzydzieści lat stara—a woman thirty years old
kaplica Pełnej Ewangelii—(Full Gospel Tabernacle)
wziąłem zdjęcie—I took a picture
kobieta do wszystkich prac domowych—a woman for all household work

Compound loans where only a part of the expression is translated are rather rare in Canadian Polish.

po-graduacyjny	for post graduate
stereo-szafka	for stereo-cabinet

Such loans are much more common in Standard Polish. In the last decade a marked tendency was observed to replace some of the translation loans by independent Polish forms where the English term only prompted a hybrid Polish creation:

księgowy przysięgły	chartered accountant
herbatka ogrodowa	garden party

Conclusion

The general amount of interference of English on Polish is not so pronounced as it may seem at first sign. The greatest influence of English can be felt in the domain of vocabulary, with nouns forming the most important part of all the loans. It is the comparatively high incidence of loan-words that produces the effect of strangeness on recent arrivals and accounts for difficulties in communication between the Polish Canadians and their relatives in the old country.

Phonic influence of English is only pronounced among the children of immigrants. English grammar relations exert a much greater influence on Canadian Polish than the English phonemic system. However, grammar relations and categories based on the English patterns are not permanently established. Their frequency varies from group to group and speaker to speaker, and they very often alternate in the speech of the same individual with Polish patterns. In general, in comparison with American Polish, Canadian Polish displays a much greater fluctuation of forms and a greater number of co-existing alternate patterns.

In the last few years under the impact of closer contact with Poland, visits of relatives and greater availability of Polish books and papers, certain Polish speech patterns and items of vocabulary have become reinforced. Many terms which practically disappeared or were on the verge of disappearance about ten years ago now have made a comeback. Words like *parcela, hipoteka, komisowe*, which ten years ago had almost become obsolete in Canadian Polish have now reappeared. The most recently recovered words are *śródmieście* for *downtown*, and *tapetowanie* for *wallpapering*. The forms created under the influence of English seem in such cases to be either slowly receding or manage to co-exist, as for instance in the case of *kotary* and *drapes*. A conscious effort appears to be made by bilingual immigrants to keep the two language systems more apart. There has been a considerable reinforcement of Polish patterns in the press and radio programs. Since this is a fairly recent development it is still hard to tell what influence it is going to exert on Canadian Polish.

Some General Conclusions concerning Russian, Polish and Ukrainian

Studies of three Slavic languages spoken in Canada testify to similar patterns of development in Ukrainian, Polish and Russian. The most conspicuous trait is the influence of English vocabulary. All three languages have acquired a considerable number of English loan-words which are subject to various degrees of integration. Integration is affected chiefly by means of suffixation, although prefixation and derivation are also fairly common processes.

Both phonology and morphology of Ukrainian, Polish and Russian has been influenced by English. English allophones are used chiefly by the first generation speakers to replace native phonemic distinctions, and English phonemes felt to be "similar" are introduced into the Slavic languages. In morphology, apart from the tendency toward borrowing unbound morphemes, the influence of English is manifested also in an indirect manner, such as confusion in the gender of nouns, reduction and redistribution of infinitive, conjugational, case and plural markers. In syntax there is a tendency to replace synthetic constructions by analytic ones as well as to use syntactic translations from English.

Of all the Slavic languages of Canada, Ukrainian has the most established patterns at variance with standard Ukrainian and displays the strongest influence of English. This is due mainly to two causes: a) the length of time Ukrainian has been used in Canada, and b) the number of people of Ukrainian origin (surpassing that of any other Slavic group), many of them settled in closely-knit communities.

Canadian Polish shows fewer established patterns differing from Standard Polish. In comparison with Canadian Ukrainian and American Polish, Canadian Polish displays a considerable degree of syntactic and morphological fluctuation. Multiple forms coexist and are used alternatively.

Canadian Russian, due to the fairly short period of contact, displays comparatively few signs of established forms and a minimal amount of integration of loans. The changes in Canadian Russian due to the English influence vary almost from person to person.

The influence of the new waves of Ukrainian, Polish and Russian immigrants has strengthened the three languages and made them less prone to interference. However this reinforcement of speech patterns can probably be looked upon as temporary.

NOTES

[1] The most important among these are Doroszewski's *Jezyk polski w Stanach Zjednoczonych*, published in 1938; and two Ph.D. theses, one by W. Sklodowski, "O niektórych faktach fonetycznych języka polskiego w związku z czynikami kształtującymi język emigracji" (University of Ottawa, 1951), and the other by Franciszek Lyra, "English and Polish in Contact" (Indiana University, 1962).

[2] Group 1 shall be referred to in this paper as immigrants, group 2 as the first generation. Although technically people who came to Canada at an early age should be classified as immigrants, they are considered in this paper as members of group 2, for linguistic reasons, since they switch very early to English as their primary language system.

[3] In this manner English consonants become identified with Polish hard consonants, and English "short" vowels with the Polish vowels.

	English	Polish
Thus:	(ph)	(p)
	(th)	(t)
	(r)	(r)
	(ɔ)	(o) etc.

[4] Unfamiliar clusters of consonants also become reduced: /stšela/ becomes /ščela/, and /čsima/ becomes /čima/.

[5] For *one way street*.

6 There is one exception to this rule in Canadian Polish, which has been already noticed by Doroszewski, the suffix *-ista*, polonized from English *-ist*, independently from Standard Polish: *radykalista, fotografista, profesjonalista, unista, unionista, byznesista.*

7 The gender of the loanword in Canadian Polish may differ from the gender of the same word in American Polish: *piczes* and *piczesa, boks* and *boksa.* American Polish shows a stronger tendency towards supplying a one-syllable English loan with a feminine ending which acts as a support vowel.

8 In such cases usually the feminine gender is undeclinable: Byłem na /kotedžu/, *bez własnej* /kotedž/ *nie da rady.*

9 The singular of /d'ip'isy/ has two forms: /d'ip'is/ and /d'ip'i/; the second is undeclinable.

10 The only two exceptions observed are *sfedupieć*, a verbal derivation from *fed up*, and *dropnąć* from *to drop* to indicate a short isolated action.

11 Standard Polish has created about the same time its own forms in the last two cases: *misjonarski* and *millennialny.*

12 This is a practice much more common in Canadian than in American Polish, especially among educated speakers.

2 Education & Religion

AN INTRODUCTION TO EDUCATION AND ETHNICITY

C. J. Jaenen
Department of History
University of Ottawa

The following are two very interesting and important papers in the area of the educational experience of select ethnic groups in Canada. The groups under discussion are located in Quebec and in British Columbia. From an educational point of view this is rather significant because these provinces are the extremities, so to speak, of the spectrum of educational philosophy and practice. Quebec has a dual confessional system with no non-sectarian state schools, and it operates both English and French public schools — that is at one end of the spectrum. British Columbia, at the other end of the spectrum, has by its own declaration in the latest Public Schools Act "separation of church and state" (a doctrine enunciated nowhere else in Canada and probably unconstitutional), and you are all familiar with Premier W.A.C. Bennett's remark concerning bilingualism in B.C.: it could refer only to English and Chinese.

What we want to know now is simply this: how do minority groups and small ethnic communities fare under these very different systems? It is probably appropriate that for the western Canadian region, which is generally regarded as being multi-ethnic, Professors Dahlie and Wilson have elected to study three groups, not one minority. By the same token, it is appropriate that Dr. Kage should focus on one of the English-speaking minorities in Quebec. In each case religious, ethnic and other socio-cultural factors are involved; in the case of the Jewish minority some very basic political rights are also involved. In all the cases there are also aspects of immigrant group problems, established ethnic group problems, provincial idiosyncrasies, upward social mobility, etc. But it is not my task to do what the participants have been invited and have graciously agreed to do.

Professors Dahlie and Wilson described the educational experience of three groups they have selected in British Columbia — namely, the Negroes, Finns, and Sikhs — as one of "boundary maintenance". I would have to comment that their experience, unfortunately, has been the experience of most minorities in Canada. The public school systems have not been sufficiently comprehensive to encompass the diversity of the community. This, in spite of the fact that the rationale of the compulsory and state education system is that it should serve the needs of the whole community. Because of this deficiency in public education the minorities have had to struggle to hold on to their legitimate cultural and social practices.

I am particularly interested in their comments on Negroes in Vancouver

Island and mainland British Columbia colonies. Negroes have been in Canada since 1606, first as slaves, later as Loyalists, then as fugitives, deportees and settlers. The reception they found in Upper Canada, Nova Scotia and the Pacific coast colonies more closely resembled attitudes in the American South than we care to admit. The fact is that most Canadians are ignorant of the Negro school problems of the nineteenth and early twentieth centuries and that most Canadians have never imagined the depth of prejudice and discrimination that was directed against this easily recognizable minority.

Professors Dahlie and Wilson see the Negro immigration to Vancouver Island as substantially different from the Negro immigration to Upper Canada in the mid-nineteenth century. What strikes me, however, is the similarity of the experience of the Negroes once they arrive in British North America — in all cases their expectations of British liberty and equity are disappointed. They were subjected to much discrimination and the majority of them returned to the United States after Emancipation where, at least in the Northern states, they believed with reason, there was less prejudicial discrimination directed against them than in British North America.

What is significant about British Columbia is that, although the Negroes formed an unusually large proportion of the population of Victoria for a decade, separate Negro schools were never legislated into existence as they were in Nova Scotia, New Brunswick and Ontario and bolstered in the latter case by numerous court decisions. Professors Wilson and Dahlie suggest that some whites resisted the discriminatory tendencies of some of their compatriots and that the Negroes provided a few outstanding leaders in the community. These facts are correct, but I wonder if the more significant factor might not have been the explicit directives of the British Colonial Missionary Society and the Lord Bishop of London — the BCMS forbade the segregation of Negroes in churches and schools of Vancouver Island "as utterly at variance with the principles of the Christian religion, as well as contrary to the usages adopted by their agents in every part of the Colonial Empire where a mixture of races is found". If the B.C. Negroes escaped the discrimination and persecution meted out at the same period in Upper Canada and Nova Scotia, was it because the Negro community in Victoria was small and its numbers soon dwindling and that the colony on Salt Spring Island was an isolated settlement which presented no economic or social threat to any established community? Is it being too cynical to suggest that the real difference between the Canadian and American experiences with the Negro is not more tolerance in Canada but the fact that the Negroes are too small a minority in Canada to be powerful politically or economically and that they have never formed a cohesive and united group?

Our B.C. colleagues' study of the Finns I find a very fascinating tale, not only as the experience of an immigrant group but especially as the account of a Utopian colony on Malcolm Island and its decay. What I did notice was the pattern of Anglo-conformity which rapidly transformed the

Finnish community. This is reminiscent of the experience of other white, Northern, Protestant immigrant groups — the Icelanders, Norwegians, Swedes, Germans, Dutch, Mennonites, for example — who have found it relatively easy (compared to Latins or Slavs) to identify with and assimilate into the Anglo-Saxon or Anglo-Celtic host and dominant society in western Canada.

The experiences of the Sikhs are probably fairly typical of the assimilation problems of non-European groups. Their problem is quite different from that of the Finns: they are considered unassimilable by some sections of the host society. Much of the experience of the Sikhs in B.C. parallels the story of the Japanese or Chinese or other immigrants from the Indian subcontinent. Professor Wilson spoke of these problems two years ago to the Comparative and International Education Society of Canada and Professor Dahlie recently published a study on the Japanese in *B.C. Studies.*

The three studies (Negroes, Finns and Sikhs) have been well chosen from the viewpoint of different experiences of immigrant groups and different problems of integration in what is supposedly a pluralistic society but which has strong indications of Anglo-conformity. The study raises numerous questions and observations.

In Dr. Kage's paper we have to grapple with a number of terms which are sometimes confused in the public mind but which are never confused by Dr. Kage. First of all, Quebec has (and Manitoba until 1890 had) a *dual confessional* public schools system; Ontario, Saskatchewan and Alberta have a *separate schools* system. Quebec's minority schools are *dissentient schools*; Ontario's are *separate schools.* The essential difference is that a separate schools system is a segregated confessional system which is centrally controlled along with the common non-sectarian public schools by the Department of Education and its agencies and officers in matters of curriculum, teacher training and certification, programs, etc. The dissentient schools control their own curriculum, teacher training, programs, etc. through their confessional section of the Council of Public Instruction and its successors. Quebec's system is confessional, not denominational: it has two streams, Catholic and Protestant representing the two confessions of Western Christianity. Newfoundland, on the other hand, had a truly denominational system: Anglican, Roman Catholic, United Church, Salvationist and Pentecostal schools represent the religious denominations of the province.

Dr. Kage says that the Act of 1869 defined the concepts of "religious majority" and "religious minority" in Quebec. Actually, prior to Confederation in the consolidated statutes of 1861 provision was made for "common schools" under Boards of Commissioners and "dissentient schools" under Boards of Trustees (syndics). What needs to be emphasized, to my mind, is that in neither Montreal nor Quebec City were there any dissentient schools. The situation remains unchanged to this day — all schools in Quebec City and Montreal are "common schools" administered by School Commissioners. The two existing school corporations, Catholic and Protestant, have exclusive control and management of the schools each represents. All provincial schools in Montreal are thus both "confessional" and "public" — none are "dissentient". Therefore, the protective Section 93, sub-section (3) of the BNA Act for dissentient schools cited by Dr. Kage does not apply to any "classes of persons" in Montreal.

What is significant about the Jewish minority studied by Dr. Kage is that it is restricted to Montreal. Were it located in rural Quebec where dissentient Protestant schools exist, the Jewish children would have to attend the Catholic public school. In other words, it may be said that if Jewish children have attended Protestant schools in Montreal it is because these are public schools, not dissentient schools. The complaints of Protestant parents and administrators concerning Jewish participation in their education would otherwise have resulted in their expulsion because dissentient schools are constitutionally protected from accepting "persons of religious faith different from that of the dissentient minority".

I am not quite certain I understand the statement in the paper that none of the education acts prior to 1863 made reference "to specific religious beliefs" nor do I know how to reconcile that statement with the assertion made later that separate schools came into existence at the time of the Union of the Canadas in 1841. The Education Act of 1841 established a dual confessional system designed primarily to protect the English minority in Lower Canada, and provided specifically "that whenever any number of Inhabitants of any Township or Parish professing a religious faith different from that of the majority of the Inhabitants of such Township or Parish, shall dissent from regulations, arrangements and proceedings of the common school commissioners . . . it shall be lawful for the Inhabitants so dissenting . . . to establish and maintain one or more common schools . . . " The Act of 1846 added " . . . they shall be entitled to receive such sums out of the general or local School Fund as shall be proportionate to the dissentient population they represent". It also provided that in the cities of Quebec and Montreal the Board of Examiners of fourteen persons be chosen "in as fair and equitable a manner as possible from among the different religious denominations". Those are surely clear references to religion in school legislation prior to Confederation and prior to 1863.

In 1903, as we have been told, a Jewish lad named Pinsler was refused a scholarship and his father took legal action against the Protestant School Commission. The courts said:

3. A resident of the Jewish faith, who although an owner of real estate has not opted as to his school tax, or who does not own real estate, cannot claim as of right to have his children admitted to the public school. [N.B. Quebec had no compulsory education law yet!]

4. If such admission is given it is by grace and subject to whatsoever conditions the commissioners choose to impose, inclusive of non-eligibility for the scholarship in question.

The paper gives us a rapid overview of the status of Jewish pupils in

Montreal schools. It indicates that as a result of the *Pinsler case* (1903) a provincial act providing that Jewish children "shall be treated in the same manner as Protestants for school purposes" failed to satisfy the Jewish community on such matters as the franchise, staff appointments, etc. Dr. Kage might have added that the Act of 1903 was sufficiently vague to permit several interpretations. It said "children professing the Jewish faith shall have the same right to be educated in the public schools of the province as Protestant children". (Section 6.) Did the Act mean that Jews had the same right to schools of their own as did Protestants, or did it merely mean that Jewish children should attend Protestant schools? This question was not definitely answered until the *Hirsch case* in 1926. Dr. Kage refers to the litigation after 1922 but he does not mention specifically that the courts upheld the idea that the 1903 Act had intended Jewish children to attend Protestant schools. The courts also pointed out that the Quebec legislature was the competent authority to create "separate schools for persons who are neither Roman Catholic nor Protestants, if so framed as not to affect prejudicially any right or privilege with regard to education enjoyed by either Roman Catholics or Protestants at Confederation".

When the Jewish community decided against a third school commission in Montreal some Protestants felt that in order to preserve the Protestant flavour of their schools, the Jewish children should be segregated in specially designated Jewish schools within the Protestant school system. This administrative device would have been the only way to maintain a Protestant milieu. Since its creation in 1930 the Jewish School Commission has signed a fifteen-year agreement, renewed in 1945 and 1960, with the Protestant School Commission to take in Jewish children.

Dr. Kage indicates at the end of his paper that some 60% of Jewish children in Montreal do not benefit from Jewish education and he terms this "a denial of their group cultural rights". I understand that in Montreal today about 75% of the Jewish pupils attend Protestant schools and about 25% are in Jewish day schools. However, the 25% in Jewish day schools can benefit from some state support since the Act of 1961 recognized "independent schools" at the secondary level for financial aid, since *Bill 37* of 1967 permitted some Jewish schools to become "associate schools" in the Protestant sector and since *Bill 56* of 1968 re-classified some of them as "schools in the public interest" qualifying for financial support. This is not to say that there is no work still to be done before achieving a truly equitable position, as the paper argues.

Jewish education has obviously had a tough course to run since Rabbi Jacob Cohen came to Montreal to teach in 1778, and since Dr. Abraham de Sola opened the first Jewish school in 1848.

The following papers confirm the historical fact that the public school has been regarded and employed as a basic institution for the assimilation of immigrant groups. The papers suggest that the schools can become the instrument by which the rich human resources of a multi-ethnic community are developed and elevated to the level of a multicultural society.

NEGROES, FINNS, SIKHS:
EDUCATION AND COMMUNITY EXPERIENCE
IN BRITISH COLUMBIA

J. Donald Wilson
Department of History
Lakehead University

Jorgen Dahlie
University of British Columbia

Any serious discussion of ethnicity today will, of necessity, acknowledge the sharply increased interest and attention being paid generally to the study of ethnic and minority groups. And careful examination of the research reveals much that is stimulating in the formulation of new conceptual models, theories, and explanations.[1] Similarly, published works of certain scholars, prompted by the new formulations and the quickened pace of inquiry, have brought about reassessment of earlier views of ethnic contributions to society, and, in a recent instance, interest in ethnic groups has even prompted legislative action by provincial governments.[2]

The following study of ethnic experiences and education in British Columbia deals with three ethnic communities and the varying degrees of success they had with "boundary maintenance", that is, with holding on to their cultural and social practices.[3] To an extent, the study focuses on the social history[4] of the Negroes, Finns, and Sikhs, considering each as a distinct community in the province (not necessarily in the geopraphic sense) and points out the particular institutional and ethnic response to education which each group made. We have been guided in the presentation by some distinctions Milton Gordon makes concerning "behavioural assimilation" and "structural assimilation" and his description of the "characteristic ethnic group experience" as embodying a "network of organizations and informal social relationships which permits and encourages the members of the ethnic group to remain within the confines of the group for all of their primary relationships . . ."[5]

Negroes

Unlike the case of south-western Ontario where American Negroes came in the first half of the nineteenth century via the "Underground Railroad", Negro immigration into British Columbia was largely a result of the Fraser River Gold Rush of the late 1850s and the proscriptive measures taken against California Negroes at the same time. In the first case the gold rush produced a severe labour shortage in Victoria which led to the publication of notices in the California press that caught the interest of the San Francisco Negro community.[6] In the second case, attempts were made in the late 1850s to bar Negro immigration into California and to resolutely rebuff efforts designed to enable Negroes to testify in court cases where white men were also involved. A further cause of concern to California

Negroes was the discrimination shown against their children by the state's all-white public school system. In the circumstances many Negroes decided to leave the United States, and after considering emigration to Mexico finally settled on Vancouver Island whose governor, James Douglas, had extended a cordial invitation to them through an advance party.[7]

From April 1858, the California Negroes began arriving in Victoria. Most settled there and took up various occupations: tradesmen, such as blacksmiths, boat builders, ship caulkers, bricklayers, plasterers; business-men engaged in bake shops, restaurants, livery stables, draying, shoe stores, tailoring, even a tinshop and a salmon cannery.[8] Others, estimated at approximately fifty, headed for the Fraser River Gold Rush.[9] A few dozen eventually settled on Salt Spring Island, some forty miles north of Victoria. All told, approximately 400 Negroes took up residence in what was to become British Columbia.[10]

One of the Negroes' closest friends in Victoria, the Church of England minister, the Rev. Edward Cridge, recorded their declared reasons for coming shortly after the arrival of the first group of settlers: "They sought the freedom to wh. they tho! they were entitled in common w[ith] y[e] [abbreviation for *the*] white man."[11] They also told Cridge they did not intend to settle in a district by themselves nor did they intend to establish a distinct church organization. Rather, although members of the American Wesleyan Episcopal Church, they wished to join "some Ch[urch] already in existence here".[12] Cridge welcomed them to his church.

The welcome, however, was not appreciated by all of Cridge's parishioners. One of them, Henry Sharpstone, a white American by origin, complained bitterly in the local newspaper of the church sexton's practice of "crowding negro men into the same seats with white and respectable ladies" with the result that "the little chapel resemble[s] a chess board". The complainant found the previous Sabbath, "an unusually warm day", to be excessively abusive to his sensitivities:

> The little chapel was crowded as usual with a "smart sprinkle" of blacks, *generously* mixed in with the whites. The Ethiopians *perspired!* they always do when out of place. . . . Several white gentlemen left their seats vacant, and sought the purer atmosphere outside; others moodily endured the *aromatic luxury* of their positions, in no very pious frame of mind.[13]

Furthermore, Sharpstone strongly disapproved of Cridge's contention that the white man should acknowledge the black man as his equal, socially and politically, and should observe toward the Negro "the same social respect that we do toward our own race". Sharpstone asked rhetorically:

> Do you mean to say that we shall admit him to our houses, take him into our confidence, confer with him in intimacy, introduce him to our wives and daughters, *sit beside him in the same church,* and subscribe to his desires of propagating a mixed blood? . . . The negro has his proper place among created beings. To make him our equal, he must submit to being skinned, renovated, "born anew", or

any other process of change to make him white.

But not all of Cridge's parishioners agreed with Henry Sharpstone. Another American colonist took him to task for his "mean", "malicious" and presumptuous letter which created the same effect on him as "a dead polecat".[14] He corrected many of Sharpstone's assertions and made plain that Sharpstone in no way represented all or even a majority of Americans living in Victoria. It seems clear, however, that the Negroes did not find in Victoria "the freedom to which they thought they were entitled". One Negro correspondent of the Victoria *Colonist* described their position in the colony as "a degrading one". "We have not conquered," he continued, "that mildew-like feeling of prejudice." To prove his point he cited cases of his people being barred from hotels, inns, whiskey shops, concerts, even steamer cabins, on grounds of colour alone. He went so far as to allege the existence of a secret association of whites "whose ostensible purpose is to keep colored men out of the jury box, and from serving on the Grand Jury".[15]

"The fancied liberality of British laws" was further underlined in terms of political rights. Although, like other British subjects, Negroes on Vancouver Island possessed the right to vote, they were only eligible for election at the municipal level, not in the provincial parliament. The pertinent law, recently passed, excluded from that latter body all except subjects of the British Empire by birth. But as one Negro pointed out in William Lloyd Garrison's anti-slavery weekly *The Liberator:*

 . . . since 1858 only 4 white persons have become naturalized; whereas, about 150 colored persons have taken the oath of allegiance. It is not very probable a colored person will ever be elected to either body [city council or provincial parliament][16] . . . Prejudice is too strong in Vancouver Island. We have brighter prospects of political elevation under our own Government, than in any British colony on this coast.[17]

Despite unfavourable public opinion the same correspondent in *The Liberator* admitted that churches and schools were exceptions to the general policy of exclusion and outright discrimination. But, he emphasized, "our leading men had to fight hard to obtain their rights in both". The equality which he found in those institutions "was grudgingly and unwillingly awarded; but they claimed it as their right as British subjects, and finally succeeded".[18]

A few Negroes, newly arrived in Victoria, decided they would prefer the rural life of the countryside to the bustling town life of Victoria. Because of the gold rush farm lands around Victoria were expensive. Moreover, surveyed lands required down payments in excess of what many settlers could afford. These Negroes therefore attached themselves to a group of men led by a Scottish immigrant, John Copland, who had formed a "Committee for Settlement of Salt Spring Island". The group was composed of English, Scottish, Irish and Australian immigrants, as well as Negroes. Official approval for the settlement was received on July 26, 1859, and the next day the first party of seventeen settlers made the short trip from Victoria to the heavily wooded island in the Gulf of Georgia.[19] By the end of the year there were forty settlers on the island.[20]

Over the next few years settlers came and went. A visiting minister, the Rev. Ebenezer Robson, reported in 1861, however, that by far the majority of settlers were Negroes. "I preached," he continued, "in the house of a colored man in the evening to about 20 persons all colored except 3 and one of them is married to a colored man." Robson commented also on the virtual absence of racial prejudice.[21] As the years passed, a great deal of intermarriage took place on the island — white and Negro, Negro and Indian and whites with Indian common-law wives. As Pilton remarks, "the Island became such a racial melting pot that discrimination because of colour could hardly flourish".[22]

As to schooling, the first teacher on the island was a Negro named John C. Jones. Born in Ohio of an Irish father and a Negro mother, he was a graduate of Oberlin College and holder of a first class teaching certificate from Ohio.[23] For six days a week beginning in 1861, Jones taught both white and Negro children. He spent three days a week at Vesuvius (then called the Central Settlement) and three days at the north end of the island. In 1864 Jones himself and F. D. Lester, also a teacher and later named Road Commissioner for the island, petitioned Governor Kennedy of Vancouver Island in the name of the "settlers of Ganges Harbour" for government support to establish a school. Their petition mentioned the presence in the neighbourhood of eighteen children between the ages of five and sixteen "who are destitute of any opportunity of attending day school". A small schoolhouse had been provided, but "being poor and few in number [we] are unable to support the teacher".[24] Governor Kennedy's reply expressed sympathy for their cause and the hope that "their reasonable requirements will in a short time be complied with".[25]

Five years passed and still no government aid was received. Then in 1869 the three-man Board of School Trustees made a second appeal to Victoria.[26] This time under the Common School Ordinance of 1869 a government grant of $480 was forwarded. So after ten years of teaching Jones finally received a salary. That year (1870) the school had an enrollment of fourteen boys and six girls.[27] Jones remained on the island only a few years longer before returning to Oberlin, Ohio.[28]

Following the American Civil War many B.C. Negroes returned to the United States. In the early 1870s reliable figures place the entire Negro population of the province at less than 500.[29] In his study, Pilton also notes the "rapidly diminishing negro population as the result of emigration" back to the United States, and accounts for it in this way: "After Lincoln's Emancipation Proclamation and the end of the Civil War there was no longer any need to continue their self-imposed exile."[30] As to Salt Spring Island, a newspaper report in 1963 estimated that about twenty Negro families were resident on the island, almost all of them descendents of the original settlers.[31]

Finns

Although the first Finnish settlers in British Columbia came from Alaska shortly after that territory was sold to the United States by Russia, the first major immigration occurred between the years 1880 and 1905. As with many Scandinavian immigrants to British Columbia, most of these Finns had originally emigrated from their homeland to the United States. In B.C. the Finnish settlers engaged in coal mining at Nanaimo and Wellington on Vancouver Island, and in railroad construction in the interior after which they took up homesteads at Salmon Arm, Solsqua and White Lake. Finnish agricultural settlements were also established in the lower Fraser Valley near Vancouver in 1905 and five years later fishing settlements were begun at Lund and Sunbury on the west coast.

The Sointula experiment in utopian socialism resulted from the discontent with their lot of the Finnish miners of Nanaimo and Wellington.[32] Working conditions were dangerous and exploitative in the extreme. Wages were kept low by the employment of Chinese, Japanese, and east Indian workers. In their reading of Finnish newspapers and journals, some of these settlers were inspired by the articles of one Matti Kurikka, a man so radical in his social theories he had been forced to leave Finland. From his exile he dreamed of founding an all-Finnish colony on socialist and anti-clerical lines. "In this colony," he wrote, "a high, cultural life of freedom would be built, away from priests who have defiled the high morals of Christianity, away from churches that destroy peace, away from all the evils of the outside world."[33]

Known in Finland as a dramatist, novelist and labour newspaper editor, Kurikka first considered the remoteness of Queensland, Australia, to be ideal for his projected colony. There, however, the Finns were treated as semi-barbarous and objects of cheap labour, and so Kurikka quickly lost interest.[34] About this time, though, in April, 1900, he received an invitation from the Nanaimo Finns to attempt such a venture in British Columbia. A collection was taken to cover Kurikka's travelling expenses. In October Kurikka arrived in British Columbia and assumed the presidency of a colonizing company called the Kalevan Kansa Colonization Company. Efforts to locate a suitable site for the colony eventually led the company in the spring of 1901 to approach the provincial government for land. The request was met with favour from the provincial authorities with the result that from several possibilities Malcolm Island, almost 200 miles north of Vancouver between Vancouver Island and the mainland, was chosen.

Late in 1901 the first settlers began to arrive at Rough Bay on Malcolm Island. They named the place where they chose to settle *Sointula* – "the place of harmony". They were the vanguard of an eventual population by 1903 of 238 inhabitants including eighty-eight children.[35] Not all settlers were able to cope with the rugged pioneer conditions of the isolated island. During the first year of settlement thirty-seven left, and the following year, 1903, eighty-five left of whom two were forced to leave as undesirable members of the colony.[36]

The colony attracted great attention from Finns and non-Finns alike. The sanguine Kurikka anticipated the early arrival of 2,000 settlers — Finns from the homeland as well as the United States.[37] The Victoria *Colonist* was even more hyperbolic on first hearing of the scheme. An article concerning it was headed "Two million People Ready to Immigrate — Desirable Class of Settlers";[38] it was fully expected that the bulk of the Finnish population was prepared to pick up stakes and head for British Columbia "in order to escape the tyranny and oppression of the Russian government".[39] Sointula was to be the nucleus for what the newspaper editors saw as "a vast immigration, which would fill up the waste places of northern British Columbia and turn the fertile valleys of Cassiar and Cariboo into prosperous agricultural communities".

While waiting for arrangements to be made for their transfer from Nanaimo to Malcolm Island, the Finns established a newspaper called *Aika* (Time), which not surprisingly was edited by Kurikka, a newspaperman with previous experience in Finland.[40] To raise funds to purchase a press and help pay for printing, ten-dollar shares were sold. Kurikka made use of the pages of the *Aika* to promote his utopian dream for Sointula. Published fortnightly and with its motto of "Freedom with Responsibility", it soon became the main cultural organ of the community. Publication ceased between late 1902 and November of the following year while the paper's press awaited transport to Sointula. The delay was caused by virtue of there being no building at Sointula in which to house it.[41] By the end of 1903 criculation reached 1,500 copies.[42]

No copies of the *Aika* could be located in the British Columbia Archives or Legislative Library,[43] but according to Kalervo Oberg's account of the colony, its editorial policy favoured articles advocating socialism, harmony and fellowship and astutely avoided voicing any religious bias. The continuing influence of the paper's editor Matti Kurikka is clearly apparent since these aspects were the hallmarks of his social philosophy. When one considers the range and scope of articles in a typical issue, one can only conclude that the *Aika* was intended as a powerful agent of adult education. In such an issue Kurikka authored three articles on "Socialism and Social Philosophy" (a 2,000-word discussion of the growth of socialist thinking from Rousseau to Marx), "The Question of Marriage" (a topic that may well have been of immediate concern as well as philosophic interest to the predominantly male population of the colony),[44] and "Current Events". A translation of an article by R. J. Ingersoll on Voltaire and a sketch of local interest, "A Night in Alert Bay", rounded out the main articles. So *Aika* readers in this issue were taken from the intricacies of socialist philosophy through the life and work of the greatest of the *philosophes* to a humorous sketch on a neighbouring Indian village — all this in the wilderness of northern British Columbia at the turn of the century.[45]

The socialist principles underlying the colony's operation are evident from the fact that all meals were taken in common in one large building. All food was prepared there and no kitchen was to be found in the individual buildings. The same rate of pay was extended to all — in 1905 one dollar per day plus board — but the hours of labour were gauged in proportion to the work done. Thus in more arduous and dangerous labour the hours of work were shortened. A fisherman, for example, might work four hours a day while a man engaged in clerical work might work nine. Both received the same pay. The original agreement was that shareholders in the company would receive five per cent on their investment, half of which went into a common fund for education, music, and the like, and the other half to be divided among the workers both men and women. A contemporary report in 1905 revealed, however, that no colonist had actually drawn his wages.[46]

The lack of interest in established religion at Sointula, if not outright hostility, is underlined by the fact that no church was ever established until several years ago.[47] The original working principle was that "each man worships or not as he pleases".[48] The same 1905 report observed that "there is no public worship nor any church established in the colony", and contrasted this state of affairs with Alert Bay, six miles away, where the "most pretentious buildings in the settlement containing, it would appear, most of the wealth spent on the settlement, were two large churches, one with stained glass windows in front and in the chancel".[49]

The original agreement between the provincial government and the Kalevan Kansa Colonization Company signed on November 27, 1901, provided that children of the colonists were to attend an English school. The Company diary for 1903 makes it plain that "in spite of renewed applications the government has as yet not set to work to get us a school house and teacher of the English language".[50] In the fall of 1904, however, the colonists' persistence was crowned with success as a new school was opened with an English teacher in charge. Up to that point the children had been taught only in Finnish.

The new teacher was an Englishwoman by the name of Miss J. M. Cleveland.[51] In 1905 she received a salary of $60 per month. She reported to a Vancouver visitor that "the [thirty-nine] children are gradually learning the English language and adopting our mode of speech, even to the loss of their own tongue in some instances".[52] Miss Cleveland left Sointula after one year.[53]

The Company diary for 1903 also called for the construction of a large nursery and children's building where mothers could leave their children while working. This idea, however, did not meet with the success anticipated for it. According to Anderson, "mother's [sic] being unwilling to have their children away from home" was the principal reason for the demise of the project.[54]

In addition to the *Aika,* the colony provided other means of adult education and entertainment. On Sunday evenings, regular discussions were held, Finnish plays staged, and band and choral music presented. Saturday night was reserved for folk dances and musical entertainment. A library was begun in 1902 and the following year "classes in English language, mechanics and other subjects [were] also under way".[55] The origins of the library owed a great deal to a group of Finnish people in Australia who not only provided the library's first books but also made the first cash donation. The library today consists of over 2,000 Finnish and 1,000 English books.[56]

Over the years formal schooling for children progressed in Sointula. In 1914, the B.C. Minister of Lands reported that the island supported an "excellent school having an average attendance of forty-seven pupils".[57] The original building consisting of two rooms was replaced in 1928 by a three-room building. Around 1955 a two-room annex was added. Now a new elementary school has been built to accommodate the first seven grades. High school students travel by ferry each day to Port McNeill on Vancouver Island where they attend a consolidated secondary school.

From a population of 238 in 1903, the colony's ranks were severely depleted by the departure of Matti Kurikka and half the members in October 1904. The ostensible issue concerned a difference of opinion over the topic of free love,[58] but the colony was already experiencing difficult times. Neither logging nor fishing proved profitable; distance from markets ruined the chances of converting shoemaking, tailoring, brick-making, or foundry work into profitable ventures. The sawmill held some promise for a time, but an ill-conceived contract to build bridges over the Capilano and North Seymour rivers in North Vancouver resulted in disastrous losses from which the colony never recovered. A long-time friend of Kurikka, A. B. Mäkelä, attempted to rally the remaining population. The last annual meeting of the Colonization Company was held on February 5, 1905, with a mere fifty shareholders present. An act of embezzlement on the part of the manager of the colony and the seizure of a large shipment of lumber destined for Vancouver by the colony's creditors finally brought the enterprise to its knees. The Colonization Company was finally liquidated and went into receivership.

To cover the colony's debts, the trust company sold all the colony's property. Those people who stayed on purchased land, built their own homes, and formed the basis for a settlement which has continued to this day. In an article in the Vancouver *Province* in April 1905, J. Edward Bird, commented very favourably on the state of the "Finnish Communistic Colony" despite its numerous setbacks. He listed as residents forty-five men, twenty women, and forty children.[59] In 1914 the population consisted of "about 250 people, chiefly members of the original Finnish colony".[60] In the early thirties the population stood at 450. By 1958 it had increased to 570 and today exceeds 700.[61]

From a totally Finnish-speaking community Sointula has become a mainly English-speaking one. The population is much more transient. Ironically some recent arrivals have been following the very pattern established by the original settlers: they seek an escape from "civilization" and a "return to the land", both prominent goals among Kurikka's followers. But Sointula is no longer isolated from "civilization" as it was in the past. The telephone, automobile, and television have made their mark on Malcolm Island as elsewhere. It is reported that the large library of Finnish books is rarely consulted by the younger generation whose parents "communicate only in English with their children".[62]

So the factors which held together the original colony despite adversities have now disappeared. The common ideological base of socialism, the vision of a Kurikka, and the ethnic homogeneity are absent. Even the opposition to established religion has been overcome with the founding a few years ago of the Sointula Community Church. Nonetheless the original colony contained within it elements of the old and the modern. It harkened back to numerous utopian socialist experiments in the nineteenth century, such as New Harmony and Brook Farm, but also in a strange way predated the current drive to escape from the unpleasantness of modern civilization.

Sikhs

In August 1970 the Sikhs in Vancouver held ceremonies to mark the opening of their new temple in the south-eastern area of the city.[63] For these immigrants from the Punjab in north central India, the dedication of the temple represented a remarkable achievement, given the unique history of the Sikhs in this province over the past six decades. The pattern of immigration itself, the disruption of family and social institutions, and the long-standing prejudice and discrimination against Sikhs, make all the more exceptional the accomplishments of this vigorous ethnic group. One finds in examining their history that the Sikhs fit no "typical" category of ethnic group and this seems especially true with respect to their educational experience and the degree of their social or cultural adaptation to Canadian life.

Sikh immigration began after the turn of the century but there were only two periods when significantly large numbers arrived: from 1905-1907 when 5,000 immigrants entered and post-1947, following the establishment of an annual quota of 300 for the East Indians. From 1918 to the outbreak of World War II annual entry was less than thirty-five and there were some years when no Sikh immigrants landed in the province.[64] By 1939 the B.C. population had dropped to 1,100, predominantly adult single males, with one estimate indicating that no more than fifteen family units were resident in the Vancouver area that year.[65] By 1970 the total had grown considerably, to approximately 12,000,[66] a result of the quota system and the re-establishment of the normal family pattern in the communities throughout the province.

The precipitate decline in the number of Sikhs from the peak year of 1907 to the low figure in 1939 (the number remained almost constant until 1946) and the virtual absence of the family, had significant implications for the Sikhs. Most of the early immigrants were able-bodied men seeking economic gain and hopefully the opportunity to send for wives or families once they had been established. Such hopes were crushed through discriminatory legislation passed by the federal and provincial governments.[67] The proviso that all East Indians intending to become landed immigrants had to have $200, and that they must make a direct and continuous voyage from India to British Columbia (most ships made stops at Hong Kong or other ports en route) practically excluded all Sikhs from entry after 1907.[68] *The Aryan,* published in Victoria by East Indians, carried a report in the August 1911 issue of the plight of one Hira Singh who was victimized by the legal restrictions. Singh had worked for three years in Vancouver and had carefully saved his money to enable him to make the journey to India where he made arrangements to bring his wife and children to Canada. On his return he was forcibly separated from them and they were compelled to sail for home while Singh was left in Vancouver.[69] *The Aryan,* citing the fact that over 6,000 East Indians had invested millions in Canada, petitioned the government, pleading "that the home life, dear to the heart of every being, should be made possible to them by the removal of the legal, but altogether unjustifiable exclusion of wives and families".[70]

At first such pleas were not heeded and it was not until 1918 that restrictions were relaxed. By this time the decision had become meaningless: in the next six years a total of eighty-four Sikhs arrived,[71] and it was evident that the return of many Sikhs to India, the migration of others to the United States, notably California, and death of some who were in the 1905 vanguard had seriously depleted the ranks of the Sikh community.[72] Those who were left were single or, if married, without wives and children. For them, it is fair to assume that their "home" was the temple, their "family" the Khalsa Diwan Society, their solace the Sikh faith. And it is to these institutions one must look to account for the social and educational influences in their lives. Not all by any means emulated the remarkable Kartar Singh who found his energies absorbed by the task of educating the adult members of the community,[73] but the great majority had shared his experiences otherwise, especially through associations in those institutions which underscored the solidarity and ethnic-spiritual homogeneity of the group.

From the initial settlement to the present, the Khalsa Diwan Society and the temples have been the main institutions binding the Sikhs together. The first immigrants who, through "an historical accident"[74] became mill and lumber workers rather than farmers, settled in Duncan, Fraser Mills, Ocean Falls and Abbotsford, in addition to the main cities of Vancouver, Victoria, and New Westminster. The Khalsa Diwan Society was established as early as 1907,[75] and permanent temples were soon erected in most of these communities.[76] The traditional association of Sikhs with the lumber industry was recently emphasized with the opening in 1962 of a new temple at Port Alberni, large enough to hold some 500 people.[77] Since the Sikhs were so closely involved in the Khalsa Diwan Society and the temples it is instructive to discover the special meaning these institutions had for the group.

Mayer, on the basis of his discussion with leading Sikhs and visits to their meeting places, has noted that the "word 'temple' is perhaps misleading as a translation of the term *gurdwara;* for it implies merely a centre for religious worship. Actually the *gurdwara* contains more than a hall of worship."[78] It also comprises dining halls, offices, kitchens, rooms for transients and a dwelling for the resident priest: "The temple premises are thus in constant use as a 'hotel' for the entire community in British Columbia – this applying especially to those at 2nd Avenue, for the largest number of transients or people coming to visit Vancouver from country districts."[79]

In this connection it is interesting to note, too, that the word *guru,* after the founder of the Sikh faith, Guru Nanak, has a wider meaning than that of priest. Dalip Singh Sadhu, university-trained in India and leader of the Sikh Temple on Topaz Street in Victoria, explained in an interview that in the Sikh religion "their priest is not so much a priest as a teacher . . . . the Punjab word for the priest is *gani* which, literally translated, means teacher. Mr. Sadhu . . . stressed most strongly that he regards himself as a teacher first and foremost."[80] Incidentally, the Topaz Street temple was built in 1912, has been in continuous use since that time and has had as its primary function "teaching" or educating the Sikh members.

The kinds of activities in the temples are indicative of the pervasive educational function that this institution performs. First there are the religious ceremonies which, in keeping with the simplicity of the temple, emphasize the "lack of elaborate ritual and underline . . . the essential message of Sikhism as a religion of belief rather than formalism".[81] The reading aloud of the Holy Book (in Punjabi) is a regular feature and is performed at the request of any Sikh, either over a forty-eight-hour period (*Akhand Path*) by a team of men, or during a full week (*Sadharan Path*) by the priest. Often a *bhog* will follow the *Sadharan Path;* it is essentially a ceremony of thanksgiving by an individual and can in turn involve a *jor mela,* or gathering of several hundred Sikhs to take part in traditional East Indian food and fellowship.[82] These gatherings have the effect of keeping alive the old culture with its emphasis on Punjabi (spoken language) and Gurmukki (script) and the more formal education carried on in the temples includes evening classes in the language. Most Sikhs hold that the Holy Book is not translatable and therefore a sustained effort is made, particularly by the India-born and educated to insure that the tradition is upheld.[83]

In other ways the Sikhs demonstrated from time to time their concern for education, in India as well as in Canada. As early as 1911 *Sikhs* in Victoria raised over $1,000 for a night school in Vancouver and sent some $6,000 back to the Punjab to assist in educating Sikhs who were to follow their brethren to Canada.[84] The records of the Khalsa Diwan Society show that in the years 1921-1952 the Sikhs donated almost $300,000 to philanthropic cases, with half of this earmarked for educational and religious institutions in British Columbia and India.[85] The concern for education in the Punjab by B.C. Sikhs seems to have been peculiar to this ethnic group from the earliest years of immigration. In a 1914 issue of *The Hindustanee,* there is a strong appeal by one Rajah Singh entitled "Education Among the Sikhs". He asked the B.C. Sikh Education Committee to lend its full support to get schools established in the Punjab and cited the examples of Germany and Japan as countries that have progressed through education.[86]

The career of Kartar Singh also reflected a life-long involvement in education in his native region and in British Columbia. Singh was a teacher, journalist, and editor in Punjab and when he arrived in British Columbia in 1911 he put his talents to work. He initiated three separate Indian journals, and lectured and taught at night schools as a member of Khalsa Diwan Society. His journals were short-lived, a result in part of the vicissitudes of Sikh immigration and general economic conditions. But he used them to good advantage in sounding the call for education among Sikhs throughout the province.[87]

Sikh newspapers and publications may not have been too effective as educational organs in the Sikh community because of the very close association of almost all Sikhs in the temples and the influence of the Khalsa Diwan Society. Nevertheless, for a time *The Hindustanee, The Aryan,* and later, *The Canadian Sikh,* contributed in educating East Indians to the Canadian way of life. Accounts entitled "Canada as a Hindu Saw It" carried reactions of a peripatetic East Indian to various aspects of life in Vancouver. He reported his amazement at the splendid cafés (as contrasted with eating places in India), commented on the presence of "commercialized vice" despite "strict monogamous laws", and remarked how the Canadian five cents "or a nickel as it is called" was worth thirty times as much "in gold value as the smallest coin circulating in India". He was also observant enough to note that there was high unemployment, and large numbers of vagrants in the city.[88]

The Canadian Sikh saw as part of its mission the need to educate non-Sikhs in the truth about Sikhism but it too stressed the priority to be given to teaching Gurmukki, "not only because it appears at all religious functions but also because it opens the way for a deeper appreciation of Sikh history and culture".[89] The editor called for the establishment of a school where university students in particular could have the opportunity to learn Hindi, Urdu, as well as Punjabi.[90] But this call for an institution beyond the temple and the Khalsa Diwan Society was premature and with the establishment of larger temples supported by a united ethnic group there is little likelihood of such a venture being pursued.[91]

A number of generalizations about the Sikh experience in British Columbia are suggested by the foregoing. The fact that over ninety percent of the Sikhs are adherents of Sikhism, that there have been no conversions to other faiths,[92] and only rare instances of marriage between Sikhs and non-Sikhs, attests to the unusually pronounced ethnic solidarity of these people.[93] Furthermore, as a group Sikhs have had no significant exposure to the public system of education in the province until recent years. In many respects, they have taken little from Canadian culture other than the "material way of life", which, Mayer contends, allows them freedom from involvement with outsiders.[94] There are some signs now that the characteristic disagreements between first and second generation might also affect the Sikhs. For example, girls are staying longer in school — they formerly left by age fourteen. But there seems to be no general weakening of the ethnic structure despite the non-Sikh behaviour patterns and attitudes to which the young people are being exposed. One Sikh leader, born and educated in India, summed up the prevailing mood of the East Indians some years ago: " . . . a man must be what he is, he cannot regret his ancestry if he is to be mentally healthy . . . . most people here think that you can either be East Indian or a white Canadian, but not both at once."[95]

Notes

[1] See, for example, Frank G. Vallee *et al,* "Ethnic Assimilation and Differentiation in Canada", *The Canadian Journal of Economics and Political Science,* Vol. XXLII, No. 4 (November, 1957), pp. 540-549; Milton M. Gordon, "Assimilation in America: Theory and Reality" in Richard M. Abrams and Lawrence W. Levine, eds., *The Shaping of Twentieth-Century America* (Boston: Little, Brown and Company, Inc., 1965), pp. 296-316; Nathan Glazer, "Ethnic Groups in America: From National Culture to Ideology" in Morroe Berger, Theodore Abel, and Charles H. Page, eds., *Freedom and Control in Modern Society* (New York: D. Van Nostrand Company, Inc., 1954), pp. 158-173; Tamme Wittermans, "The Frisians: An Ethnic Group in the Netherlands", *Sociology and Social Research An International Journal,* Vol. 52, No. 1 (October, 1967), pp. 88-100, and John A. Hostetler and Calvin Redekop, "Education and Assimilation in Three Ethnic Groups", *Alberta Journal of Educational Research,* Vol. VIII, No. 4 (December, 1962), pp. 189-203. These writers have attempted more precise definitions of ethnicity and have argued that certain concepts such as the "melting pot" and "cultural pluralism" have not been adequate to the task of explaining the social interaction of ethnic groups.

[2] Illustrative of the new work being done is Timothy Smith's "Immigrant Social Aspirations and American Education, 1880-1930", *American Quarterly* XXI (Fall 1969), pp. 523-543. For a recent indication of the effect that studies of ethnic groups might have on provincial governments see "Alberta Planning for Multi-culture", *Vancouver Sun* (April 26, 1971), p. 15.

[3] Hostetler and Redekop, *op. cit.* Their paper set out to prove the hypothesis that "the degree of assimilation is an index to the degree to which the ethnic group is dissolving". They compared the Amish, Hutterites, and Old Colony Mennonites and indicated that all ethnic groups with pronounced religious views, cultural attitudes, or ideologies had to contend with "the 'imperialistic' nature of the educational institutions" of the host society.

[4] Although there are specific ethnic groups in British Columbia, whose educational experiences have been more closely identified with the interaction of politics and education, this is not the case with the Blacks, Finns, and Sikhs. For examples of the former refer to F. Henry Johnson, "The Doukhobors of British Columbia", *Queen's Quarterly* LXX No. 4 (Winter, 1964), pp. 528-541; Jorgen Dahlie, "The Japanese in B.C.: Lost Opportunity? Some Aspects of the Education of Minorities", *BC Studies,* No. 8 (Winter 1970-71), pp. 3-16, and J. Donald Wilson and Jorgen Dahlie, "Characteristics in B.C.", *The Comparative and International Education Society of Canada Papers: 1969: Communications,* pp. 28-37.

[5] Gordon, pp. 312-313.

[6] Rudolph M. Lapp, "Negro Rights Activities in Gold Rush California", *California Historical Society Quarterly,* Vol. XLV (March 1966), p. 14.

[7] For details on the preliminary discussions, see F. W. Howay, "The Negro Immigration into Vancouver Island in 1858", *British Columbia Historical Quarterly,* Vol. III, No. 2 (April 1939), pp. 110-13.

[8] B.C. Archives, W. D. Anderson to J. S. Matthews, August 29, 1934.

[9] A "colored miner" in *The Cariboo Sentinel* (Barkerville, June 25, 1866), estimated "50 colored men in and about Cariboo, the greater portion of whom are miners". It is interesting to note that these men were not unanimous in support of the "Liberator of the Slaves", Abraham Lincoln. A report in the same newspaper (January 15, 1867) made this clear: "The colored people celebrated the anniversary of their liberation on the 1st instant; they were not unanimous on the subject however. The admirers of Abe Lincoln met at the Parlor Saloon; the apologists of Jeff Davis held forth in

front of Dixie's shop. Characteristic speeches were delivered by speakers on each side."

[10] Matthew Macfie, *Vancouver Island and British Columbia* (London: Longman, Green, Longman, Roberts & Green, 1865), p. 388; Howay, p. 113; J. S. Matthews, typed insert opposite p. 110 in Howay; *British Colonist,* February 2, 1958.

[11] B.C. Archives, Diary of the Rev. Edward Cridge, April 26, 1858, typescript, p. 92.

[12] *Ibid.,* p. 94.

[13] *Daily Victoria Gazette,* August 24, 1858.

[14] "M.W.G." in *Daily Victoria Gazette,* August 25, 1858.

[15] *British Colonist,* June 13, 1859. Whether as a result of this "secret association" or not, it is recorded that no Negroes sat as jurors in the province between 1860 and 1872. *Ibid.,* November 27, 1872.

[16] Actually, one Mifflin Wistar Gibbs, an outstanding figure among California Negroes in the 1850s and prominent Victoria merchant, was elected to the City Council in 1868. Upon his return to the United States in 1869 Gibbs occupied a number of official positions and was eventually appointed United States Consul to Madagascar. See J. W. Pilton, "Negro Settlement in British Columbia, 1858-1871" (unpublished M. A. Thesis, University of British Columbia, 1951), ch. IV. Also Gibbs's autobiography, *Shadow and Light* (Washington, D.C., 1902).

[17] A correspondent of the *Pacific Appeal* (organ of the coloured people at San Francisco), *The Liberator* (Boston, April 15, 1864). Included in Philip S. Foner, "The Colored Inhabitants of Vancouver Island", *B.C. Studies,* no. 8 (Winter 1970-71), pp. 29-33.

[18] *Ibid.*

[19] The land office authorization and list of petitioners seeking land is included in Pilton, pp. 130-1. But Pilton cautions: "Who the first negro colonists were, it is impossible to say, for the majority of those who made application never actually went there, and Island tradition does not correspond at all with the scanty official records that do exist." *Ibid.,* p. 134.

[20] *Victoria Gazette,* November 22, 1859.

[21] B.C. Archives, Diary of the Rev. Ebenezer Robson, February 21, 1861; December 21, 1861.

[22] Pilton, p. 135.

[23] B.C. Archives, W. D. Anderson to J. S. Matthews, September 12, 1934. Anderson was himself a student of Jones's for twelve years between 1861 and 1873.

[24] B.C. Archives, Colonial Correspondence, Jones and Lester to A. E. Kennedy, May 18, 1864.

[25] Kennedy's opinion appended to original incoming letter on May 23, 1864.

[26] B.C. Archives, Colonial Correspondence, J. P. Booth to Colonial Secretary, October 26, 1869.

[27] B.C. Archives, *Blue Book* for British Columbia, 1870, p. 167.

[28] The last mention of his name in the Department's annual reports occurs in 1875. British Columbia, Department of Education, *Annual Report of Public Schools, 1875,* p. 39.

[29] *Victoria Directory,* 1871 accounts for 439 Negroes as of April 1871 (excluding Salt Spring Island). See App. J. in Pilton, p. 237. *Lovell's Gazetteer of British North America* (Montreal, 1873), p. 47, lists a Negro population in British Columbia of 462.

[30] Pilton, p. 110; p. 1.

[31] Vancouver *Province,* August 6, 1963.

[32] One contemporary report noted that the Finns "do not take kindly to work in the mines. They are a pastoral people, combining the pursuit of agriculture with fishing . . . ." Victoria *Colonist,* April 11, 1901.

[33] Quoted in Aili Anderson, *History of Sointula,* (n.p., n.d.; 1958), p. 2. Said to be based on a longer work published in Finnish in 1936 by Matti Halminen, one of the original pioneers. Its title is *Sointula, Kalevan Kansan ja Kanadan Suomalaisten Historia* (Helsinki, 1936).

[34] Victoria *Colonist,* September 8, 1901.

[35] Of the hundred men, forty-seven were married, fifty-three unmarried; of the fifty women only seven were unmarried. Kalervo Oberg, "Sointula, a Communistic Settlement in British Columbia" (graduating thesis, U.B.C., 1928), p. 24.

[36] *Ibid.*

[37] Vancouver *Province,* April 9, 1901.

[38] Victoria *Colonist,* June 27, 1901. Kurikka himself expected "up to a million" might immigrate. *Ibid.,* April 4, 1902.

[39] The local press made repeated reference to the despotic nature of Russian rule which was leading the "freedom-loving" Finns to seek emigration. For example, *Province,* April 9, 1901; *Colonist,* April 11, 1901.

[40] There Kurikka edited the Finnish labour paper *Työmies* (The Worker) and became recognized leader of the working class movement. John I. Kolehmainen, "Harmony Island, A Finnish Utopian Venture in British Columbia", *British Columbia Historical Quarterly,* Vol. V, no. 2 (April 1941), p. 113.

[41] Anderson, p. 8.

[42] Oberg, p. 23.

[43] It is reported that an incomplete file of the newspaper is housed at the Cleveland Public Library, Cleveland, Ohio. Kolehmainen, p. 111, fn. 1. (A more complete file has since been acquired on microfilm by the Finnish-Canadian Archives, Lakehead University.)

[44] According to Anderson, Kurikka even wrote articles on free love, a topic which, not surprisingly, drew the attention of the outside world. Kurikka's advocacy of free love lead to the outbreak of a bitter dispute late in 1904 which split the colonists into two camps. The ensuing controversy accounts, in part, for Kurikka's resignation and hasty departure from the colony. Anderson, pp. 11, 12.

[45] Concerning the contents of the *Aika,* I have relied on the research of Kalervo Oberg, "Sointula . . .", p. 28.

[46] *Province,* April 9, 1901; April 22, 1905. *Colonist,* September 8, 1901.

[47] Mrs. Aini Tynjala, "Sointula, Past and Present" (mimeographed supplement to A. Anderson, *History of Sointula.* Dated April, 1969), p. 3.

[48] *Province,* April 22, 1905.

[49] *Ibid.*

[50] Diary dated February 15, 1904. Quoted in Oberg, p. 24.

[51] British Columbia, Department of Education, *Annual Report of Public Schools, 1905* (Victoria, 1906), Tables B and C.

[52] Province, April 22, 1905.

[53] British, Columbia, Department of Education, *Annual Report of Public Schools, 1906 (Victoria, 1907), Table C.*

[54] Anderson, p. 10.

[55] Kalevan Kansa Colonization Company Diary, February 15, 1904. Quoted in Oberg, p. 24.

[56] F. E. Leach to the Surveyor-General, November 16, 1914. In British Columbia, *Report of the Minister of Lands . . . 1914* (Victoria, 1915), p. D168.

[58] Kolehmainen lists some other areas of disagreement among the colony's members: questions of policy, the constitution of the colony, the status of private property, the position of women, and the education of children. Kurikka always seemed to be

front and centre in these disputes. Kolehmainen, p. 121.

[59]*Province,* April 22, 1905. In Bird's view, "the colonists have in fact in a very short time done probably what many other communities in this country have taken many long years to accomplish".

[60]Leach to Surveyor General, November 16, 1914. *Report of Minister of Lands . . . 1914,* p. D168.

[61]Anderson, p. 16; Tynjala supplement, p. 4.

[62]Tynjala supplement, p. 2.

[63]The Vancouver *Sun,* August 1, 1970, p. 6. The new temple is reported to be the world's largest outside India, as well as the biggest church in the city. Sikhs have contributed $750,000 to the project and will advance a further $500,000 to make this a fully integrated community centre.

[64]Adrian C. Mayer, *A Report on the East Indian Community in Vancouver.* Working paper. Institute of Social and Economic Research, UBC, 1959, pp. 1-4 and Appendix A, p. 34. Typescript copy in Special Collections, UBC.

[65]Mayer, p. 2. As late as 1944 there were no more than 400 East Indian women in the province. See Marion W. Smith and Hilda W. Boulter, "Sikh Settlers in Canada", *Asia and the Americas,* Vol. 44 (August, 1944), pp. 359-564.

[66]Vancouver *Province,* November 16, 1967, p. 36. The figure of 12,000 was estimated by Ram Strivastava, Simon Fraser University. See also Vancouver *Sun,* August 1, 1970, p. 6. Census records do not specify totals except for Chinese and Japanese with the remaining Asians classified as "other".

[67]Khushwant Singh, *A History of the Sikhs 1839-1964* (Princeton: Princeton University Press, 1966), pp. 169-175.

[68]*Ibid.,* p. 173, n. 14. Two regulations, P. C. 2642 (1913) and P. C. 23624 (1914), passed by the B.C. government allowed them to exclude all "artisans or labourers, skilled or unskilled" and this conveniently permitted discrimination against East Indians – and incidentally to exclude all women and children.

[69]*The Aryan,* Vol. 1, No. 1 (August 1911), p. 3. This monthly publication carried the following message: "Devoted to the spread of the Eastern View of the Truth; the Interests of the Hindus in the British Dominions; and the Cause of the Present Unrest in India." Issues to March-April 1912 are in the Provincial Archives, Victoria, B.C. The chief concern of *The Aryan* was to correct false allegations made by officials on the "unsuitability" of East Indians as immigrants.

[70]*Ibid.,* pp. 5-6.

[71]Mayer, Appendix A.

[72]The ill-fated *Komagata Maru* incident in 1914 had contributed to a hardening of opposition to Asian immigration and intensified the grievance of the Sikhs. For details see *India, Report of the Komagata Maru Committee of Inquiry,* Calcutta: 1914; G. H. Lowes, "The Sikhs in British Columbia", (Graduating Thesis, Dept. of History, UBC, 1952); Robie L. Reid, "The Inside Story of the 'Komagata Maru' ", *British Columbia Historical Quarterly* Vol. V, No. 1 (1941), pp. 1-23; and Fred Lockley, "The Hindu Invasion, A New Immigration Problem," *Sunset, The Pacific Monthly* (1916?), pp. 584-595. These items are in Special Collections, UBC.

[73]Kartar Singh arrived in Canada in 1911, aged twenty-two. A teacher in Punjab, he followed this profession in Canada where he also started three publications. See *India and Canada, A Journal of Interpretation and Information,* Vol. 1, No. 1 (June 1929) in Special Collections, UBC.

[74]Vancouver *Province,* November 16, 1967, p. 36, and Mayer, *passim.* Sikhs in the Punjab were primarily peasant farmers and had not had any experience working in the woods.

[75]Khushwant Singh, p. 174; Lowes, pp. 37-40. Lowes cites Khalsa Diwan proceedings which place the date of the founding in 1909, and mentions Coombs and Abbotsford as additional places where the society had branches.

[76]Lowes, pp. 37-40.

[77] *The Canadian Sikh*, Vol. 2, No. 1 (July 1962). This is a special issue dedicated to the Port Alberni temple ceremonies. A previous reference to the Alberni Valley Sikh Community noted that among the guests of honour at the initiation were S. Bachint Singh, president of the Sikh Education Board of Vancouver and S. Arjan Singh, secretary of Vancouver's Khalsa Diwan Society. *The Canadian Sikh*, Vol. 1, No. 6 (November 1961), p. 17.

[78] Mayer, p. 8.

[79] *Ibid*. The 2nd Avenue temple has since been replaced by the new one at Ross Street and Southwest Marine. See note 1 supra.

[80] Margaret S. Belford, "Punjab in Victoria", *The Daily Colonist*, April 14, 1968, p. 2.

[81] Mayer, p. 6.

[82] *Ibid.*, pp. 6-8.

[83] *Ibid.*, p. 29. Mayer noted that evening classes in Gurmukki were in progress while one that was started for English instruction was in danger of failing as it lacked serious students. When the Sikhs launched their sawmill enterprise at Barnet — Kapoor Sawmills — they also erected a building at the mill to house cultural records, books, and musical instruments. Vancouver *Province*, July 18, 1942, Magazine Section, p. 5.

[84] *The Aryan*, Vol. 1, No. 2 (September 1911), p. 3.

[85] Lowes, p. 40, n. 9.

[86] *The Hindustanee*, April 1, 1914, p. 8, a monthly publication of the United India League, Victoria. Copies March 14-June 14, 1914 are in the Provincial Archives, Victoria, B.C.

[87] R. A. Francis, "B.C.'s Turbaned Tribe", *Canadian Business* (February 1952), pp. 44-45, 124. Singh started *Sansar* (World) in Victoria in 1912, *Canada and India* in Toronto in 1915 and *India and Canada. A Journal of Interpretation and Information* in Vancouver just as the Depression came and made financial success impossible.

[88] *The Hindustanee*, March 1, 1914, p. 11 and April 1, 1914, p. 10.

[89] *The Canadian Sikh*, Vol. 1, No. 3 (August 1961).

[90] *Ibid*.

[91] The Vancouver *Sun*, August 1, 1970, p. 6.

[92] Lowes, p. 37; Mayer, p. 5.

[93] Mayer, p. 28. He notes the consistent stand of the Sikhs on opposing inter-marriage with Caucasians, despite several decades when women were not available.

[94] *Ibid.*, p. 26.

[95] *Ibid.*, p. 28. In an interview last year Charan Gill, U.B.C. graduate in Education stated that while she no longer had a permanent association with her ethnic group she understood Punjabi and had memories of discrimination to which her family had been subjected, including her mother particularly, who worked as a translator for the Immigration Department in Vancouver. Miss Gill said her generation had a deep pride in the Sikh tradition and it was her assessment that this was not likely to fade and would perhaps be fortified in the years ahead. Interviewed by Jorgen Dahlie, Prince George, B.C., May 5, 1970.

THE EDUCATION OF A MINORITY —
JEWISH CHILDREN IN GREATER MONTREAL

Dr. Joseph Kage
Jewish Immigrant Aid Services of Canada (JIAS)

Preamble

Minority is not a narrowly-defined term and may have several connotations. In Europe, for example, it usually implied a folk or national group which, through war or political arrangements, found itself within a larger political unit inhabited by a dominant population. *The Random House Dictionary of the English Language* defines minority as "a group differing in race, religion, or ethnic background from the majority of a population, especially when the difference is obvious and causes or is likely to cause members to be treated unfairly." *A Dictionary of Sociology* (H.P. Fairchild, ed., 1944) defines a minority as a sub-group within a larger group, ordinarily a society, bound together by some special ties of its own, usually race or nationality, but sometimes religion or other cultural affiliation.

Canada is a nation of immigrants, but also a society of minorities because every group comprising the Canadian mosaic is a minority somewhere: the English are a minority in Quebec; the French in Ontario, etc.

It has been aptly said that the question of education is crucial in the area of minority rights. The majority of Quebec's population are French-speaking Roman Catholics. English Protestants are a minority. Jewish children, for purposes of education, are deemed to be Protestant. This paper will discuss the relationship between two Quebec minorities, the Protestant and the Jewish, as reflected in the specific area of education of Jewish school-age children within the Protestant school system. In addition, we shall consider the impact of this relationship on the issue of Jewish education, namely, the education of the Jewish school-age child as a member of a cultural and religious group.

BNA Act — Section 93

Prior to Confederation there were a number of Acts passed in Canada relative to education. In none of them was reference made to specific religious beliefs. The only exception was the Act of 1863 which relates to restoring in Upper Canada (now Ontario) certain rights to Roman Catholics. In all the legislation there is consistent mention of "common schools" as applied to "any religious denomination".

The British North America Act of 1867, sometimes designated as the Canadian Constitution, has given the different provinces the right to legislate in school matters. Section 93 of the Act reads:

In and for each Province the Legislature may exclusively make laws in relation to education, subject and according to the following conditions:

1. Nothing in any such law shall prejudicially affect any right or privilege with respect to denominational schools which any class of persons have by law in the Province at the Union;

2. All the powers, privileges, and duties at the Union by law conferred and imposed in Upper Canada on the Separate Schools and School trustees of the Queen's Roman Catholic subjects shall be and the same are hereby extended to the dissentient schools of the Queen's Protestant and Roman Catholic subjects in Quebec;

3. Where in any Province a system of separate or dissentient schools exists by law at the Union as is thereafter established by the Legislature of the Province, an appeal shall be made to the Governor-General in Council from any Act or decision of any provincial authority affecting any right or privilege of the Protestant or Roman Catholic minority of the Queen's subjects in relation to education.

In general, it can be said that in all provinces of Canada, with the exception of Quebec, there seems to be no difference in the status of the children of any religion.

Separate Schools

Separate schools came into existence when Lower (Quebec) and Upper (Ontario) Canada were united in 1841. This arrangement was a political compromise to alleviate difficulties caused by district between the two major religious groups, the Catholics and Protestants.

In provinces where separate schools existed at the time of entrance into Confederation, the right of religious minorities to maintain such schools is guaranteed by Section 93 of the BNA Act of 1867. In that year the provinces now known as Ontario and Quebec had separate schools.

In provinces where in addition to the common or undenominational schools there exist separate schools for children of Protestant or Catholic parents, these are in fact state schools maintained and supported by the authorities, administered by school boards elected by tax-payers, and follow the curriculum of the public schools. Children who are neither Catholic nor Protestant have complete access to the schools and their parents are eligible to be elected as trustees of the public schools.

Quebec Educational System

The situation in the province of Quebec is completely different. While systems of education differ somewhat from province to province, the

Quebec system is unique. It provides for a confessional structure divided along Roman Catholic and Protestant denominational lines. It also provides for private initiative to organize schools especially at the level of secondary, college, and university education.

In 1869 the Quebec Legislature adopted an Act which defined the concepts of religious majority and minority. The Act states: "The words 'religious majority' and 'religious minority' in that and any other statutes in force concerning public instruction, shall mean the Roman Catholic or Protestant majority or minority, as the case may be."

The same Act established a Council of Public Instruction divided into two committees: Protestant and Catholic. Both committees meet periodically to discuss and govern all matters related to the elementary schools.

Local school boards – except in Montreal and Quebec City where special charters were issued more than a century ago to the school commissions – are elected locally by property owners; they administer the schools in their communities. In Montreal the Catholic School Commission is administered by a board composed of persons appointed by the cabinet and by the archbishop of Montreal. A similar situation exists in Quebec City. The Protestant School Board of Greater Montreal administers the schools of Montreal and surrounding municipalities.

There is no personal provincial tax for education, but there is the Education Fund, made up of taxes levied on certain companies and industries utilizing the natural resources of the province, namely, the hydro-electric, pulp-and-paper and mining industries. Such funds are used to help the local school boards in meeting their financial obligations and to grant special sums for building public schools. School taxes are levied locally and wherever a Catholic and Protestant school commission exist in the same area, each collects its own taxes and administers its own budget. In Montreal, every proprietor is assessed by the city and his name and assessment of his property are put on one of three lists or panels: Catholic, Protestant or Neutral. Each of the two school commissions (or boards) fixes the mill rate that suits its purpose. The city collects the taxes, remitting to each in the following way: to the Catholic School Commission, the tax levied on all Catholic property plus a percentage of the tax on the neutral panel in proportion to the Catholic population of the city; to the Protestant School Board all the proceeds of the tax levied on the Protestant-owned properties plus a percentage of the neutral tax proportional to the Protestant population. The same procedure, except for collection by the city, applies to all other communities in the province of Quebec.

It should be noted that the above provisions apply to the cities of Montreal and Quebec. In all other school districts of the province, minority populations, whether Catholic or Protestant, have had the right to establish and maintain with their taxes separate schools; taxpayers of other denominations residing in the district, paying their taxes to the "common" or majority schools.

The Jewish Community

The first Jewish settlers appeared in Canada about 1760. During the first century of settlement, the number of Jews was very small. In 1831 there were 147 Jewish residents in Upper and Lower Canada; in 1841 — 154; in 1851 — 451.

A change came about the middle of the nineteenth century when Jewish immigrants began to arrive from overseas. The growth of the Jewish population since 1851 for Canada and the province of Quebec can be gleaned from the following table:

Census Year	Canada	Quebec
1851	451	348
1861	1,195	572
1871	1,333	549
1881	2,456	989
1891	6,586	2,703
1901	16,717	7,607
1911	75,838	30,648
1921	126,201	47,977
1931	156,726	60,087
1941	170,241	66,277
1951	204,836	82,701
1961	254,368	104,727
1971	275,000 (est.)	125,000 (est.)

The above data clearly indicates that Quebec's present Jewish inhabitants are either immigrants themselves, or descendents of immigrants who migrated to Canada principally within the last seventy years.

While Jews can be found in many Quebec communities, the vast majority, about 122,000, reside in greater Montreal, which includes the various cities and municipalities surrounding the metropolis, such as Outremont, Westmount, Hampstead, Ville St. Laurent, etc. Therefore, in discussing Jewish education in Montreal, we are dealing with almost the total Jewish population in the province.

Children of non-Catholic and non-Protestant parents attend, as a rule, the Protestant schools. In 1870, at the suggestion of the Protestant Panel, Jewish taxpayers who paid their taxes to the Neutral Panel, were entitled at their option to pay either to the Catholic or Protestant Panels. There was evidently some division of opinion on this matter within the Jewish community, but it was resolved in a decision that the Jewish taxes be paid into the Protestant Panel. Jewish children attended the Protestant schools and on the surface, at least, there were no unusual difficulties until 1902, when for the first time the blatant inequality of the Jewish child in the Protestant school system became apparent.

The Pinsler Case

A Jewish high school boy, Pinsler, was admitted to a scholarship competition and having won the scholarship, was denied it on the grounds that the boy's father was a tenant, not a proprietor, paid no taxes to the Protestant School Panel and, therefore, had no right to the scholarship. This raised the question of what were the rights of Jews in education in the province of Quebec. A test case was made and a mandamus was taken against the Protestant School Board.

The case was tried before Mr. Justice Davidson, who came to a decision that the Protestant School Board was within its rights in refusing the scholarship. In rendering his judgment, Justice Davidson stated that the earlier common schools of the province had been superseded by separate schools in subsequent legislation which designated, in fact, the population of the province as either Roman Catholic or Protestant. Thus, the religious equality of all citizens did not apply to school laws. The injustice was glaring. The Jewish community, other segments of the population, and the press decried a system which made possible a court decision leaving Jewish children without school rights. There were at that time 1,775 Jewish children attending Protestant schools.

Mr. Justice Davidson himself added the following rider to his decision:

> There are now (1903) over 10,000 Jews in the City, and besides a great many property owning taxpayers who are neither Protestant nor Roman Catholics. These numerous and important groups of our population create problems which did not exist when the foundations of our present education school system were laid. Their solution by the Legislature, if this judgment correctly interprets the law, has become of pressing importance.

The decision also meant, of course, that Jews had no legal right under existing legislation to elect or be elected or appointed to any school board.

Jews as "Protestants" Without Rights

The Jewish community was ready to appeal the court judgment. The Protestant School Board, however, suggested an understanding regarding the education of Jewish children. As a result, in April 1903, an Act was passed that Jews shall be considered as Protestants for purposes of education and be accorded all rights and privileges. Section I of the Act reads in part: "Persons professing the Jewish religion shall, for school purposes, be treated in the same manner as Protestants, and for the said purposes, shall be subjected to the same regulations and shall enjoy the same rights and privileges as the latter."

The passing of the Bill, in 1903, solved the problem only partially. Jewish children were admitted to school and Jewish taxpayers paid their taxes to the Protestant School Panel. However, all attempts to secure representation on the school boards were denied. Thus, the promise of "equal rights and privileges" was largely ignored. It may also be added that until 1913 not a single Jewish teacher was engaged by the Board, although 23 per cent of children attending the Protestant schools were of the Jewish faith. In 1924 the Protestant Schools in Montreal numbered about 19,000 Protestant and 12,000 Jewish students. Yet, out of the one thousand teachers employed by the Board, only seventy were of the Jewish faith, and not one Jewish teacher was admitted on the staff of the high schools. There was also a definite attempt at segregation: in schools with parallel classes, all the Jewish children were placed in the same classroom or diverted to the same school.

Grievances were also voiced by the Protestant School Board. There was evidently fear that with growth of the Jewish population and therefore the proportion of Jewish children in the schools, there was likely to be greater demand for representation. The Board also indicated that Jewish holidays interfered with the regular operation of the schools and therefore ways and means to remedy the situation had to be found; this was probably related to the charge of segregation. Financial issues were also a factor.

Litigation

In 1922 the Board made application to the Legislature for a new law to repeal the Act of 1903; to designate the Jews as neutrals and to charge the education of the Jewish children to the Neutral Panel. Such legislation, in effect, would further segregate Jewish children and deprive the Jewish parent from the rights implicit in the Act of 1903.

The Jewish community objected to the proposed legislation. The Quebec government refused to accept the proposal as requested by the Board and introduced temporary compromise measures.

The negotiations in the meantime continued. There were cleavages of opinion among the Jewish representatives as well as among the members of the Protestant Board. One section of the Jewish community requested the application of the 1903 Act in spirit and in fact, and demanded to be treated as Canadian citizens on a level of equality with other citizens. Another Jewish group stated that they did not want to have their children educated under humiliating conditions and therefore preferred the establishment of separate schools. Even some members of the Protestant community pointed out the intolerant attitude of the Protestant Board and called upon the Protestants of Quebec to demonstrate that they "are as ready to exercise toleration towards a Jewish minority as they are anxious to receive toleration from the Roman Catholic majority".

In 1925 the issue was carried to the Court of Appeal and then in 1927 to the Supreme Court of Canada which ruled that:

a) Jews could not be appointed or elected as School Commissioners on the Protestant Board;

b) The Protestant Board could not be obliged to appoint Jewish teachers in its schools;

c) The Provincial Legislature had the right to establish Jewish separate schools;

d) Jewish children could be educated in Protestant schools as a matter of right in Montreal and as a matter of grace in rural schools;

e) Jewish children were to be excused from the study of the New Testament;

d) The Protestant Board pledged not to discriminate against employment of Jews as teachers.

In April 1931, the Quebec government passed a new Act incorporating the agreement between the Protestant and Jewish representatives. At the same time, however, it repealed the provision entitling the establishment of separate schools. This was done without consulting the Jewish Board who, as a result, resigned in protest.

World War II Aftermath

The upheaval of the Second World War, the impact of the vast social and economic changes which took place in Canada, the national and social ferment in the province of Quebec, legislation against discrimination, the quest for human rights, changes of attitudes and relationships, and societal democratization processes — all of these also exercised their impact in the area of education of Jewish children in Quebec. Many of the former grievances have either disappeared or certainly diminished. The fact remains, however, that to all intents and purposes, the Jewish school-age child is still subject to the provisions of the 1903 and 1931 Acts. These provisions are now being practically interpreted in a much more liberal fashion, but the legal disenfranchisement still exists.

In 1967 Jewish representatives were appointed to the Protestant School Board of Montreal, and a Jewish candidate was elected, uncontested, to the Protestant School Board of Chomedy, a suburb of Montreal, now part of the City of Laval. These are steps forward, but tolerance, even if well-meaning and genuine, does not represent equality. The present confessional school system in Montreal, confined to the Catholic and Protestant denominations, places Jews in an unequal position in the province of Quebec. As long as Jews are not given intrinsic rights of suffrage on an equal footing with all Canadians, and are considered for purposes of education as Protestants, without in fact being Protestants, there is a denial of equality. This is the situation which in 1970 affected 19,624 Jewish children of whom 14,584 attended Protestant schools of Greater Montreal, including Chomedy.

In March 1971, the Quebec Minister of Education announced a proposed amendment to the Education Act, partially modifying Jewish disenfranchisement. Legislation is also pending with reference to reorganization of the school administration on the Island of Montreal which would, hopefully, remove the previous anachronistic legislative provisions.

The amendment to the Education Act was adopted by the National Assembly of the Province of Quebec on March 30, 1971, and reads as follows:

1. Section 580 of the Education Act (Revised Statutes, 1964, Chapter 235) is amended by adding the following paragraph:

   This section shall not be interpreted as depriving a person professing the Jewish religion of the right conferred by other parts of this act, to vote and to be a school commissioner for any school municipality contemplated in section 46 or 49, except as regards the Protestant Board of School Commissioners of the City Montreal, the Protestant Board of School Trustees for the City of Outremont and the Protestant Board of School Trustees of the City of Verdun.

2. This act shall come into force on the day of its sanction.

It should be noted that the cities of Montreal, Outremont and Verdun are excluded. In effect the amendment applies to the Jewish residents of St. Laurent, Town of Mount Royal, Hampstead and a few other municipalities.

An editorial in the *Montreal Star* of March 24, 1971, states:

   In view of forthcoming legislation to reorganize school administration on the Island of Montreal, it might have been easy for the provincial government to have avoided a decision on the contentious issue of Jewish disenfranchisement in local school board elections. Recognizing, however, that reorganization of the entire system will take time, and refusing to tolerate further this long-standing discrimination, the government, to its credit, has decided to bring an end to the anomaly of taxation without representation in several areas under the jurisdiction of the Protestant School Board of Greater Montreal.

   If the proposed historical amendment to the Education Act is enacted in time, it will permit Jewish residents of such communities as Hampstead, Town of Mount Royal and St. Laurent to vote and stand for school board office as soon as June of this year. Because of a judicial ruling dating back fifty years, the amendment will still not apply to three other local school boards: Montreal (which also, for school purposes, includes the municipalities of Côte St. Luc, Anjou and St. Léonard), Outremont and Verdun. But the principle of universal suffrage to be embodied in the reorganization bill, also scheduled to be tabled in the near future, should eventually correct the continuing discrepancy in those particular school districts.

While the issue has focussed in recent years on discrimination against Jewish taxpayers and residents in most of the Greater Montreal area, it is not confined to that group alone. Neither Protestants nor Catholics, for example, exercise a school vote in the City of Montreal, where both Boards remain appointive. The denial of universal suffrage in 1971 is more than an anachronism; it is a prejudice, sanctioned by law, which a democratic society should act quickly to remove in its entirety.

Jewish Education

Education of Jews and Jewish education are not synonymous terms. Education of Jews refers to the participation of Jews, their rights, privileges and obligations within the general educational system of the country or area in which they reside. Jewish education relates specifically to the transmission of religious and cultural values, and the historic traditions of Judaism. The biblical command *V' shinantom l' vonecha* (and thou shalt teach tradition diligently unto thy children) has been a holy command for every Jewish father throughout history. In essence, Jewish education is deemed to be the birthright of every Jewish child.

As among other people, the form and content of educational institutions within the Jewish community are basically variables of the prevailing social conditions, economic possibilities, ideological trends, intro- and inter-communal and personal attitudes. It is not within the framework of this paper to discuss the historical evolution of Jewish education. It should be noted, however, that since the very inception of Jewish settlement in Canada, Jewish education was deemed to be a basic part of the communal structure. The Jewish schools of Montreal mirror the kaleidoscope of Jewish life in its various shadings. They vary in their religious philosophies, cultural interpretations, organizational affiliation and intensity of programs. Some are regular day schools which in addition to Jewish studies follow the prescribed curriculum of the general school program of the Protestant schools; some are supplementary afternoon schools or Sunday classes; there are also some private classes and itinerant teachers for religious instructions.

According to 1970 data, there are 19,624 Jewish children of school age attending the Protestant and Jewish day schools in Greater Montreal, including Chomedy.

The distribution of Jewish pupils among the Protestant and Jewish day schools on the elementary and high school levels is as follows:

Auspices	Elementary	High	Total
Protestant – Greater Montreal	6,084	5,665	11,749
Protestant – Chomedy	1,960	875	2,835
Jewish Day School	4,278	762	5,040
	12,322	7,302	19,624

Thus, 5,040 Jewish children in Montreal attend Jewish day schools where they receive their secular and Jewish training. The language of instruction in the secular subjects is English with French assuming greater importance. The language of instruction in the Jewish subjects is Hebrew and/or Yiddish. Until recently such schools received no tax support. As of 1968, however, certain schools have been recognized as having "associate" status with the Montreal Protestant School Board and received a per capita subsidy for secular studies. The Jewish studies costs are borne by the schools which derive their revenues from fees and charitable appeals. The day school fee per child for Jewish studies alone amounts to $350-400 per year.

Under the prevailing conditions, only a certain percentage of children can attend the day schools. Apart from the very high cost of day school education, which makes it financially prohibitive for the majority of parents, only the intellectually capable and motivated child can cope with the heavy curriculum, combining within almost the same number of school hours both the general secular and Jewish studies.

The fact remains that for many years about 25-30% of the Jewish children of school age attending day schools were thus not taking advantage of the Protestant Board schools. Yet, the Protestant School Board was receiving school taxes on their behalf, which really means that Jewish taxpayers were subject to double taxation.

In a study based on the 1958-9 school year, it was shown that if the number of children attending Jewish day schools were added to the Protestant Board schools, all facilities and costs to the Protestant Board would be increased by at least 10 per cent – an estimated four million dollars for new school buildings and about one million on yearly operating expense.

There are also Jewish afternoon schools for children who receive their general education in the Protestant schools. It is estimated that in 1970 about 2,600 children were registered in such schools. The afternoon schools are geared primarily to elementary grades and the curriculum is entirely devoted to Jewish studies. The schools are financed entirely from fees and contributions: the average cost per child is about $125-150 per annum.

Under existing conditions only about 40 per cent of Jewish children of school age in Montreal receive some form of Jewish education. Conceivably, if the Jewish community had not been subject to double taxation for school purposes, the funds thus saved could have been utilized to permit a higher percentage of children to benefit from a program of Jewish education; the existing system, furthermore, would have been relieved from heavy deficits, overcrowded facilities and other impediments to a decent Jewish educational program.

Summary

The specific conditions of the BNA Act have established a particular, two-confessional Catholic and Protestant school system in the province of Quebec. Jews, for purposes of education, have been classified as Protestants. However, their rights to equality were denied. No matter what the Fathers of Confederation had in mind when drafting the educational provisions of the BNA Act, it is very unlikely that they wished to preclude Canadians of the Jewish faith from equal educational rights and subject them to the existing undignified legal status. In a sense, it may also be argued that for Jews to ask for a voice in the affairs of the dissentient Protestant schools may be an infringement on the rights of Protestants: Jews are not Protestants, and a Protestant or Catholic school, by definition, is not a neutral school.

The Jewish community of Greater Montreal numbers about 122,000 persons and forms the vast majority of the total Jewish population of Quebec.

The community has a particular interest in the private sector of education, as evidenced by the fact that 5,040 Jewish children attend Jewish day schools. They are not operated for private gain and admission is open to all children of the Jewish faith. In the specifics of the Quebec educational program they are in fact confessional schools within the same ambience as Quebec Catholic or Protestant confessional schools. Legally, however, they are considered as private schools. It was not until very recently that the Jewish day schools that have been accorded "associate" status have benefited from a per capita subsidy from the Protestant School Board for ongoing operational expenses. The Jewish studies part of the curriculum, however, have not been receiving such support nor are funds allocated capital expenditures. Thus, Jewish children remain disadvantaged and their rights denied in terms of whatever aid, tax support and grants are provided to the established confessional schools.

Group identity is a must for every individual and many forms of personal pathology are ascribed to alienation from such membership. It is also consonant with the proclaimed aims of Canada as a multi-cultural society, where alongside the two main cultures, English and French, other cultural values are encouraged.

About 60 per cent of school age Jewish children in Montreal do not benefit from Jewish education: in essence, this means a denial of their group cultural rights. The Montreal Jewish community, as a voluntary association, is faced with the need to maintain its cultural and religious identity in an active and vital form. This requires extensive effort on the part of the Jewish community of Montreal, but it is also imperative that Jews obtain equal civic rights and tax support in educational matters which would assist the private voluntary efforts in creating a more supportive structure for Jewish cultural development. Equality implies that the constitutionality of guaranteed rights, privileges and obligations with regard to schools must apply to all segments of the population. This equality with reference to primary and secondary education has been denied to the Montreal Jewish community.

RELIGION AS A SOURCE OF PERPETUATION
OF ETHNIC IDENTITY

David Millett
Department of Sociology
University of Ottawa

One observation occurs repeatedly as one studies various ethnic groups in Canada: of all the institutions supporting the survival of distinctive cultures, the church is usually the strongest and the most active. I would like first to document the ethnic diversity of the churches; then to enquire whether this diversity simply reflects Canadian society or is also cultivated by the churches; and finally to examine what the decline of religion in Canada means for the future of ethnic diversity.

The Documentation of Diversity

I have confined my attention here to some census material, to information from the annual reports of certain churches, and to a small survey I carried out in connection with a doctoral thesis.[1]

Taking language differences as an indicator of ethnic diversity, it is apparent that the variety of languages of worship in Canada is truly amazing. In 1968, when I conducted a survey of languages of worship, I found that Roman Catholics worshipped in twenty-one languages, the United Church of Canada in fourteen, the Anglicans in twelve, the Presbyterians in five, the Lutherans in nine and the Baptists in thirteen. Orthodox churches usually worship in their own tongues, with the exception of the Syrians of certain parishes. Altogether I found 118 Roman Catholic parishes worshipping in languages other than English or French, and 502 Protestant congregations worshipping in languages other than English, in the above-mentioned denominations. To these must of course be added hundreds of Orthodox, Mennonite, Hutterite, Doukhobor, and other parishes and congregations.

Notwithstanding the diversity of languages available, each of the major denominations of Christianity in this country, as well as the major non-Christian religions, displays a heavy concentration of adherents claiming the same national origin, the same language, or both. Roman Catholicism, for instance, ranged from 63.6% to 58.3% French, and 15.5% to 19.9% British in the period 1931-71. The most recent breakdown of the British population (1941) indicated 52.4% Irish, 28.0% English, 19.1% Scottish, and 0.5% "Other". Therefore I consider it legitimate to speak of the French and Irish wings of the Catholic church. Even with the heavy immigration of German and Italian Catholics after World War II, their combined force in 1961 was less than that of the Irish (if we assume that half the British were still Irish).[2]

To take another example, the United Church of Canada is essentially British in origin, though its Britishness has declined from 88.4% in 1931 to 78.6% in 1971. The latest breakdown (1941) of those claiming British as national origin showed 49.5% English, 27.8% Scottish, and 21.3% Irish.

In the Orthodox Church, the Ukrainians steadily increased their dominance from 54.1% in 1931 to 64.5% in 1951, but began to be challenged by the Greeks and Romanians in the 1950s. By 1971 Ukrainians constituted only 36.9% of the Orthodox, while Greeks alone accounted for 35.4%.

Figures on the origins of Jews are complicated by the fact that "Jewish" was offered as an ethnic origin as well as a religion until 1961. This response, however, has been increasingly rejected by Canadian Jews. It was given by 99.8% of the respondents in 1931, but dropped to 66.3% by 1961. In 1971 all persons answering "Jewish" by religion were assigned Jewish origin, no matter what response they actually gave. The 1961 figures give a vague (but unreliable) suggestion of the composition of Canadian Jewry. They report 10.7% Polish, 9.2% Russian, 2.0% Hungarian, 1.6% Austrian, 0.8% German, and 2.7% British. It seems, then, that East European (Ashkenazic) origins are dominant. (Presumably the majority of other respondents gave Canadian, American, or Israeli as their origins.)

These studies suggest two things: First, that the number of languages used in Canada's religious institutions is immense; and second, that these institutions, in their linguistically-defined or origin-defined structure, encourage and perhaps permit the survival of a great many ethnic groups. Churches appear to be more ethnically diverse than schools, political groups, or any other major Canadian institution.

Is This Diversity Intentional?

A key question is whether the churches' diversity is merely a reflection of Canada's diversity, or whether the churches purposely maintain this diversity. An argument can certainly be made that churches are a repository of diversity by default; that is, other institutions which normally would be diverse are denied this possibility by Canadian law. The public and separate school systems, the courts and the political systems operate only in the official languages of the country, except in individual cases where this is clearly impossible. The language of work is nearly always English or French. This leaves the churches, the family, and certain recreational institutions as the only places where people seeking those of their own race, national origin or language can gather and feel at ease. And to feel "at ease", in this case, means primarily to feel that one's language, attitudes, and references to other times and places are understood.

One of the functions of the identifiably ethnic parish or congregation is precisely to make its members "feel at ease" in this sense. It provides them with words of understanding and familiar rituals which, at least once a week, free them from the tension of speaking another language or of being continually misunderstood, and from the isolation of knowing that one's deepest convictions are not shared by anyone else at work, or at school, or on the street.

Once having set up such an environment, church authorities feel they must maintain it, certainly through a sense of responsibility to those they describe as "the faithful", but also because it is in their own bureaucratic self-interest. One is easily tempted to count heads at the end of each year and to interpret an increase as strictly the work of the Holy Spirit. Conversely, a decrease must be interpreted as the work of forces contrary to the Holy Spirit, such as forced assimilation by a majority group, or the yielding of the faithful to the temptation to assimilate.

Once this line of thought is indulged in, it is very easy for the preservation of ethnic identity to become the *first* priority of an ethnic church, and for strictly religious considerations to be used as *justifications* of ethnic survival. The church then begins to attract primarily those interested in ethnic survival and to alienate those with genuine religious convictions. And the church becomes a generator and guardian of ethnic diversity rather than simply reflecting the diversity of the Canadian population. It takes under its wing those national associations, cultural groups and mutual aid societies which are not strong enough to survive on their own, and sponsors language courses, dancing classes, and political activities.

All this happens to different degrees and with varying effectiveness depending on the size of the ethnic population, the number of generations that have been in Canada, the regularity of the flow of immigrants, and whether a whole church is involved (the Orthodox case) or only an ethnic parish of an English-language or French-language sponsoring church.

The result of this is the hyphenated Canadian, who identifies himself by religion and language (French Jew, English Catholic, French Protestant), or by religion and national origin (Ukrainian Orthodox, German Catholic, Scotch Presbyterian, Swedish Lutheran).

The Future of Religion and Ethnic Diversity

In 1971 Canadians affiliated themselves with nine principal religious bodies,[3] comprising 88% of the Canadian population. All of these are growing more slowly than the national population, and complaining of a decline in religiosity. I do not propose to discuss the theological reasons for this decline, but simply to suggest that there are also other reasons which are related to problems of ethnic identity.

The generation of Canadians which has grown up since the advent of television has had an opportunity never before available to experience visually the events and the people of all parts of the country. This experience has tended to break down their regionalism as Maritimers, Central Canadians, Westerners and Coast-dwellers, and at the same time has separated them from older people who still think in regional terms. Internationally, television has brought them into visual contact with many countries of the world, no longer confining them to English-speaking Commonwealth countries, as the CBC radio programs tended to do in the past. Canada, in their eyes, thus becomes less and less a child of Britain, and more and more a self-determining country with a truly international approach to the world. The fact that Canada is less Britain-oriented externally helps destroy the myth that it is essentially British internally. But whereas for the older generations the destruction of the British myth leads to the notion of a mosaic, the young people have a different experience. Not being raised with a British myth, they define themselves and the country as simply Canadian. Their definition of themselves is based on the country *as it is,* and not on a lot of other countries which have sent people to live here. Thus they oppose or ignore any institution which seems to perpetuate old traditions, including prejudices brought from other lands.

The most obvious perpetuator of old traditions and prejudices is the ethnic church. As we have seen, *all* major denominations in Canada are ethnically identifiable, and this is reinforced by parish traditions.[4] Churches are also the repository of dying languages, spoken by increasingly elderly people, and directed by increasingly elderly clergy, as recruitment to seminaries and theological colleges drops drastically from year to year. To the young Canadian, then, churches are institutions for old people with old languages and old prejudices which divide people on a very petty basis. For him there are much more serious kinds of division to be overcome, such as rich and poor, rural and urban, Indian and white, and French and English, and independence versus American domination. The Church, far from uniting Canadians under God, divides them into Protestant, Catholic, Orthodox and Jew, so that they are even discouraged from marrying one another.

If the best of our many ethnic traditions are to be preserved, then, they must be removed from the churches and located in other institutions which are more acceptable to young people, and divorced from the old battles and prejudices which are so often used to justify them. They must be shown to be relevant to the present, in the context of a pan-Canadian identity expressed in two official languages. They must also be shown to be of practical use internationally.[5] People under thirty years of age will no longer study Ukrainian because their father is Ukrainian; they will only do it if the Ukrainian language is shown to be useful to them *in* Canada, *now, as* Canadians, and in Canada's relation to the rest of the world.

Those languages and sub-cultures which will survive will probably be those whose countries of origin are most important on the world scene, and they will survive because our school systems will begin to point out their importance for *all* Canadians, rather than simply for those whose families come from this or that country, and attend an ethnic church.

NOTES

[1] An updated version of the thesis is presently being considered for publication by MacMillan of Canada under the title, *The Age of Organized Religion in Canada.*

[2] By 1971, however, the Italians, with 6.8% of all Catholics, were approaching the Irish (7.5%), and 61.7% of Catholics were neither British nor French in origin.

[3] In order of size, these were: Roman Catholic 9,974,895; United Church of Canada 3,768,800; Anglican 2,543,180; Presbyterian 872,335; Lutheran 715,740; Orthodox 316,605; Greek Catholic 227,730. The total is 19,087,530, out of a national population of 21,568,310.

[4] As recently as 1962 I attended a Saint Andrew's Day banquet at a United Church in Montreal, where the guest speaker gave a tongue-in-cheek explanation of "Why the Scots are God's Chosen People".

[5] I find it rather unfortunate, for example, that with some 70,000 persons of Chinese origin in Canada, a few years ago we should have sent still another elderly Anglo-Saxon abroad as Ambassador to China, however acceptable his credentials.

THE UKRAINIAN CATHOLIC CHURCH
AS A NATIONAL INSTITUTION

Dr. Bohdan Z. Kazymyra
University of Saskatchewan, Regina campus

The Ukrainian Catholic Church was originally known in Canada as the Ruthenian Greek Catholic Church. This Church was founded by Volodymyr the Great, the prince of Kievan Rus'. During the twelfth to the fourteenth centuries there was an alienation from the Apostolic See. By the Act of Union during the National Synod (i.e. ecclesiastical council) of the Ukrainian Church at Brest in 1596 the hierarchy recognized the supremacy of the pope. The Church accepted all dogmas pertaining to Catholicism but retained certain privileges which resulted in the development of a distinctive character in such areas as rite and church language; separate church organization and hierarchy; own church calendar (Julian); married clergy and distinctive canon law concerning church administration, discipline, etc. Receiving these privileges the Church obtained its own specific identity which vested it with particular national characteristics.

Ukrainians are religious people by nature. Their Church and religion have become, throughout the centuries, a source of strength and courage in fighting for religious and national identity.

Due to geo-political circumstances the Church as a national institution guided the people in their struggle for religious, cultural and national survival. From the beginning of the Tartar invasions in the thirteenth century to this day the church leaders have remained inseparable from the populace. The metropolitans from Kiev or Galicia (Halych) were efficient opponents to political invaders of Ukraine.

The majority of Ukrainians belong to the Orthodox Church, and a minority to the Catholic Church. Both churches have persistently strived to preserve their religious and ethnic identity.

The Ukrainian Catholic Church in Canada is an offspring of the mother Church in Western Ukraine. This Church although universal, i.e. catholic, is also a typical national institution with its own identity.

The Ukrainian settler establishing himself in the Prairie provinces, found well-established Catholic and Protestant church organizations. Under the impulse of their profound religious beliefs and strengthened by the influence of the environment, the Ukrainians started to build up their organizational life in Canada around their two national churches: Catholic and Orthodox.

There are four distinct periods in the development of the Ukrainian Catholic Church in Canada, namely: the pioneer era; the period of Bishop

Budka; the development under Bishop Ladyka; and the establishment and growth of the Metropolitan See.

Each era is characterized by the strivings of various laymen, clergy and hierarchy to build up the Church as a national institution as a means to preserve and develop religious and ethnic identity.

During the pioneer era there was a shortage of Ukrainian priests to serve the immigrants and provide necessary leadership. Only a few priests from the United States moved to Canada to temporarily serve their country-men. The arrival of the first Basilian fathers in 1902 and the apostolic understanding of the Latin hierarchy in western Canada was a turning point.

During that period a few Ukrainian churches were built, a number of chapels erected, Russian Orthodox propaganda was repudiated, church institutions such as schools, choirs and dramatic societies evolved to help the newcomers in their adjustment.

When Bishop Budka arrived in Canada in 1912 he found that his countrymen had made noticeable progress and were somewhat organized. The bishop, a young and vigorous man, managed in a short time to normal-ize religious life for his people. One of his first achievements was to make his church a chartered institution. Further he paid proper attention to organizing parishes, schools, economic institutions and in obtaining new priests. New parishes and other church institutions helped a great deal in integration but protected from assimilation.

In 1929 a Basilian monk, Father Ladyka, was nominated bishop. His main goal was to strengthen Bishop Budka's notable achievements, to keep close ties with the hierarchy in Western Ukraine and to expand his activ-ities into new pastoral fields. He increased the number of clergy, started to organize the lay element on the principle of catholic action and paid due attention to publishing. The Ukrainian Catholic Church was steadily ex-panding. Therefore in 1948 this vast diocese was divided into three exar-chates. The Church was strikingly fortified by the arrival of the new im-migrants.

With the establishment of the Metropolitan See in 1956 and Bishop M. Hermaniuk as the first Archbishop-Metropolitan, the Ukrainian Catholic Church in Canada obtained a structural entity similar to that in Kiev or Western Ukraine. Although the Ukrainian Catholic Church in Western Ukraine is now oppressed and confined to the catacombs, it is flourishing and further expanding here in Canada. This Church serves Ukrainian Canadians as a truly ethnic institution and contributes to preserving their religious, cultural and national heritage. Some 200,000 persons belong to the Church. It has the complete Church hierarchy (one archbishop-metro-politan and three bishops), adequate number of clergy, church institutions, lay organizations, etc. Rite, canon law, organization and discipline are observed.

In recent years Ukrainians in the free world are requesting the Apostolic See to establish the patriarchate for Ukrainian Catholics with Major-Archbishop Joseph Cardinal Slipyj as the first patriarch. This is regarded as a vital means of strengthening and uniting scattered forces. The Ukrainian hierarchy in Canada is supporting this plea.

The Ukrainian Catholic Church, this transplant from the Old Country, did not lose its charm and vitality. The institutions established and developed by the church preach love and loyalty to the new country as well as love and loyalty to their religion, traditions and ethnicity.

BIBLIOGRAPHY

Balch, Emily Greene. *Our Slavic Fellow Citizens.* New York, 1910.

Bozyk, P. *Church of the Ukrainians in Canada.* Winnipeg: Canadian Ukrainian, 1927.

Canada. Royal Commission on Bilingualism and Biculturalism. *The Cultural Contribution of the Other Ethnic Groups.* Ottawa: Queens Printer, 1970.

Darcovich, William. *Ukrainians in Canada: The Struggle to Retain Their Identity.* Ottawa: Ukrainian Self-Reliance Assn., 1967.

Elliott, Jean Leonard (ed.). *Immigrant Groups.* Scarborough: Prentice-Hall, 1971.

Inter University Committee on Canadian Slavs. *Slavs in Canada.* Proceedings of Conferences held at Banff (1965), Vol. I; University of Ottawa (1967), Vol. II; and York University, Toronto (1969), Vol. III.

Janiw, Volodymyr (ed.). *Material for History of the Ukrainian Church.* Munich, 1969 (Scientific Memoirs of the Ukrainian Free University, no. 9-10, 1967-1968).

_____ *Religion in the Life of the Ukrainian People.* Munich, 1966 (Memoirs of the Shevchenco Scientific Society, v. 181, 1966).

_____ *The Ukrainian Layman in the Life of the Church, Society and Mankind.* Paris: 1966 (Collected Material of the Ukrainian Christian Movement Study-Conference, v. 3, 1966).

Kazymyra, Bohdan Z. *Development of the Ukrainian Catholic Group in Canada.* Toronto: Basilian Press, 1965.

_____ *First Basilian in Canada.* Toronto: Basilian Press, 1961.

_____ "Metropolitan Andrew Sheptyckyj and the Ukrainians in Canada", *Canadian Catholic Historical Association. Report 1957.* Ottawa. (pp. 75-86.)

_____ *Obstacles and Achievements of a Great Undertaking: Two Aspects of Metropolitan Sheptycky's Plan for the Settling of Ukrainians in Canada.* Rome: Bohoslovia, 1969.

Kaye, Vladimir Julian. *Early Ukrainian Settlements in Canada 1895-1900.* Toronto: University of Toronto Press, 1964.

Kubijovyc, V. (ed.). *Ukraine: A Concise Encyclopaedia,* 2 vols. Toronto: University of Toronto Press, 1963-71.

Marunchak, Michael H. *The Ukrainian Canadians: A History.* Winnipeg: Ukrainian Free Academy of Sciences, 1970.

Nahayewsky, Isidore. *History of Ukraine.* Philadelphia: America, 1962.

Piddubcheshen, Eva. . . . *And Bless Thine Inheritance.* Schenectedy: Eric Hugo Printing Co., 1970.

Pospishil, Victor J. and H. M. Luznycky. *The Quest for an Ukrainian Catholic Patriarchate.* Philadelphia: Ukrainian Publications, 1971.

Slipyj, Joseph. *Blahovisnyk—Litterae—Nuntiae Archiepiscopi Maioris Ritus Byzantino-Ukraine.* Rome, 1965-1970.

Skwarok, J. *The Ukrainian Settlers in Canada and Their Schools, 1891-1921.* Edmonton: Basilian Press, 1958.

Trosky, Odarka S. *The Ukrainian Greek Orthodox Church in Canada.* Winnipeg, 1968.

Woycenko, Olha. *The Ukrainians in Canada.* Winnipeg: Trident Press, 1967.

Yuzyk, Paul. *Ukrainian Canadians: Their Place and Role in Canadian Life.* Toronto: Ukrainian Canadian Business and Professional Federation, 1967.

_____ *The Ukrainians in Manitoba: A Social History.* Toronto: University of Toronto Press, 1953.

ESSAI D'HISTOIRE COMPARÉE:
RELIGION ET NATIONALISME

Michel Brunet
Département d'histoire
Université de Montréal

Face aux mystères de la nature et de sa propre existence, l'homme pré-historique s'est posé de troublantes questions sur l'origine de la vie, sur l'action des déterminismes auxquels it était soumis, sur le sens de la mort, en particulier de la sienne. Ses interrogations et les réponses qu'il leur a données ont engendré les diverses religions primitives. Quelques-unes d'entre elles ont évolué pour finalement constituer un corps de doctrine s'iden-tifiant avec une civilisation particulière. Dans d'autres cas, les grandes religions organisées ont intégré les cultes avec lesquels elles étaient en concurrence et facilité ainsi l'assimilation des groupes culturels qui les pratiquaient.

Toute religion peut se vivre à deux niveaux du comportement humain. Si une religion est d'abord un itinéraire individuel, des circonstances par-ticulières la transforment souvent en une expression d'action collective. La religion devient alors un phénomène politique. Dans plusieurs sociétés primitives, le pouvoir s'exerçait à l'intérieur des structures religieuses. Dans d'autres cas, l'autorité politique jugeait nécessaire d'imposer un culte officiel afin de prévenir plus facilement tout mouvement d'opposition. Des chefs religieux ont également usé de leur autorité pour mettre sous leur coupe le pouvoir civil. De même qu'on a vu les puissances impérialistes se servir des Eglises avec lesquelles elles s'étaient associées pour consolider leur domination, ne doit-on pas être surpris de constater que les groupes dominés ou minoritaires ont privilégié leurs institutions religieuses dans un geste spontané de conservation afin de protéger leur existence comme collectivités distinctes.

A titre d'expérience personnelle poursuivie isolément ou en groupe afin d'atteindre à un certain équilibre émotif qui favorise le plein épanouissement de l'individu et lui assure la maîtrise de soi, la religion est un objet d'étude qui appartient principalement aux théologiens, aux philosophes et aux psychologues. L'historien en tient parfois compte surtout quand il étudie certains personnages qui ont directement influencé l'évolution historique chez lesquels le sentiment religieux a joué un rôle particulier. Il doit alors devenir temporairement psychologue.

Mais l'historien ne raconte pas d'abord l'histoire des individus. Sa tâche c'est de décrire, de comprendre et d'expliquer la vie des collectivités. Comment se sont-elles formées? Quel fut leur développement? Quels déterminismes ont agi sur celui-ci? Quelles furent les causes de leurs échecs et de leurs succès? Comment leur présent et leur avenir sont-ils liés à leur passé? Pour répondre à ces questions, l'historien doit déceler et évaluer tous les gestes que pose un groupe dans son agir collectif. Si la religion devient une partie de celui-ci c'est parce qu'elle a cessé d'être exclusivement un itinéraire individuel et a pris une dimension politique. Elle s'est alors transformée en un instrument d'affirmation ou de revendication nationaliste. Dans ce cas, la religion entre directement dans le champ d'observation de l'historien.

Ce sont les luttes au sujet de l'exercice du pouvoir qui ont influencé l'histoire des religions comme cultes organisés. Chaque fois que les dirigeants d'un Etat ou d'une collectivité ont cru qu'une religion particulière servait leurs fins politiques, ils l'ont nationalisée. Si, au début, l'Empire romain a persécuté les chrétiens parce qu'il les soupçonnait de menacer son hégémonie, Constantin comprit que le christianisme contribuerait à faciliter l'établissement de son autorité. Charlemagne sut utiliser l'Eglise pour bâtir son Empire. La confusion qui prévalut en Europe entre le IXe et le XIVe siècle permit aux dirigeants ecclésiastiques d'étendre considérablement leur pouvoir politique. Leur prééminence ne pouvait être que temporaire.

La formation des Etats nationaux mit fin à la suprématie du Pape et de ses représentants. La France de François Ier se donna une Eglise nationale en signant le Concordat de 1516 avec Léon X. Les populations de l'Allemagne, de la Confédération helvétique et des Pays-Bas, humiliées et provoquées par l'arrogance des émissaires de Charles-Quint, de Pape et de Philippe II, affirmèrent leur volonté d'indépendance nationale en se déclarant favorables aux nouvelles religions réformées. En Angleterre, le pouvoir royal et le nationalisme de la bourgeoisie s'affirmèrent en consommant la rupture avec Rome. Les Ecossais censurèrent le caractère ambivalent de leurs souverains francophiles en s'inventant une religion nationale. En Irlande, la population vit dans la pratique du catholicisme un moyen de proclamer son droit à une existence collective distincte. Les souverains scandinaves se convertirent au protestantisme qui leur fournit l'occasion d'affirmer leur autorité et de s'enrichir des biens ecclésiastiques. Les régions pauvres de la France ou qui se jugeaient négligées par le pouvoir central s'opposèrent à celui-ci en se déclarant calvinistes. En Espagne, Philippe II se servit de la Sainte Inquisition pour unir sous l'autorité de Madrid les habitants de la péninsule ibérique. Derrière toutes les professions de foi de cette époque, il faut chercher les motifs politiques qui les inspirèrent.

La religion fut également mise au service de l'expansionnisme européen en Amérique, en Asie et en Afrique. L'Espagne, le Portugal et la France prétendirent vouloir augmenter le nombre des membres de l'Eglise romaine en évangélisant les populations aborigènes qu'elles soumirent à leur domination. Celle-ci s'appuyait sur la force militaire et sur l'action des missionnaires qui devinrent, sans toujours s'en rendre compte, les agents d'un pouvoir étranger. Les Anglais se reconnurent la mission de faire échec au papisme partout où leurs navires les conduisirent, particulièrement en Amérique du Nord où ils s'opposèrent à la Nouvelle-France. De leur côté, les Amérindiens, les Asiatiques et les Africains virent dans la conservation de leurs pratiques religieuses ou dans leur opposition au culte proposé par les missionnaires de l'occupant un moyen de contester le joug des envahisseurs. La plupart des anciens peuples colonisés qui ont récemment conquis leur liberté collective semblent peu intéressés à conserver les institutions religieuses que leur ont laissées les Occidentaux. Ils les identifient naturellement avec l'époque de leur mise en servitude.

A l'intérieur du monde occidental des XIXe at XXe siècles, les institutions religieuses ont joué un rôle déterminant chez les minorités nationales soumises à la domination d'une autre collectivité lorsque celle-ci pratiquait une religion différente de celle du groupe minoritaire. La résistance des Irlandais à l'oppression britannique se confondit avec la lutte du catholicisme contre le protestantisme. Dans la partie de la Pologne divisée soumise à la Russie, les nationalistes polonais purent compter sur l'appui au moins tacite du clergé catholique. Celui-ci se montra beaucoup plus docile dans les régions polonaises annexées à l'Autriche. En Italie, les nationalistes durent s'opposer à l'Eglise pour réaliser leurs ambitions politiques. En Afrique du Sud, une commune allégeance au protestantisme ne favorisa pas l'union entre les Britanniques et les Boers. Ceux-ci s'appuyèrent sur leur Eglise luthérienne jusque'au jour où, devenus la majorité de la population blanche, ils obtinrent le contrôle du gouvernement de Pretoria. Ils mirent alors l'Etat au service de leurs fins nationales.

Aux Etats-Unis, les immigrants qui sont parvenus à former, durant une certaine période, des groupes culturels distincts ont trouvé dans les institutions religieuses qu'ils administraient eux-mêmes un cadre leur assurant temporairement un minimum de survivance collective. La plupart de leurs membres finissent, cependant, par s'intégrer à la majorité blanche dès que celle-ci se montre prête à les accueillir. Deux minorités nationales sont appelées à se manifester de plus en plus comme collectivités distinctes disposant d'un pouvoir de marchandage dans la société américaine contemporaine: les Noirs et les Hispano-Américains. Ceux-ci n'ont jamais été des immigrants comme les autres et ne semblent pas destinés à s'assimiler à la majorité des Américains. Il faut préciser, toutefois, que les institutions religieuses ont joué un rôle très restreint dans l'évolution de leur nationalisme. Il en est de même pour les Amérindiens.

Au Canada, les groupes ethniques qui maintiennent encore une existence collective distincte sont ceux que certaines circonstances historiques ou la discrimination pratiquée par la majorité ont amenés à vivre en circuit fermé. Quatre grandes communautés culturelles, ne s'identifiant pas complètement avec la majorite *Canadian,* se détachent de la mosaïque pancanadienne: les Amérindiens, les Juifs, les Slavo-Ukrainiens et les Canadiens français.

Le sort des Amérindiens est le plus tragique. Victimes d'une discrimination absolue qui dure depuis plus de trois siècles, dépouillés de leur territoire, privés des moyens de conserver leur ancienne culture, convertis aux religions de leurs conquérants français et britanniques, ils ont été complètement aliénés. Il est peu probable que le Pouvoir Rouge a un avenir mais il constitue une force de contestation qui devra être canalisée vers des objectifs réalistes qu'auront eux-mêmes choisis les membres de la communauté amérindienne.

Les Juifs se sont longtemps repliés sur leurs traditions religieuses pour expliquer et légitimer leur survivance comme collectivité distincte. En fait, la discrimination générale exercée contre eux ne leur laissait aucun autre choix. La diminution de la pratique religieuse chez les nouvelles générations de la communauté juive et le caractère pluraliste de la société urbaine contemporaine forcent les Juifs canadiens à se poser de nouvelles questions sur leur itinéraire collectif et sur les options individuelles qui leur sont dorénavant offertes. La création de l'Etat d'Israël et le dilemme que celui-ci présente à la conscience des citoyens canadiens d'origine juive qui reconnaissent le Canada comme leur seule et unique patrie ont rendu urgente cette réévaluation globale. En particulier, les Juifs du Québec, où vit la communauté juive la mieux organisée en Amérique du Nord, traversent actuellement une période difficile de transition au cours de laquelle ils doivent choisir le milieu culturel national avec lequel ils s'identifieront. La religion ne peut pas résoudre ce problème qui est essentiellement politique.

Les Slavo-Ukrainiens immigrés au Canada ont longtemps vécu dans un certain isolement. Le genre de vie qu'ils menaient en milieu rural, leur langue, leurs institutions religieuses et l'attitude réservée des WASPS à leur égard ont favorisé une cohésion qui explique la vitalité relative de ce groupe culturel. L'exode rural, la mobilité sociale des nouvelles générations auxquelles une instruction plus poussée ouvre de nouveaux canaux de promotion, la laïcisation de la société contemporaine et son pluralisme ont pour conséquence de mettre à jour la fragilité des institutions sur lesquelles s'appuyait autrefois la communauté slavo-ukrainienne. Celle-ci est engagée dans une nouvelle étape de son évolution historique en territoire canadien. La plupart de ses membres prendront désormais des décisions individuelles qui s'accorderont avec la nouvelle échelle de valeurs qu'ils se seront donnée.

Quant aux Canadiens français, leur association avec l'Eglise catholique a une longue histoire. Cependant, la place qu'ont occupée les institutions religieuses dans leur vie collective a varié selon la conjoncture et en relation avec leur itinéraire comme entité nationale distincte en Amérique du Nord. A l'époque de la Nouvelle-France, l'Eglise était simplement un département de l'Etat. Ainsi l'avaient voulu les rois de France depuis François ler. Louis XIV et Colbert n'ont jamais eu l'intention d'encourager l'établissement d'une théocratie dans la vallée laurentienne. La ferveur mystique de quelques missionnaires, de certaines âmes pieuses et des fondateurs de Ville-Marie ne fut pas un phénomène collectif mais une forme d'action individuelle qui influença très peu l'ensemble de la société coloniale.

En guerre contre les colonies anglaises, les Canadiens du XVIIIe siècle se firent dire par leurs dirigeants ecclésiastiques et laïques qu'ils luttaient pour prévenir l'introduction "dans ce diocèse, dont la Foi a toujours été si pure, [des] erreurs détestables de Luther et de Calvin". En réalité, s'ils étaient prêts à risquer leur vie au combat, c'est parce qui'ils voulaient protéger leurs biens et leur patrie contre un envahisseur qui avait proclamé sa volonté de les écraser comme collectivité distincte en Amérique du Nord.

Immédiatement après la Conquête et jusqu'à la fin du XVIIIe siècle, l'Eglise catholique devint un symbole, un cadre, un point de ralliement pour les Canadiens vaincus, conquis et occupés. Réclamer la nomination d'un évêque, défendre la liberté de culte, afficher avec ostentation leur catholicisme se révélèrent pour les Canadiens des moyens commodes d'action politique, une forme de résistance efficace, un instrument de propagande nationaliste en face d'un conquérant qu'ils ne pouvaient pas défier sur d'autres terrains mais qu'ils forcèrent à négocier avec eux comme collectivité distincte en invoquant le fait qu'ils pratiquaient une autre religion que celle de l'occupant. La situation aurait été bien différente si celui-ci avait été lui-même catholique. Pour affirmer leur identité collective, les Canadiens français auraient dû alors abandonner la pratique religieuse ou fonder une Eglise schismatique.

L'introduction des institutions représentatives, après la mise en vigueur de la Constitution de 1791, fournit à la population francophone de la vallée du Saint-Laurent de nouveaux et puissants moyens d'action collective. Ses représentants à l'Assemblée législative du Bas-Canada ne tardèrent pas à constituer un pouvoir parallèle dans la société coloniale de la première moitié du XIXe siècle. Le parti de Louis-Joseph Papineau, chef incontesté de ses compatriotes, s'opposa aux autorités britanniques et à l'Eglise. Celle-ci fut réduite à un rôle très effacé durant les années où le nationalisme de la collectivité canadienne-française s'exprima à l'Assemblée du Bas-Canada. Les chefs laïques n'avaient-ils pas proclamé que celui-ci était la patrie des Canadiens? Maîtres d'un Etat, ils n'avaient plus besoin de privilégier leurs institutions religieuses pour s'affirmer comme collectivité distincte.

La suspension de la Constitution de 1791, la proclamation de la loi martiale, l'intervention de l'armée britannique, les raids conduits par les troupes de choc formées par les membres les plus fanatiques de la minorité anglaise du Bas-Canada, la création du Conseil spécial, l'exil et la pendaison de plusieurs chefs politiques et la suppression du Bas-Canada rappelèrent brutalement aux Canadiens français que la Conquête de 1760 n'était pas un simple souvenir historique. Ils s'étaient tragiquement trompés en s'imaginant qu'ils avaient le droit de nationaliser le territoire qu'ils habitaient depuis le XVIIe siècle. Un grand rêve politique s'écroulait et les chefs laïques qui l'avaient entretenu perdirent toute crédibilité auprès d'une partie importante de la population. Un nouvel équilibre des forces économiques, politiques et idéologiques obligea celle-ci à se donner de nouveaux objectifs, à se chercher des raisons de vivre et d'espérer sans risquer de s'engager dans un cul-de-sac, à maintenir sa présence collective sans s'exposer aux représailles de la majorité britannique triomphante. Spontanément, comme durant les années qui suivirent immédiatement la Conquête, le peuple se tourna vers ses institutions religieuses.

Quelques dirigeants ecclésiastiques particulièrement lucides, doués d'un sens politique supérieur à celui de Louis-Joseph Papineau et de ses principaux lieutenants, avaient prévu cette minute de vérité, ce revirement de la conjoncture. De 1840 à 1880, l'Eglise québécoise se transforma en une institution puissante dont l'influence déterminante se fit sentir à tous les niveaux de l'agir collectif des Canadiens français. Ceux-ci exprimèrent leur volonté de survivance nationale au sein de structures et d'institutions multiformes que s'était données ou avait suscitées une Eglise omniprésente: paroisses, diocèses, archidiocèses, communautés religieuses d'hommes et de femmes, écoles, collèges, universités, hospices, hôpitaux, entreprises commerciales, industrielles et financières, coopératives de crédit, de consommation et de production, associations professionnelles et ouvrières, mouvements d'éducation populaire, journaux et revues, groupes de pressions, etc. Porte-parole d'une collectivité qui avait dû renoncer — temporairement du moins — à sa vocation nationale sur le territoire laurentien, agents de coordination au sein d'une population momentanément désorientée et privée d'instruments politiques d'action commune entièrement sous son autorité, les dirigeants ecclésiastiques avaient profité des circonstances pour imposer leur autorité. Le peuple lui-même leur en était reconnaissant. Finalement, un Grand Compromis s'établit entre les représentants des principaux groupes qui se partageaient le pouvoir dans la vallée du Saint-Laurent: les grands entrepreneurs capitalistes, les hommes politiques et les chefs religieux. Chacun de ces milieux avait intérêt à préserver l'équilibre qui se constitua au Canada après 1850. Ce Grand Compromis de la vallée laurentienne s'est maintenu jusqu'à la fin de la Deuxième Grande Guerre.

L'instabilité politique que connaissent le Québec et le Canada depuis vingt ans démontre que l'ancien équilibre des forces qu'avait consacré la Constitution de 1867 a été définitivement rompu. Depuis les luttes autonomistes de Maurice Duplessis, les Franco-Québécois ont redécouvert la dimension politique de leur nationalisme séculaire. La nouvelle conjoncture a ramené les institutions religieuses au rôle qui leur revient dans une société laïque et pluraliste. Seules les minorités francophones des provinces anglaises maintiennent l'ancienne alliance de la religion et de la survivance collective. Leur statut, même s'ils ont le droit d'acheter en français des timbres bilingues, ressemble à celui de tous les groupes d'immigrants qui cherchent à prolonger une existence autonome dans un milieu qui ne la favorise pas. Les nouvelles générations sont soumises aux mêmes pressions qui minent toute résistance culturelle qui ne s'appuie pas sur le nombre et sur les instruments politiques que celui-ci permet d'acquérir. Tout agir collectif qui ne conduit pas à la nationalisation d'un Etat et d'un territoire est condamné à demeurer une manifestation de nature folklorique. Héritage de la société paysanne, le folklore est devenu un mode d'expression artistique et un article de musée à l'âge de la cybernétique.

Ce trop court essai d'histoire comparée aura atteint son but s'il aide à faire comprendre que la religion n'est pas, selon Toynbee et ceux qui pensent encore comme lui, "the serious business of the human race".

Chaque individu est seul devant son destin personnel et il lui appartient de donner aux inconnues que celui-ci soulève les réponses que la foi en la vie éternelle ou l'idéal de la perfection lui inspire. Comme membre d'une collectivité, l'homme fonctionne à un autre niveau et rencontre des problèmes qui ne sont pas religieux. Leur solution relève de la politique. Si la religion y est mêlée c'est parce que la vie politique de cette collectivité est incomplète et que les institutions religieuses y exercent un rôle de suppléance.

L'histoire contemporaine du Canada révèle également que la religion est très marginale dans les conflits qui opposent les collectivités. Il fut longtemps admis chez certains historiens et par ceux qui ne demandaient qu'à les croire que les différences religieuses avaient été, depuis la Conquête, la cause principale de l'antagonisme qui existait entre les Canadiens anglais et les Canadiens français. Les premiers ont abandonné le militantisme protestant du XIXe siècle et les seconds ont rejeté les postulats cléricaux qui avaient guidé l'action collective de trois générations de dirigeants ecclésiastiques et laïques. Cette accession commune et parallèle au pluralisme religieux et au laïcisme a-t-elle subitement mis fin aux divisions d'autrefois? Bien naïfs ceux qui l'avaient espéré car celles-ci sont plus profondes que jamais auparavant. Débarrassées des échos des anciens débats théologiques qui en camouflaient la véritable nature, elles ont pris toute leur dimension politique. Ce n'était pas deux religions qui s'opposaient au Canada mais deux nationalismes. Il en a toujours été ainsi dans l'histoire de l'humanité chaque fois que des collectivités se sont disputé l'exercice du pouvoir.

3   Ethnic Identity

CONSTITUTIONAL ASPECTS OF ETHNIC IDENTITY IN CANADA

Dr. Mark MacGuigan M.P.
Windsor — Walkerville
(House of Commons, Ottawa)

In my capacity as joint chairman of the Special Joint Committee of the Senate and House of Commons on the Constitution of Canada, I have been listening for the past eight months to presentations made by others on the theme I have chosen for discussion. From the procedural viewpoint, then, this paper might well be entitled "The Tables Turned" or "The Listener Speaks". However, I want to emphasize that what I say here is not to be taken as an indication of the position of the Parliamentary Committee on the matters treated. I am speaking not as a chairman of the committee, but as a simple Member of Parliament, or better still as a citizen of Canada. Nevertheless, as a member of a committee which has not yet presented its report and is indeed still holding public hearings on this and other subjects, I must keep my remarks somewhat more general than would otherwise have been necessary, so as not to anticipate the recommendations of the committee.

Every constitution has the twofold purpose of expressing as fully as possible the multidimensional reality of a people and of dividing the powers of government according to the views generally accepted by that people. It is usual for lawyers to stress the technical aspect of the division of powers in speaking about constitutions, but this is really secondary in importance, even though it is the most obvious aspect. More important than technical considerations are the values and goals of the people which underlie the division of powers and express the national life of the community in its most fundamental dimensions.

The national realities which are of particular concern to us here are those of an ethnic nature. Let me begin, then, by stating the statistics. The ethnic origin of the Canadian population as of the 1961 census, when the total population was counted as 18,200,000, breaks down as follows: British, almost eight million or 43.85%; French, more than 5,540,000 or 30.38%; other origins, more than 4,700,000 or 25.77%. Among the other origins the predominant are German, with slightly more than one million or 5.75%; Ukrainian, with just under 475,000 or 2.59%; and Italian, with 450,000 or 2.47%. It is interesting to note that the French proportion of the population has remained almost constant since 1871, declining from 31.07% in that year only to 30.38% in 1961, whereas the British proportion declined from 60.55% in 1871 to 43.85% in 1961. The great increase, of course, has come in the category of other ethnic groups, rising from 8.38% in 1871 to 25.77% in 1961.

It will already be obvious that I am using the term "ethnic" in the broad sense of national origin and not in the restricted sense in which it is sometimes used to identify Canadians of the so-called "third force". I believe that this is more than a question of words and is rather one of approach, for it carries the implication that it is impossible to treat the constitutional position of any ethnic minority adequately without putting it in the context of all other ethnic groups. It entails, for example, the conclusion that multiculturalism can be properly considered only in rela-tion to bilingualism. I am not, of course, forgetting the audience I am addressing, but I must be even more mindful of the makeup of the national community. We must, therefore, approach the subject of ethnic identity in its constitutional aspects with the knowledge that the largest ethnic groups in Canada are the British and the French.

These groups are already recognized by the Canadian constitution. Even though the British North America Act did not establish any official language as such, it did confer special rights as to the use of the English and French languages in the legislatures and courts of Canada and of Quebec (Section 133). Moreover, in the amending formula adopted in 1949 for federal matters (Section 91 (1) the English and French lang-uages are put beyond the reach of the Federal Parliament alone. Then, too, the British Empire is specifically referred to in the preamble and in the treaty power (Section 132), and the preamble also expresses the desire of the four provinces which united in 1867 "to be federally united into One Dominion under the Crown of the United Kingdom of Great Britain and Ireland, with a Constitution similar in Principle to that of the United Kingdom".

At the constitutional conference in February (1971) the governments of Canada reached tentative agreement to take a giant step beyond the existing situation and to recognize English and French as the official lang-uages of Canada, with whatever further consequences might be agreed upon. There seems to be little doubt that this tentative agreement will be confirmed at a later constitutional conference, perhaps at the conference in Victoria in several weeks (June 1971). For all practical purposes Canada would now appear to be an officially bilingual country.

The British have always held a position of special recognition in Can-adian government and life both in law and in fact, but in recent years Canadians have come to see that this state of affairs was unfair to the French. The Quiet Revolution which marked the political and social awaken-ing of Quebec soon led to the establishment of the Royal Commission on Bilingualism and Biculturalism in 1963. This commission has only this year wound up its work, but in the eight years of its existence was in undeterminable measure responsible for the enlargement of the French role in our national life. The principal milestone to this point has been the Official Languages Act passed by the Parliament of Canada in 1969, which provided that "the English and French languages are the official languages of Canada for all purposes of the Parliament and Government of Canada". (Section 2.) We have recently had the report of the Bilingual Districts Advisory Board set up under this Act, and in all likelihood the federal Government will within the specified three-month period proclaim bilingual districts, again for purposes only of the Parliament and Government of Canada. And, as I have already mentioned, we appear to be on the verge of constitutional entrenchment of two official languages.

In my opinion the time has now come to raise the question whether there should not also be some form of constitutional recognition of other-ethnic groups. The fact that we have not seriously considered this question before 1971 should be no more of a deterrent to action than was the fact that we had not seriously thought before 1961 of additional recognition of the French fact.

I have already said that a constitution should recognize the multidimensional reality of a people. Such reality includes, perhaps preeminently, the realm of symbols.

Symbolically, Canada has traditionally appeared to be a British country. The constitutional provisions I have already mentioned, the Crown, the general predominance of the English language, the use until recently of the British flag, have all combined to create an impression, at the level of symbol and of feeling, of Canada as distinctively British.

We have now realized that, if we expect French Canadians to feel at home in Canada as a whole and not only in Quebec, Canada's image must be one which includes a French projection as well, and we have moved to achieve that purpose, largely through the medium of language. Canada is therefore in the process of projecting an English-French ethnic image.

Canadians must now consider whether this is where they wish to stop in image-making, or whether they wish to take another step. About 26% of the population (on the 1961 figures) are not able to identify with English-French symbols, except insofar as they have lost consciousness of themselves as members of other-ethnic groups. Should this portion of the population be made to accept symbols which have no resonance for them or should the symbols be augmented so as to provide a broader basis for response?

The Royal Commission on Bilingualism and Biculturalism evaded this issue on the intellectual plane by interpreting their terms of reference "as limiting constitutional change exclusively to the country's two official languages". (Report, Book IV, pp. 13-14.) However, they add that "measures adopted at the provincial level in the spheres of administration and education will be more appropriate for meeting the linguistic requirements of the various cultural groups than a constitutional formula advanced by federal authorities". (*Ibid.*, p. 14.) But the constitutional issue will not go away, even if the commissioners are right in thinking that the most effective measures are those taken at a sub-constitutional level.

One of the ten commissioners, J. B. Rudnyckyj, by a somewhat ingenious interpretation of the terms of reference, succeeded in justifying, in his Separate Statement to Volume I, a proposal for constitutional change concerning regional languages. He recommended that "any language other than English and French used by 10% or more of the population of an appropriate administrative district of a province or territory shall have the status of a regional language; the legislation of the provisions for regional languages shall be vested in the governments concerned". (Volume I, p. 168.) It might well be argued that this proposal is primarily a symbolic one since the definition of the status of a regional language would be left entirely within the discretion of the governments concerned (presumably both federal and provincial).

It appears to me that the case against the constitutional recognition of other-ethnic groups rests on two large fears. The first fear is that such recognition might bring about a Balkanization of our country through a cultural separatism which could effectively negate the building up of a spirit of political and social unity. If constitutional recognition were to turn the country, or at least the other-ethnic parts of it, into a discrete series of ghettoes, such an unfortunate result would demonstrate the folly of the premise. But I see no reason why recognition should not now be equally consistent with integration.

Perhaps I should make it clear that I use the term "integration" in the same sense as the B & B Commission. As their Report states:

> Integration, in the broad sense, does not imply the loss of an individual's identity and original characteristics or of his original language and culture . . . . Integration is not synonymous with assimilation. Assimilation implies almost total absorption into another linguistic and cultural group. (Volume IV, p. 5.)

On the positive side integration implies an adequate adaptation to the character of Canadian society. Of course, the measurement of such things is a matter of degree and of subjective judgment, but it is useful to know the ultimate objective.

Perhaps at an earlier stage of Canadian development Balkanization might have been a legitimate fear. The great wave of other-ethnic immigration came to Canada in the early part of the century, just as the west was being settled. Before the pattern of life in Alberta and Saskatchewan was formed, it conceivably might have been disastrous for Canada to have been inundated with non-assimilable groups which insisted on a relatively distinctive life in largely separate communities. But in the Canada of today, with an ever-increasing majority of people thrown together in the close quarters of urban life and with the powerful uniformity-creating effect of the mass media of communication, it strains credulity to imagine the development of a large-scale problem of Balkanization.

The second fear is of a diminution in the newly-acquired status of the two official languages. This is a more substantial fear, especially in the light of the initial reaction in some other-ethnic (and English) communities to the new policy of official bilingualism, but I nevertheless believe that it, too, is unwarranted. I cannot recall any other-ethnic witness who appeared before the Parliamentary Committee on the Constitution who was not prepared to accept, with greater or lesser degrees of enthusiasm, the official status of the English and French languages. The following statement by the Canada Press Club of Winnipeg, representing some twenty-four other-ethnic publications printed in Manitoba, is typical:

1. Canada is a bilingual country.

2. Our Canadian nation is made up of peoples of many cultural backgrounds. Therefore, it must be recognized that Canada is a multi-cultural country. This multiculturalism must be given recognition in any new Constitution or amendment to the present Constitution. (*Proceedings,* September 10, 1970, no. 8, p. 39.)

Similarly the Montreal branch of the Baltic Federation in Canada declared:

We recognize and respect the historical priority of what have been called the two founding races, which have given Canada its two official languages and its legal and political structure . . . . Nevertheless . . . we would . . . urge that greater official recognition be given to the growing one-third of the Canadian population whose extraction is neither English nor French.
(*Proceedings,* April 28, 1971, no. 71, p. 21.)

The consistent theme of other-ethnic witnesses before the Constitution Committee has been the compatibility of multiculturalism with official bilingualism. I myself can see no likelihood that a constitutional recognition of Canada's actual multiculturalism would in any way diminish the position of the official languages, since they would retain their legal priority.

The case for recognition is not merely the absence of the foregoing fears. I would adopt as a principle the following statement by the B & B Commission: "Canadian society, open and modern, should be able to integrate heterogeneous elements into a harmonious system, to achieve 'unity in diversity'." (Book. IV, p. 7.) In other words, because Canadian society is demographically open, it can integrate heterogeneous cultural groups into a harmonious system for the purpose of creating unity, even while maintaining diversity.

Such a national goal would not mean that unity was the only goal of national policy. Provided that unity was respected, diversity might also be an objective actively fostered by government policy. Such diversity might well serve the purpose of further distinguishing our country (and its cultures) from the United States, although the theories of the melting pot are less popular in the U.S. than they used to be. But the principal reason for recognition is simply that it would recognize the country as it is, and the constitution must symbolize the country. Canada is some twenty-six per cent other-ethnic, and it is unrealistic, as well as somewhat inequitable, to use symbols for Canada which do not reflect this large and important aspect of its character. It might accomplish constitutional recognition explicitly by a statement in the preamble acknowledging the multicultural nature of Canadian society, and implicitly by the adoption of such measures as a constitutional Bill of Rights which would have the effect of protecting minority rights.

Constitutional recognition need not be limited to the symoblic plane. Language use and education are two practical areas which might well be included. However, because of the multiplicity of languages in Canada and the fact that other-language groups are comparatively small, it might be preferable to have such matters dealt with by provincial governments, with perhaps only an empowering provision in the constitution to this effect. If it were necessary, the federal Government could assist the provinces financially in carrying out these duties, as it is now doing with respect to education in the official languages, though there is a strong case also to be made for making the provinces solely responsible.

The Government's aim should be, not to assure the survival of every ethnic group, but to give them all a reasonable opportunity to survive, by providing the necessary pre-conditions. For every ethnic group, and every member of every ethnic group, must be left the freedom to choose either assimilation or integration. This advocacy of freedom may seem inconsistent with my earlier stress on the social need for the preservation of other-ethnic groups, but it is obedient to a higher rule, that of human freedom. Nor indeed is it necessary for the well-being of society that the ethnic distinctness of every individual and every ethnic group be preserved. It is in my opinion beneficial to society to preserve cultural distinctiveness on the whole because of the richness of a society in which cultures mix, but this does not demand the infinite continuation of every group, still less the removal from an individual of his freedom to choose his culture.

Moreover, the principal reason for the constitutional recognition of other-ethnic groups would remain valid even if all of these groups in the country were to become wholly assimilated. The constitution of a country must reflect reality. If the reality is multicultural, this should appear in the constitution. If it is not, or no longer so, then there is no need for constitutional recognition.

So indeed I am not here today to sing the praises of multi-ethnicity per se. I am rather here to say that I see a great role in the Canada of today and in the Canada of tomorrow for other-ethnic groups. If I am right in my perception of this reality, then that fact ought to be acknowledged in the constitution if it is truly to mirror the multidimensional nature of Canadian society.

THE PROCESS OF MAINTENANCE OF ETHNIC IDENTITY: THE CANADIAN CONTEXT

Wsevolod W. Isajiw
Department of Sociology
University of Toronto

Very broadly, ethnic identity may be defined as commitment to a social grouping of common ancestry, existing within a larger society of different ancestral origins, and characterized by sharing of some common values, behavioural patterns or symbols different from those of the larger society. Defining ethnic identity in this sense allows for distinguishing a variety of ways in which a person may be committed to an ethnic group. This, in turn, makes possible a distinction of types or forms of ethnic identity. Differentiation of forms of ethnic identity is necessary if we are to understand fruitfully the process of its maintenance. Much of the literature on ethnic communities and their persistence makes the study of ethnic group maintenance as a process difficult because of its failure to deal with the problem of forms of ethnic identity.

Essentially, the problem of maintenance of ethnic identity is the problem of retaining some form of commitment to an ethnic group over the span of generations. The conventional approach to this question has been by means of (a) the concept of assimilation and (b) the various factors which either hasten or retard it. The concept of assimilation itself, largely due to Milton Gordon's efforts, has been submitted to a somewhat moot division into structural and cultural assimilation. Analytically, the division is clear enough. Reformulating it a little, it can be said that structural assimilation, also referred to as integration, means inclusion of members of an ethnic group into the role and group system of society. This can be either in the area of secondary or primary relationships, that is, either those of the instrumental (economic, occupational and similar) character or those of friendship and the family and community. Cultural assimilation, on the other hand, is the opposite of inclusion. It is the internalization of the overt or covert patterns of behaviour characteristic of the larger society by the members of the ethnic group.

Useful as this distinction may be in assessing the type of inclusion or exclusion of members of ethnic groups in the larger society, the problem with it is the difficulty in assessing empirically how precisely these two forms of assimilation vary independently. There is enough literature to support Gordon's argument that the two forms of assimilation are not necessarily conditioned by one another, that is, that a member of a racial group, an immigrant or his son can become culturally assimilated, yet structurally remain unintegrated. Studies of Negroes, Jews, Italians and others in the United States have shown this.[1]

On the other hand, policy oriented literature upholding the idea of cultural pluralism has claimed that structural assimilation or integration also can take place without necessarily implying full cultural assimilation.[2] In any case, many empirical studies, although not done with the aim of testing the concepts of assimilation, leave the reader uncertain as to the empirical applicability of the distinction.[3] This is especially true of the data on the second and third generation Ukrainians presented in a recent study by B. Bociurkiw.[4] All this does not mean that the distinction between the two types of assimilation is of no use. It does have to be rethought.

One attempt to understand the factors slowing down or speeding up assimilation have been the theoretical formulations dealing with what has been called "ethnic institutional completeness"[5] and similar to it "ethnic community closure".[6] Breton's carefully collected data led him to conclude that the more institutionally complete an ethnic group is, the more members of that group will tend to contain their interpersonal, informal relations within the group and the less will they develop personal contacts with members of the society at large. Also associated with this is language orientation and the type of occupation predominantly held by the members of the ethnic community. That is, ethnic communities with a high degree of institutional completeness tended to have a high proportion of persons ignorant of the language of the dominant society and a high proportion of persons engaged in manual occupations.

If we relate these findings to the question of maintenance of ethnic identity, it can be said that institutional completeness of an ethnic group, by reinforcing ethnic interpersonal ties, functions as a mechanism of maintenance of ethnic identity. In other words, the more institutions an ethnic group has, the more organized it is, the greater its chance of maintaining its identity.

Max Weber's argument of community closure as applied by Neuwirth to ethnic groups seems to be similar. As translated by Neuwirth, community closure refers to the process by which community members, once they have formed communal relationships, tend to monopolize economic, political and/or social advantages. This, however, does not mean that a closed community is necessarily the dominant community. Closure, states Neuwirth, may be attained by communities located at various positions along the stratification continuum.

When applied to ethnic communities, the assumption made in this concept is that ethnic community closure, if nothing else, functions to attain or maintain at least a positively esteemed form of ethnic identity.

I have no argument with either the institutional completeness theory or the ethnic community closure theory. Both theories direct our attention to important categories of factors involved in the process of maintenance of ethnic identity, one referring to interpersonal relations, the other to power, privilege or prestige. But it may be legitimately asked, how about those whose interpersonal relations tend to be outside of the ethnic community, or those whose language of discourse has become that of the larger society? Or again, excluding for the moment the Weberian notion of ethnic honour, how about those members of ethnic groups who do not maximize, or try to maximize, ethnic monopoly on opportunities for increasing status?

The implicit logical answer would be that they are being assimilated, be it culturally or structurally, into the surrounding society at whatever level of the social stratification ladder this may be taking place. In other words, they are experiencing a loss of ethnic identity.

This answer, however, is not satisfying, especially in the face of the evidence of the second, the third, or the fourth ethnic generations whose conversational language is English, whose involvement in ethnic institutions may be minimal, whose opportunities are not related to ethnic boundaries, yet who show interest and feelings for their ancestral heritage. Important as the studies of factors favouring or impeding the maintenance of ethnic identity are, they can be meaningful only if they are made to bear on the different forms of commitment to ethnic cultures, i.e., different forms of ethnic identity.

Methodologically, therefore, what seems to be needed and what this paper will attempt to do in an outline form is the following: (1) The problems of retention or loss of ethnic identity will be defined as a process in which the various forms of commitment to ethnic cultures can be recognized and seen as emerging, disappearing and reemerging, as it were, at different times, depending on specific conditions; (2) Among the conditions to be considered should be both the structural and cultural state of the ethnic groups under consideration at any given time, and the structural and cultural state of the societal system as a whole at the same time. The times involved here should be both past and present; (3) Relative to the conditions, both within the ethnic group and the society at large, the process of maintenance of ethnic identity should be related to other processes within society, especially those of social mobility and solidarity formation.

Too often it has been assumed, both popularly and by sociologists, that the question of ethnic identity is, on the one hand, a temporary question, i.e., that in time all "ethnics" assimilate and the ethnic group boundaries disappear, and on the other hand, that it is primarily the problem of the ethnic groups themselves rather than the problem of the system and the processes inherent in the society at large. Neither of these assumptions can be justified.

Structural Context of North American Ethnic Groups

In both Canada and the United States, ethnic groups are constituent groups; they are part of the basic structure of society. In European societies, with several notable exceptions, ethnic groups are more or less peripheral to the structure of society. It is unrealistic, for example, to speak of Canadian or American higher or lower classes without any reference to ethnic groups. It is never simply upper or lower class, it is upper or lower "ethclass". For this reason the problems of social integration of North American societies are inherently bound up with the problems of ethnic groups.

Both Canada and the United States have developed a form of pluralism; the forms, however, differ. As a rule, Americans have been reluctant to give any legal recognition to ethnic groups. In Canada, the precedent for such recognition has been established early, in particular by the Quebec Act of 1774. The role of the governments in regard to the immigrants has also differed. The Canadian government has had a much more direct and active role in both recruiting and bringing over immigrants than did the American government.

The Canadian variety of pluralism, however, should in no way be seen as a policy of extending equal opportunities to all ethnic groups. In fact the contrary is more true. The Quebec Act itself can be seen as yet another case of the British pattern of "indirect rule" over its colonies, a pattern followed in the British African and Asian colonies.[7] According to this pattern, a policy of non-assimilation made possible a more rational yet more effective control over potential tensions arising from cultural differences by containing the demands of the differing cultural groups within the bounds of established autonomies. Thus the preservation of native or other cultures ensured that equal rights would not be extended to them.[8] As the historian A. G. Dorland put it, the Quebec Act "did achieve its main objective: it kept Canada British by allowing it to remain French-Canadian".

Structural and ideological factors within ethnic groups themselves have contributed also to an uneven opportunity structure among other ethnic groups. The most important among these factors have been the occupational and educational background of the immigrants and the values related to achievement motivation.

All these variables, originating both in the core society and within ethnic groups, have molded a setting for ethnic histories in Canada and the United States to which the term pluralism can be applied only in a very qualified manner. Specifically I would call it pluralism of ethnic stratification, implying an unequal access to both structural and cultural opportunities.

Patterns of the Ethnic Identity Maintenance Process

It is in the context of such conditions that the process of maintenance of ethnic identity has to be considered. Three patterns of the process can be singled out: (1) pattern of "transplantation" of the old culture, (2) the rebellion pattern, and (3) returning or rediscovery pattern. The assumption made is that these patterns are discernible under the conditions of pluralism of ethnic stratification.

The pattern of "transplantation" refers essentially to the attempts by the immigrants to reestablish and follow the same institutional ways which they have known before arrival in the new country. It is the problem primarily of the first generation, i.e., the immigrant generation. It is the process of building ethnic ghettos, of establishing relations with people whose sympathy and loyalty can be assumed. Transplanted things, however, never grow the same. The transplantation pattern is not really a continuation of the old ways. Reestablishment or establishment of relations even with persons sharing the same heritage under different conditions of existence cannot result in simply continuing the old ways. Even in rather isolated areas the characteristics of the new society impinge on the immigrant. In a colourful style Oscar Handlin has described how the new church built by the peasant immigrants in the U.S. has never "felt the same", and how the old village and regional affiliations were never adequate for a group life full of "in-fellow feeling".[9] On the other hand, the organizational life of the first Ukrainians in Point Douglas, Manitoba, as described by Marunchak, was full of activities never engaged in by the villagers in their former country.[10]

Glazer has pointed out that in the New World many first generation Italians and Polish have come to feel Italian or Polish for the very first time, thus establishing a type of ethnic identity which they have never had before.[11]

Nevertheless, the essential features of the life style and the organizational patterns have remained, most of them retained from the old culture without much reflection or critical self-awareness.

It is the rebellion pattern, characteristic especially of the members of the second generation immigrants, that represents a heightened awareness of one's own cultural and social background. This type of self-awareness comes about as a consequence of psychological confrontation with the cultural ways and relational structures of the larger society. One result of such confrontation is either embarrassment, dissatisfaction with, or shame of one's own parental patterns and expectations. The reaction may be a conscious rejection of one's past, or it may be an overidentification with the dominant society, or still another form of reaction may be a commitment to ideologies or utopias involving some ideal patterns of universal justice or love. Identification with such actual movements may follow. The rebellion pattern, of course, is not necessarily unique to the ethnic communities. The concept may be applicable to any generational relationship.

The "returning" or rediscovering pattern is the most interesting and significant if we think of the process of maintenance of ethnic identity in terms of a longer span across generations. It seems to be most applicable to persons who have no confrontational problems deriving from the cultural differences of their parents. Both they themselves and their parents might have gone through the process of socialization within the culture of the dominant society and may be anywhere on the scale of social status. It can, however, be also applicable to members of the second ethnic generations who have gone through the process of socialization in the culture of the dominant society and who may or may not have gone through the rebellion pattern. The essential consideration here is that there are persons who have gone through the basic process of socialization not in the culture of their ancestors, and who might have experienced much social mobility within the larger society but whose feeling of identity with their ancestral group has actually developed rather than decreased.

The only way to attempt to explain this phenomenon is to see the pattern not in any literal sense of the word "returning", that is, picking up where some forgotten grandfather left off, but in the sense of rediscovering one's ancestral past as something with new meaning. The turn to the past is therefore symbolic. Either some elements of the heritage or perhaps the total historical heritage itself comes to be glorified, i.e., the past becomes transfigured. This may or may not be accompanied by rejection of the values of the societal culture. Empirical research is badly needed here. What is significant in this respect is that there is a process of selection of items from the cultural past and even relatively few items, such as ethnic folk art, music, can become symbols of ethnic identity. Furthermore, when recourse to the past is made, it seems to be a recourse to the remote past rather than the immediate past, e.g., the link with Africa on the part of the Blacks, the recourse to ancient Hebrew by the Jews, to ancient art forms by the Indians, etc. The remote past signifying primordial origins, the roots as it were, is a better symbol of identity than the immediate past.

Forms of Commitment to Ethnic Cultures
and Factors of Identity Maintenance

The patterns involved in the process of ethnic identity maintenance indicate at least two different forms of commitment to ethnic cultures, "traditional" and "symbolic". It is in relation to these forms of ethnic cultural commitment that the factors favouring or impeding assimilation have to be considered. Thus institutional completeness or community closure among those committed to their culture in a traditional "transplanted" way, may not necessarily mean maintenance of ethnic identity in the long run because it would exclude those who, though assimilated into the dominant culture, have an interest in their ethnic background. At the same time, institutional completeness may evoke, especially among the younger generation, the pattern of rebellion against the ethnic group.

On the other hand, a degree of ethnic community closure or institutional completeness among those whose commitment to the ethnic culture is symbolic, the "rediscoverers", may be precisely a condition of long-range identity maintenance of an ethnic group within the larger society. This, of course, may alienate those committed to the ethnic culture in a traditional manner, thus cutting the rediscoverers away from a potential source of their symbolic enrichment.

Turning the argument around, it can be said that institutional completeness may be functional for the traditionals but dysfunctional for the rediscoverers, since the ethnic rediscovery itself is in some way tied up with their participation in the institutions of the larger society. By the same token, it can be argued that the pattern of rebellion against the ethnic group and ethnic identity is in the long run potentially functional for the maintenance of this identity since it removes the person from a purely traditional commitment to his ethnic background and by bringing him closer to the larger society may increase, let us say, his son's chance of becoming a rediscoverer.

In any case, the argument suggests that the maintenance of ethnic identity, as originally defined in this paper, depends primarily upon emergence of rediscoverers rather than traditionalists. Two questions which arise from this premise are: (1) What type and degree of symbolism is necessary for a person or a group to maintain its ethnic identity?; and (2) What are the dynamics which produce the so-called rediscoverers in ethnic communities?

The number of ethnic symbols necessary to maintain ethnic identity seems to vary among ethnic groups. It appears that some groups, like the Jews, for example, may require relatively few symbols, whereas others, like many Slavic groups, may require a good number. Without empirical data it is impossible to answer this question in any satisfactory manner. Two types of symbols, however, seem to be important for most ethnic groups, namely, ethnic language and ethnic endogamy. Although all groups place a value on both means of strengthening ethnic ties, some consider one more significant in preserving their ethnic identity than the other. Jews, for example, seem to place a much higher value on endogamy than on language as a means of ethnic identity maintenance. Ukrainians, on the other hand, place a very high premium on language. In both cases other patterns, important as they may be to the ethnic group, tend to become auxiliary symbols. Relation to the country of origin and the events taking place in it may also become a significant symbol of ethnic identity in its own right. Perhaps the minimum symbolism would be simply acknowledgement of common ancestry.

Structural Sources of Ethnic "Rediscovery"

Awareness of one's own ancestry remains a basic mechanism in the ethnic rediscovery process. However, the dynamic factors involved in ethnic rediscovery in North American societies are located primarily in the structure of these societies themselves. The structure of ethnic stratification and its concomitant occupational, economic and political competition, all influence one's awareness of ancestry.[12] The rediscovery pattern may emerge when members of ethnic groups begin to realize that cultural assimilation is indeed not sufficient to achieve their economic and/or social aspirations, but that owing to the community closure of the dominant groups, their opportunities are limited. They may have the qualifications relative to the positions to which they aspire, yet be excluded from them because they are identified as members of an ethnic group. Under such conditions a degree of ethnic community closure may enable the members of the group to achieve, through concerted group action, an access to the political, social and economic opportunity structure which they, as individuals, would be unable to attain. There is some evidence to show that this may be true especially when members of ethnic groups have already been mobile in the economic structure of society.[13] Social mobility, therefore, may produce ethnic rediscoverers and thus stimulate rather than stifle the process of ethnic identity maintenance. This is one reason why the question of multiculturalism, ethnic rights and group civil rights is raised today not by the immigrant groups, but by the established ethnic communities.

An analysis of Canadian census data on occupations suggests that there may be an order in which ethnic groups enter the structure of society over a period of time involving two or more generations. The first stage, embracing the first and to some extent the second ethnic generations, involves filling positions which assure little occupational mobility. The second stage, embracing perhaps primarily the second generation, is that of assimilating into the occupational mobility structure of society, i.e., filling positions which have a promise of advancement. The third stage, involving perhaps primarily the third ethnic generation, is the stage of mobility into positions of influence or power. This may be interpreted as a reach by an ethnic group for the rights of the establishment.[14] Studies referred to above suggest that the ethnic rediscovery pattern may appear precisely between the second and the third stage.

On another level, contemporary North American societies have a deep-rooted problem of identity. Instead of inducing strong feelings of social solidarity, they tend to produce the opposite, feelings of social alienation. Search for personal identity in an alienating society is closely related to the rediscovery of ethnic identity and search for the former often results in the latter. Meaningful definition of the ego can take place only in terms of larger solidarity groupings. Since one's ancestry is a natural link to solidarity groups, search for psychological identity prevalent in our society is a significant source of emergence of ethnic rediscovery.

This is especially relevant to the contemporary Canadian attempts to develop both national identity and national unity. Northrop Frye, significantly not a sociologist, has aptly pointed out that the two goals are quite different things and in Canada they are perhaps more different than anywhere else. As he states, "identity is local and regional, rooted in the imagination and in works of culture; unity is national in reference, international in perspective, and rooted in a political feeling."[15] We should add that identity has also a dimension whereby one relates to his ancestors either in a traditional manner, in which their ways are simply a precedent, or in a symbolic manner, in which their ways, or only some of their ways, become a legacy.

Frye goes on to say that "the tension between [the] political sense of unity and the imaginative sense of locality is the essence of whatever the word Canadian means. Once the tension is given up and the two elements of unity and identity are confused or assimilated to each other, we get the two endemic diseases of Canadian life. Assimilating identity to unity produces the empty gestures of cultural nationalism; assimilating unity to identity produces the kind of provincial isolation which is now called separatism."

The problem of developing a Canadian national identity is that it is difficult to develop a unified sense of Canadian history. In the absence of a unified tradition, it is difficult to rediscover cultural elements of the past which are common to all ethnic and regional groups and not predominantly associated with only one group. There is not enough of the common and shared remote past from which to draw viable symbols. Thus the search for Canadian identity engenders by its nature an awareness of ethnic and local identities. It can be said that conscious promotion of Canadian identity will contribute to further emergence of ethnic rediscoverers.

The policy objective may well be an articulation rather than an elimination of the tension between a sense of unity and the sense of identity. The consequences of this tension, however, must also be clearly understood. One of the most significant consequences is the pressure exerted on the system of law, inasmuch as the law can be said to be the medium through which intergroup tensions are managed. From the legal perspective this question may very well be phrased in terms of group rights versus individual rights. The sociological analyst, however, will do well if he understands this as an inherent societal process.

Notes

[1] See T. F. Pettigrew, *A Profile of the Negro American* (Princeton: Van Nostrand, 1964). Also *cf.* N. Glazer and D. P. Moynihan, *Beyond the Melting Pot* (Cambridge, Mass.: MIT Press, 1963); S. Goldstein and C. Goldscheider, *Jewish Americans* (Englewood Cliffs, N.J.: Princeton-Hall, 1968); H. J. Gans, *The Urban Villagers* (Glencoe, Ill.: The Free Press, 1962); and P. A. Munch, "Social Adjustment Among Wisconsin Norwegians" in *American Sociological Review,* XIV (1949), pp. 780-871.

[2] See: H. M. Kallen, "Democracy Versus the Melting Pot" in *The Nation* (February 18 and 25, 1915); I. B. Berkson, *Theories of Americanization: A Critical Study with Special References to the Jewish Group* (New York: Teachers College, Columbia University, 1920); P. Yuzyk, *Ukrainian Canadians: Their Place and Role in Canadian Life* (Toronto: Ukrainian Canadian Business and Professional Federation, 1967).

[3] See: F. G. Vallee, M. Schwartz and F. Darknell, "Ethnic Assimilation and Differentiation in Canada" in *Canadian Journal of Economic and Political Science,* XXVII (1957), pp. 540-549; R. Breton and M. Pinard, "Group Formation Among Immigrants: Criteria and Processes" in *Canadian Journal of Economics and Political Science,* XXVI (1960), pp. 465-477; E. C. Hughes, "French and English Canadians in the Industrial Hierarchy of Quebec" in *Canadian Society,* ed. B. R. Blishen (Toronto: Macmillan of Canada, 1968); H. B. Gans, *op. cit.*

[4] B. R. Bociurkiw, "Ethnic Identification and Attitudes of University Students of Ukrainian Descent, the University of Alberta Case Study" in *Slavs in Canada,* Vol. III, ed. C. J. Jaenen (Toronto: Inter-University Committee on Canadian Slavs, 1970).

[5] R. Breton, "Institutional Completeness of Ethnic Communities and the Personal Relations of Immigrants" in *The American Journal of Sociology,* LXX, No. 2 (1964), pp. 193-205.

[6] G. Neuwirth, "A Weberian Outline of a Theory of Community: Its Application to the Dark Ghetto" in *The British Journal of Sociology,* Vol. XX, No. 2 (1969), p. 148.

[7]R. J. Ossenberg, "The Conquest Revisited: Another Look at Canadian Dualism", *The Canadian Review of Sociology and Anthropology,* Vol. 4 (Nov. 1967), pp. 201-218.

[8]W. W. Isajiw, "The Process of Social Integration: The Canadian Example" in *Dalhousie Review,* Vol. 48, No. 4 (1968-9).

[9]O. Handlin, *The Uprooted* (Boston: Little Brown and Co., 1951).

[10]M. H. Marunchak, *The Ukrainian Canadians: A History* (Winnipeg: Ukrainian Free Academy of Sciences, 1970).

[11]N. Glazer, "Ethnic Groups in America: From National Culture to Ideology" in *Minority Responses,* ed. M. Kurokawa (New York: Random House, 1970).

[12]M. Weber in *Economy and Society,* Vol. 1, ed. G. Roth and C. Wittich (New York: Bedminster Press, 1968), p. 389.

[13]See: H. Guindon, "Social Unrest, Social Class, and Quebec's Bureaucratic Revolution" in *Canadian Society,* ed. B. R. Blishen (Toronto: Macmillan of Canada, 1968); C. Taylor, "Nationalism and the Political Intelligensia: A Case Study" in *Social and Cultural Change in Canada,* Vol. 1, ed. W. E. Mann (Vancouver: The Copp Clark Publishing Co., 1970); and B. Bettelheim and M. Janowitz, *Social Change and Prejudice* (New York: The Free Press, 1964).

[14]W. W. Isajiw and N. J. Hartmann, "Changes in the Occupational Structure of Ukrainians in Canada" in *Social and Cultural Change in Canada,* Vol. 1, ed. W. E. Mann (Vancouver: The Copp Clark Publishing Co., 1970).

[15]H. N. Frye, *The Bush Garden: Essays on the Canadian Imagination* (Toronto: House of Anansi, 1971).

DEMOGRAPHIC ASPECTS OF ETHNIC IDENTITY AND ASSIMILATION

Warren E. Kalbach
University of Toronto

Canada's succession of identity crises, and the continuing concern over the problem of ethnic balance between Canada's two major ethnic origin populations, have been well documented and debated in the literature, as have the most recent arguments supporting a bilingual and bicultural society. An example of the latter is the following statement made by the Royal Commission on Bilingualism and Biculturalism:

> In particular, he (the immigrant) should know that Canada recognizes two official languages and that it possesses two predominant cultures . . . which form two distinct communities within an overall Canadian context . . . . Immigrants, whatever their ethnic or national origin, or their mother tongue, have the right and are at liberty to integrate with either of the two societies.[1]

Yet, in spite of, or because of the Royal Commission's reports, arguments continue over the nature of Canadian society, both with respect to what it actually is, and what it ought to be. The reality of the historical dominance which has been enjoyed by the British origin population is reflected both in its size relative to the other groups, and in the persistence of English as the official language for the majority of Canada's population. For example, between 1931 and 1961, the proportion speaking English only held relatively constant at approximately 67%, while the proportion of the population reporting British origins actually declined from 51.9% to 43.8%. If any further evidence is needed of ethnic inequality, the continuing and heated arguments for equality between Anglophone and Francophone societies should suffice. Demographic data also reveal the relative position of dominance enjoyed by French Canadians, as well as those of British origin, vis-à-vis the other ethnic minority groups. The dominant cultural force since Confederation for Canada as a whole, of course, has been British, with the expectation of Anglo-Saxon conformity. However, the increasing strength of the Quebec separatist movement has given a sense of urgency to the acceptance of bilingualism and biculturalism as a fact of life, and the minimal acceptable form of a cultural pluralism for Canada. Canada's other ethnic groups, with similar concern for the preservation of their unique cultural forms, have increased their efforts to obtain modification of the concept of bicultural pluralism to one of multicultural pluralism.

The Research Problem

The problem to be addressed here deals with the social and cultural realities of Canadian society, rather than with ideologies which attempt to establish the bases of Canadian ethnic identity. To this end, the following statement by Vallee, Schwartz, and Darknell is particularly relevant:

> The social structure of an ethnically plural society is more aptly characterized as a constellation of ethnic groups, which are becoming more like each other in some ways (i.e., assimilation) and less like each other in other ways (i.e., differentiating).[2]

From this perspective, the objective of the social scientist is to assess the effects of interaction between all ethnic populations at both national and regional levels. To accomplish this, it is necessary to (1) identify the members of distinct ethnic communities sharing common identities; and (2) determine the extent to which these groups differ from each other with respect to their social and economic characteristics (extent of structural differentiation), and their behaviour.

Conceptualization of Ethnic Identity and Its Measurement:

The first task presents considerable difficulty, because the Canadian government does not collect any data which deal directly with ethnic identity. If direct measurements are to be made, they must be carried out through the conduct of original and relatively costly field research. This is not meant to imply, however, that the self-identification type of data generally obtained in this manner is necessarily the answer for ethnic research. One's ethnic group origin may still have significance for his behaviour even if the person doesn't verbalize an ethnic identity consistent with his ethnic origin. This has been made abundantly clear by the use of reference group theory to explain the behaviour of upwardly mobile persons in social status systems.

The complexity of the concept itself presents certain additional obstacles to its conceptualization and measurement. Ethnic identity is only a part of that identity of self that is painstakingly acquired during the process of socialization in primary type groups (such as the family), which are themselves being shaped and influenced by the larger social and economic structures within which they are functioning. Thus, those of similar race, religion, nationality, language, national or ethnic origin, and who are members of the same generation, tend to have similar socialization experiences and to share a common social-psychological core of elements. According to Milton Gordon, it is this "common core" that constitutes the essence of ethnic groupings and the sense of "peoplehood".[3] Thus, all persons have a national or ethnic component to their "self identity", and it is this component and its relevance for the social and economic characteristics and behaviour of ethnic origin groupings that is of primary concern to those interested in the processes of assimilation in society.[4]

Indicators of ethnic identity:

Lacking direct measures, such as self-identification questions of the type used by Bociurkiw in his study of Ukrainian university students in Alberta,[5] the Dominion Bureau of Statistics collects data during each decennial census on the ethnic and cultural origins, country of birth, year of immigration of foreign born, religion, mother tongue, and official language of its population. No one question asked by the census has been found to be completely adequate for identifying all the ethnic groups, but the single question dealing with "ethnic and cultural origin" perhaps comes closest to being the best all-round measure. Even here, further data on country of birth, mother tongue, and religion are necessary if certain distinct cultural groups, e.g., the Americans in Canada, are to be identified and studied.

The utility of any ethnic indicator is determined by its ability to differentiate the population into distinguishably different sub-populations in terms of their social and economic characteristics. Failure to differentiate the population would suggest that the indicator no longer possesses social or economic relevance. This being the case, responses to the census question would tend to be random in nature, as would any differences which might appear between the categories of the particular classification scheme based on a specific question.

Since immigration to Canada from many diverse cultures has continued to make a rather significant contribution to Canada's population, it is highly unlikely that the ethnic origin question would experience a total loss of discriminatory power. However, considering the varying lengths of time that different ethnic groups have been established in Canada, it is logical to expect that "ethnicity" would have greater significance for some groups than for others. Furthermore, it would be expected that those groups whose characteristics are most distinguishable from the general population, would have the greatest potential for the expression of a unique ethnic identity. The recent emphasis on "Black is beautiful" in the United States is a good example of using a highly visible trait to strengthen a group's identity.

Assessing the significance of ethnic identity:

Having identified the ethnic groups in a population by the use of some appropriate "indicator", the problem still remains of determining the degree of similarity or dissimilarity in their social and economic characteristics, the extent of change through time, and assessing the significance of these differences for our conceptual models of Canadian society. The first two types of analyses are to be found in much of the literature dealing with Canadian society. An extensive analysis of ethnic differentials and changes which have occurred through time is included in the 1961 Census monograph, *The Impact of Immigration on Canada's Population,* published in 1970. Careful scrutiny of these and similar data and analyses will provide evidence to support, in varying degrees, the validity of each of the assimilation models to be discussed in the following sections.

Theoretical Models of Assimilation

Students of assimilation are familiar with the "melting pot", "Anglo-conformity", and "cultural pluralism" models.[6] Such models, while not necessarily representing the "real" world, do serve a heuristic purpose by giving us an idealized model against which to compare and test our observational data. Thus, the investigator may be just as interested in determining the extent to which his data fail to fit this theoretical model as he is in its closeness of fit. In either case, the model serves as an oversimplified conceptualization of reality which can then be elaborated or modified to more closely conform to, and explain, his data.

Testing the validity of the first two models for Canadian society requires the utilization of some type of convergence hypothesis, while the latter model would be validated, in part, by the lack of convergence and the maintenance of differences in characteristics over time. The crucial difference in testing the two convergence models lies in the selection of the standard, or reference population, for use in evaluating the demographic character of the particular ethnic populations under consideration.

The Anglo-conformity Model:

The population standard for testing this model is self-evident. If additional evidence were needed, a close reading of the countless debates and statements on immigration policy and legislation during the course of Canada's history would clearly show the extent to which the British origin group has served as the standard for evaluating the desirability of potential immigrants. Until recent years, the history of immigration policy has been one of restrictive legislation for the purpose of preserving the "fundamental character" of Canada's population.[7] It has been well established that the numerical dominance of the British origin population has been maintained primarily through Canada's immigration policies. Thus, the characteristics of the various ethnic groups can be statistically compared at successive censuses with the British origin population to determine the extent of convergence which has occurred with respect to their social and economic characteristics, i.e., structural assimilation. Implicit here is the assumption that structural assimilation will be followed by behavioural assimilation.

This type of model has been used in recent attempts to explain Negro-white fertility differentials in the United States.[8] Convergence of socio-economic characteristics was hypothesized to be associated with convergence of fertility as evidence of behavioural assimilation. Some support for the hypothesis was obtained after controlling for regional effects. However, their analysis suggested that minority group status might contribute an independent effect (to fertility) in those groups which have achieved structural assimilation.[9] The relevance of these findings for this discussion is its general support of the relationship between structural and cultural assimilation. The more two populations are similar in terms of their social and economic characteristics, the less important ethnic identity becomes in terms of behavioural differences.

Interestingly, the standard type of demographic analysis simply compares the characteristics of the component ethnic groups to their combined total to assess the extent of convergence. Since the British origin group has constituted the major share of the population, the results are essentially the same as they would be had the comparisons been made just with the actual British origin population. Technically speaking, however, this practice is more consistent with the procedure for testing the "melting pot" theory of assimilation.

The "Melting Pot" Theory of Assimilation:

As has already been suggested, the combined characteristics of all ethnic populations would be the standard against which each ethnic group would be compared. The implication here is that with time, each group would become identical to all others; and, again, structural assimilation to this standard would be translated into uniformity in behaviour reflecting uniformity in cultural values and attitudes. This theory is perhaps more consistent with our understanding of the assimilation process, i.e., it allows for changes in the structural and behavioural characteristics of the dominant ethnic groups as a consequence of their interaction with minority ethnic groups, and stresses the two-way nature of this interactive process. The type of "mix" that would be produced in the long run would be highly dependent upon the regional distributions of dominant and minority ethnic population, and the degree of regional economic and political autonomy.

Demographic Convergence as Structural Assimilation and Implications:

While it has already been suggested that structural assimilation, as demographic convergence, leads to behavioural assimilation, the conditions under which this occurs and the degree of assimilation which may follow need further explication. There is, however, a troublesome consequence of this acceptance of a link between structural and behavioural assimilation insofar as Canada is concerned. If this "link" is a valid one, then the implication is that the concept of cultural pluralism is essentially incompatible with structural assimilation. If this is so, then the Bilingualism and Biculturalism Commission's statement about the right of immigrants to integrate into either of Canada's two societies, while retaining their own cultures, would seem to be based more on some profession of faith than on any understanding of social processes. In this connection, it is interesting to point out that those ethnic groups which have enjoyed the greatest success in preserving their cultural uniqueness in Canadian society, such as the Hutterites, have been characterized by a lack of structural assimilation, and a maximum of social isolation.

There are additional problems associated with the selection of a standard population for use in convergence analysis. Using the dominant ethnic origin population in a nation, or region, as the standard against which to compare the minority groups, assumes that the standard population is not, in turn, being influenced by another dominant population, or that both are not responding to some superdominant economic or political presence.

This problem doesn't arise when regions are relatively autonomous (economically and politically). Immigrants arrive with low entrance status, and the pre-existing social and economic system becomes the standard against which they compare their successes and failures, i.e. adjustment. But what happens during periods of rapid industrialization, urbanization, and growth of international capitalism? Porter has shown how Canada has met its expanding needs for skilled manpower through immigration in order to maintain its high rate of economic development.[9] Since World War II, there have been immigrant ethnic populations entering the system with high entrance status, and exhibiting greater evidence of structural assimilation than some of their native-born counterparts. Some examples would be post-war immigrants of French origin, as well as those of Jewish and Asiatic origins. While not representing an ethnic group according to the census definition, post-war immigrants from the United States constitute another group of arrivals with high entrance status.

What does structural assimilation mean for those groups who arrive with high entrance status? What is suggested here is that these skilled immigrants have already achieved some structural assimilation, but to a new and evolving post-industrial social and economic system. Perhaps then, it is this structure which should serve as the standard for evaluating any particular group's level of social and economic adjustment. To share in the benefits of the post-industrial world, it may be necessary to achieve more than structural assimilation with the dominant ethnic groups within the regions of residence. The appropriate standard may be the population of the economically and technologically dominant society. Today, that may be the United States, but tomorrow it could be Japan, or in time, Russia.

Assimilation Models and the Demographic Transition

An interesting comparison can be made between the experience of immigrant groups in Canada, and the populations of underdeveloped countries at the threshhold of the demographic transition. The process of changing from a basically rural-agricultural society to a modern urban-industrial society is obviously very complex; but, as industrialization proceeds, the occupational structure undergoes change, educational attainment levels rise, incomes and standard of living rise, i.e., structural transformation occurs. This transformation may be seen as structural assimilation into the industrial-urban type of social and economic structure. As a consequence of this change, behavioural changes also occur, i.e., changes in attitudes and values which are subsequently reflected in lower levels of fertility and mortality associated with the new urban-industrial life style. Every western European country has experienced this transition in varying degrees, as have both Canada and the United States.

The immigrant to Canada, whether his decision to move was voluntary or not, most likely selected his destination on the basis of his assessment of the potential opportunity to improve his lot through economic achievement and some measure of political security. His most immediate and pressing problem is to achieve a satisfactory adjustment in his adopted country by learning whatever new skills might be necessary, and acquiring more education and training if needed; in short, to undergo a structural metamorphosis to achieve his own personal demographic transition. There will obviously be certain behavioural consequences as may be seen in the generally lower fertility of the most urbanized sections of society. Again, it is no accident that some of Canada's most ethnically distinct populations are to be found in the more rural parts of the country, i.e., those regions which have not yet fully experienced the demographic transition.

Changes in the ethnically dominant population's social and economic characteristics, i.e., structural change, will not likely stop as long as technological developments continue to affect our social and economic institutions, and the world's nations become increasingly interdependent. The only groups that would appear to be exempt from these influences are those whose strong religious convictions enable them to reject the materialistic values presently dominant in the world's viable economic and political systems. Even these groups are threatened to the extent that they too are not totally independent of the larger society in which they live.

The "melting pot" theory of assimilation in American society has been attributed to a "quietly *romantic* eighteenth century French-born writer and agriculturalist . . . who had settled in New York".[10] (Italics mine.) In the long run, the melting-pot theory may be a more realistic theory than the notion that cultural pluralism can survive for very long in modern post-industrial society. Whether one opts for change or the preservation of older and perhaps dysfunctional cultural forms — which may have been perfectly functional in an earlier era — is ultimately a matter of values and individual choice. Neither choice can be made without paying a price, but the implication here is that the cost of maintaining cultural pluralism may also include a certain degree of personal and social disorganization that may arise when it is discovered that integration into any larger and diverse cultural system is not possible without a considerable degree of behaviour assimilation.

Some ethnic groups, like the Hutterites, undoubtedly have discovered that the struggle to maintain their unique ethnic identity and culture has not been easy, but they have accepted this as the price they must pay to be true believers. The British origin population in Canada may also discover that to remain British will become increasingly more difficult. Even the Americans are beginning to suspect that their economic and industrial dominance is not a permanent feature of world society, and those who attempt to return to the good old days will join the legions of earlier ethnic and cultural dominants whose day of glory has come and gone.

Bociurkiw found that the majority of Ukrainian (descent) students at the University of Alberta "preferred neither an ethnic 'ghetto' nor complete assimilation into the dominant Anglo-Saxon group, but an integration into a multi-cultural Canadian society". Perpetuation of cultural forms may have an intrinsic value in itself and provide an important source for emotional gratification. Yet, successful retention of language and culture on the part of minority ethnic populations may impede social change by preventing their members from acquiring the skills they need to effectively compete in the ongoing industrial and technological revolution.

Notes

[1] Royal Commission on Bilingualism and Biculturalism, *The Cultural Contribution of the Other Ethnic Groups,* Book IV (Ottawa: Queen's Printer, 1969), pp. 4-5.

[2] R. G. Vallee, M. Schwartz and F. Darknell, "Ethnic Assimilation and Differentiation in Canada" in Blishen *et. al., Canadian Society,* 3rd Edition (Toronto: Macmillan of Canada), p. 603.

[3] M. M. Gordon, *Assimilation in American Life* (New York: Oxford University Press, 1964), pp. 27-29.

[4] M. Schwarts, *Public Opinion and Canadian Identity* (Scarborough: Fitzhenry & Whiteside Ltd., 1967), p. 5.

[5] B. R. Bociurkiw, "Ethnic Identification and Attitudes of University Students of Ukrainian Descent: The University of Alberta Case Study" in Jaenen, *Slavs in Canada* Vol. 3 (Toronto: Homin Ukrainy Printers, 1970).

[6] M. M. Gordon, *op. cit.,* pp. 85-159.

[7] W. E. Kalbach, *The Impact of Immigration on Canada's Population* (Ottawa: Queen's Printer, 1970), pp. 10-11.

[8] F. Sly, "Minority Group Status and Fertility", *American Journal of Sociology,* Vol. 76, No. 3 (November, 1970), pp. 443-459.

[9] J. Porter, *The Vertical Mosaic* (Toronto: University of Toronto Press, 1967).

[10] M.M. Gordon, *op. cit.,* p. 115.

[11] B. R. Bociurkiw, *op. cit.,* p. 30.

TWO TYPES OF ETHNIC COMMUNITIES

Ihor V. Zielyk
Department of Sociology
Seton Hall University
South Orange, N.J.

This paper is intended as a contribution to the taxonomy of ethnic communities, defined here as communities of immigrants in a country whose
culture and socio-historical identity are different from their own. It will
try to identify two distinct types of ethnic communities, one of which
has been rather neglected in the literature.

Over the years, sociological discussions of ethnic groups have usually
focused on the situation of the "uprooted" — rural immigrants transplanted
into an urban industrial environment in which they tried to hang on to
their peasant folk traditions and, as a rule, developed some organized
devices for mutual aid and problem-solving. The resulting community
seemed to show certain stereotyped characteristics and to follow a predic-
table course of life which ended as the second and third generation individuals were assimilated into the surrounding society.[1]

Clearly such an image of the ethnic community was determined by
certain background factors and characteristics of membership composition
which most of the groups coming to the U.S., for example, have indeed
held in common. The majority came from traditional agricultural societies,
and were attracted by economic opportunities. The great preponderance
of males meant that, for a time at least, most of the men could not carry
on family and other cultural patterns to which they were accustomed;
thus their behaviour, if not their attitudes, was bound to change rather
drastically from the beginning. Their educational level was generally very
low.[2] They showed little occupational differentiation. Finally, few of
these groups were concerned with political matters or had a highly developed "national consciousness"; most acquired it only on foreign soil.[3]

But there have been, even in the U.S., immigrant groups with background characteristics strikingly different from these. Quite a few came
from urban or urbanizing settings. Many left their homelands for political,
religious or other non-economic reasons. They migrated in family units.
They had considerable occupational and social differentiation, and a high
level of literacy. Most important, these were self-conscious groups: the
nationalists, the irredentists, those persecuted because of their religion.
Some observers were quite aware of them, but few got so far as tracing
the development, or systematically examining the nature, of their organized
life.[4]

The kind of community such groups formed in the new country was a far cry from the Gemeinschaft-like community of the uprooted. The same applies to their natural history: for example, it seems that the latter — let us call it the "folk community" — is gradually transformed into an intermediate product[5] with the original cultural traits progressively modified and ultimately disappearing, with the second generation forgetting, or at least trying to forget, the mother tongue, etc., whereas the former — I shall call it the "nationality community"[6] — is more likely to remain distinct in identification, with an eclectic mixture of traits from both cultures, and with a bilingual, if not bicultural, second generation.

To the extent that the nature of the parent society, the group's reason for emigrating, and membership composition "direct" the emerging ethnic community into distinct paths of development, knowledge about those factors may be used to predict — or to understand — certain aspects of the sociological nature and the dynamics of a given community.[7] Among these are (1) internal structure, (2) external relations, (3) actual longevity and also the members' expectations concerning the future of the community, which can be important by affecting motivation.[8]

The two types of urban ethnic communities, the "folk" and the "nationality" community, can now be contrasted in some detail. I say "urban" because groups which settled in large numbers in rural farm areas (in the United States as well as in Canada) seem to have had somewhat different experiences and distinctive problems.[9] The sketch given here is based on an examination of the literature on ethnic communities and their problems; on observations from studies of specific immigrant groups; and on the author's own research. It is thus a composite "ideal" construct, and as such may tend to sharpen certain traits, to oversimplify some problems, as well as to overlook possible empirical exceptions. Most importantly, one must remember that concrete cases tend to approximate one or the other ideal type in varying degrees, rather than to embody them fully.

The Internal Structure of the Community

The notion of *folk* community as applied here to immigrants does parallel in many ways Redfield's concept of "folk society": it is small and intimate, culturally homogeneous and isolated, and a high proportion of its members are illiterate or barely literate.[10] Its institutions and associations are survival-oriented, i.e. established to protect the individual from foreseeable crises and to guarantee minimum satisfaction of needs, especially economic ones. In time they may acquire other functions (notably sociability), but the mutual aid society remains the basic form. Such close connection with the day-to-day needs of the immigrant is one reason why these organizations have to change their functions or slowly disappear, as the subsequent generations can get along without them.

The hub of community organization is usually the church, which often doubles as a community center and is surrounded by a complement of auxiliary associations. It is likely to exert a pervasive influence on the whole community. This has an important corollary: once an individual leaves the parish or congregation, there may be little else to link him with the ethnic group.

If there is a school, it is probably run by the church and it functions mainly as an adaptive institution. Instruction, in the beginning, is in the ethnic language since the teachers may not know enough of the dominant tongue.

The family retains much of its Old World importance, and often its patriarchal authority system. Although the effective unit is nuclear rather than extended, kinship remains crucial in the organization of informal relations. The distance between generations is accentuated by the children's involvement in the outside world and frequently by their desire to disassociate themselves from the minority status of their parents.

The culture of the folk community is a "little tradition"[11] embodied in custom, song, proverb, and transmitted by word of mouth. Since it is poorly adapted to urban conditions and, on occasion, may be a source of embarrassment, it succumbs relatively easily — and in the second generation abruptly — to acculturation pressures.

The community is ultimately held together by a network of personal relations and defined in terms of particularistic traditional symbols representing the original village or region.

The homogeneity of membership composition and the lack of concern with ideologies are reflected in the low degree of differentiation, both status and political. At most, there appears eventually a quantitative socioeconomic gradation not unlike the one in the surrounding industrial society.

In the *nationality* community, one is likely to find a proliferation of associations corresponding to more diversified needs. A large community may achieve a high degree of institutional completeness,[12] including even professional services, so that most of its members do not have to go outside of it for anything except perhaps employment.

In marked contrast to the folk community, there are here many purely secular organizations (political, cultural, educational). There may be a tension between some of them, with their determined resistance against assimilation, and the church which, by comparison at least, may appear to be playing an adaptive role. In some communities, on the other hand, the church will go out of its way to provide "retentionist" leadership.[13]

The nuclear family is here important as a socializing agency rather than as a focus of social organization. The distance between the generations is reduced by a measure of egalitarianism, by the fact that the parents are better educated, and also because the young have less reason to experience their ethnicity as a stigma.

The culture of the nationality community is part of a "great tradition" whose literary, artistic, and intellectual achievements are a source of proud identification. Not only is it, as an urban, literate culture, better able to hold its own; energetic efforts are also made to perpetuate it, particularly through the ethnic school and through the network of associations, especially youth organizations.[14]

The community is integrated by a shared ideology (irredentism, messianism, etc.)[15] whose symbols are universalistic, representing the most comprehensive unit — the nation of origin or motherland. Like the "pioneer spirit" of the immigrants in modern Israel, the ideology not only cements but motivates and therefore constitutes a crucial source of vitality for the community as a whole.[16]

On the other hand, there are "second level" ideologies (partial views, political creeds, usually concerning means rather than goals) which provide a source of differentiation and, at times, of bitter internal conflicts. Another kind of differentiation results from the attempts of the higher strata within the community to perpetuate the Old Country system of invidious distinctions. In many European groups this takes the form of dichotomous stratification, setting the "intelligentsia" apart from the rest of the community and at the same time making it an object of hostile or ambivalent attitudes.[17]

Relations With the World Outside

The immigrant in the folk community remains residentially segregated and socially isolated[18] because he has to live in a low rental area, doesn't know the dominant language, and is rejected by the natives. His children will learn the new idiom, forget their mother tongue, and try to move out of the old ethnic neighborhood.[19] Their acculturation is automatic and comprehensive. So long as the young remain in the community they are subject to the strain of culture conflict which may claim a high cost in delinquency and personal disorganization.

At the same time the values of the dominant culture are experienced as an objective, external force — and in most cases as supremely desirable. To attain some of these values, the immigrant and his children must utilize what meager opportunities for participation in the larger society are open to them. Even then they participate not as individuals but as anonymous units in a voting bloc, or in a labour reservoir, or in a client population.

The nationality community as a social whole remains oriented to its mother country and maintains manifold ties with other communities of compatriots abroad. Its isolation from the surrounding dominant society is largely self-imposed.[20] This extends to intermarriage with other ethnic groups, including the dominant: while it does occur, it is consistently frowned upon.

The higher educational level produces a paradox. On the one hand, there are few practical obstacles to acculturation. Language is less of a problem for the first generation. There is less of a gap between the cultures objectively, and subjectively the ethnic tradition is not seen as a burden, nor the dominant one as an unattainable good. On the other hand, there may be little interest in acculturation, and even ideologically motivated strong opposition to it. Some acculturation will take place, of course; but it is selective and consciously instrumental.

The individual, especially second generation, participates in both societies, escaping the classical dilemma of the young in folk communities who may see themselves as either "rebels" or "in-groupers", and at the same time avoiding the passive "apathetic" solution.[21] And he participates in both as an individual.

My comments so far have been intended to bring out in high relief the contrast between the two kinds of community as analytically pure types. But "mixed" types do occur in reality, and some of them may defy easy classification. For example, Ukrainians in the United States, although over-whelmingly of peasant background, had a small but active nucleus of educated individuals who succeeded in making the entire group highly nationality-conscious.[22] Again, the nature of the group may change in time: e.g., as the second and third generation become educated, they may develop an intellectual appreciation of their heritage; or political events in the homeland may elicit a nationalistic response.

Persistence of the Ethnic Community

Most students of immigrant communities have either observed or predicted their rather early demise. Increasing differentiation corrodes cultural consensus and social solidarity;[23] acculturation takes its toll, as also does out-marriage; activities and institutions appeal less and less to each successive generation. It seems that only the influx of new immigrants can save the ethnic community.

The evidence is incontrovertible so far as the folk community (at least in the cities) is concerned. Is the nationality community any different? Are its prospects of survival better? Apart from available empirical cases, is there anything about it which would warrant a theoretical prediction of longer life? Perhaps a key to the answer lies in the *kind* of identification in the two groups.

To the uprooted peasant his ethnicity was embodied in concrete relations to his plot of land, his village, his church, the customs he practiced. These could not be transplanted to the new country, at least not without change — even the church suddenly became an impersonal institution. For his children, on the other hand, ethnicity was often identical with poverty and social inferiority; its positive and nostalgic aspects could not be experienced by them directly. Thus in folk communities ethnic identification can hardly be counted upon to motivate activities, or to maintain institutions, beyond the second or third generation — unless it is transformed into a symbolic-ideological identification.[24]

Hansen's well-known thesis of "third generation return" seems to apply to cases where a de-ethnicized third generation, no longer pressed to repudiate its roots, picks up what might be called an historical identification with its nationality and learns about its culture. Needless to say, the knowledge of culture is at this point second- or third-hand, and the historical-cultural identification of the grandsons is qualitatively as different from the concrete ethnic experience of the grandfathers as it is from the emotionally charged ideological identification which marks the offspring of nationalistic immigrants. In any case, by the time the third generation "finds itself" the ethnic folk community is either severely attenuated or simply gone.

A nationality community starts out with an ideology whose symbols can be transmitted to the young much more easily since, being abstract, they do not depend for their meaning on the concrete experience of particular people, objects, or relationships. If, in addition, it is an irredentist ideology, it will remain a source of identification at least until the political ambition of the group is attained.[25] Thus it would seem that national-symbolic identification may be capable of turning the formidable trick of maintaining the continuity of ethnic involvement through the second and third generations. On this basis, at any rate, one would expect nationality groups to survive longer than folk communities, although they may change considerably in the process. It is quite interesting that the young people in such communities visualize their continuance — given certain changes — for at least one or two generations beyond their own. In a study I did of Ukrainian youth in the U.S.A., they predicted the following modifications, among others: increasing use of English by all except a small core; de-emphasis of political (as distinct from cultural) nationalism; changes in the functions of organizations; and a psychological shift from a defensive to a more assertive stance in relations with the dominant society.

One of the obvious changes is numerical decline: attrition is bound to occur. Yet there remains a "solid, group conscious nucleus"[26] of individuals who will derive some gratification from whatever values the ethnic community has to offer at successive stages of its development. It could be organizational rewards, or material advantage, or pride in the group's heritage: different things appeal to different kinds of people. But this means that, in order to predict the longevity of a given community, one would have to know (among other things) something about its present internal differentiation, particularly about the distribution of motives to stay in the community, degrees of involvement in its affairs, and stakes in its persistence.

For example, if the "natural" leaders of the community prefer to stay in it despite attractive residential, occupational or social alternatives because they feel responsible for its continuity; if the organizational activities are modified in such a way that they offer unique opportunities for sociability or self-realization to many members, the life span of the community will be extended. Again, individuals may have business assets (including client good will) in the community which cannot very well be transferred outside, or deep personal involvement in organizational positions, or simply a circle of friends they are reluctant to give up. The longevity of the community is directly related to the incidence of such cases, just as, on the other hand, it is limited by the extent to which people who would like to stay will have no choice about it.

Other relevant variables must be sought on the community level rather than that of individual motives. Among them are the prestige that the given ethnic group enjoys in its surroundings, the political influence it can wield (because of its numerical strength or through prominent representatives), a continuous flow of events and the persistence of issues that affect or trouble the group, and perhaps most important, the habit of meeting problems collectively, as a unit.

Finally, certain developments in the larger society may have ramifications for the processes within the ethnic community. Thus the twin emphases on liberation and on ethnic power in our own day can be reasonably expected to curb tendencies toward individual assimilation and to reinforce retentionist arguments and motivations.

Let me close by recalling a question asked some years ago by an American sociologist.[27] The question was: Is the ethnic community a transitional phenomenon, or has it become institutionalized? The considerations presented above suggest that the answer — at least as regards urban groups — depends on the nature of the particular community. While a folk community in its pure form is bound to disappear once it is no longer needed by the immigrants' descendants *as individuals,* the nationality community, which serves *collective* needs and *group* ideals, has a good chance of remaining an identifiable feature of the social landscape.

Notes

[1] W. I. Thomas and F. Znaniecki, *The Polish Peasant in Europe and America* (New York: Dover Press, 1958); W. L. Warner and L. Srole, *The Social Systems of American Ethnic Groups* (New Haven: Yale University Press, 1945); C. F. Marden and G. Meyer, *Minorities in American Society* (New York: American Book Co., 1962).

[2] Julian Bachynskyj, *The Ukrainian Immigration in the United States of America* (Lviv: Balytskyj and Harasevych, 1914), pp. 74-75, Table 3;

[3] Nathan Glazer, "Ethnic Groups in America: From National Culture to Ideology" in Minako Kurokawa (ed.), *Minority Responses* (New York: Random House, 1970), p. 80.

[4] Among the exceptions are Robert E. Park, *The Immigrant Press and its Control* (New York & London: Harper and Bros., 1922); Everett V. Stonequist, *The Marginal Man* (New York: Charles Scribner's Sons, 1937); Joseph S. Roucek, "Lithuanian Immigrants in America", *American Journal of Sociology*, Vol. 41 (1936), pp. 447-453; E. K. Francis, "The Nature of the Ethnic Group", *American Journal of Sociology*, Vol. 52 (1947), pp. 393-401.

[5] Helen Znaniecki Lopata, "The Function of Voluntary Associations in an Ethnic community: Polonia" in E. W. Burgess and D. J. Bogue (eds.), *Contributions to Urban Sociology* (Chicago: University of Chicago Press, 1964), p. 205.

[6] The distinction between folk community and national community parallels that between "ethnic group" as a cultural and socio-historic category and "nation" as a politically self-aware collectivity.

[7] There might be, in this, the makings of a theory of sub-communities in which the background and social characteristics of the members would be conceptualized as "independent" and the relevant features of the community as "dependent" variables.

[8] Robert K. Merton, *Social Theory and Social Structure* (New York: Free Press, 1957), pp. 421-236.

[9] Glazer, pp. 78-80.

[10] Robert Redfield, "The Folk Society", *American Journal of Sociology*, Vol. 52 (1947), pp. 293-308.

[11] R. Redfield, *Peasant Society and Culture* (Chicago: University of Chicago Press, 1956), pp. 41-44.

[12] Raymond Breton, "Institutional Completeness of Ethnic Communities and the Personal Relations of Immigrants", *American Journal of Sociology*, Vol. 70 (1964), pp. 193-205; *cf.* also Bachynskyj, Lopata.

[13] Ruth Johnston, *Immigrant Assimilation* (Perth, 1965), pp. 39-40.

[14] See, for example, Warner and Srole, p. 264.

[15] Jacques Vernant identifies the source of many such ideologies when he writes: "Understandably, some ethnic groups in exile regard themselves as trustees of a precious national heritage and culture which they believe they have a sacred duty to preserve and foster, since in their former homeland it is being strangled and stamped out." Vernant, *The Refugee in the Post-War World* (New Haven: Yale University Press, 1953), p. 359.

[16] S. N. Eisenstadt, The *Absorption of Immigrants* (London: Routledge and Kegan Paul, 1954); *cf.* Johnston, p. 39 and Roucek, p. 452.

[17] Thomas and Znaniecki, p. 1109, fn. 1; Park, pp. 111-119; E. D. Beynon, "Social Mobility and Social Distance Among Hungarian Immigrants in Detroit", *American Journal of Sociology*, Vol. 41 (1936), pp. 423-434.

[18] O. D. Duncan and S. Lieberson, "Ethnic Segregation and Assimilation", *American Journal of Sociology*, Vol. 64 (1959), pp. 364-374.

[19] Alex Simirenko, *Pilgrims, Colonists, and Frontiersmen* (New York: Free Press, 1964), pp. 86; 126-128.

[20] Interaction with other communities of the same nationality is kept up through personal ties, superterritorial organizations, the ethnic language press, etc. Again, the nationality community is more likely than the folk community to be concerned with issues that transcend local interest.

[21] The terminology is Child's. Alternative patterns of adjustment by children of immigrants to their marginal situation have been discussed at length in the following works, among others: Irvin L. Child, *Italian or American?* (New Haven: Yale University Press, 1943), pp. 70-84; Paul J. Campisi, "Ethnic Family Patterns: The Italian Family in the United States", *American Journal of Sociology,* Vol. 53 (1948), p. 447; Warner and Srole, p. 147.

[22] Bachynskyj, pp. 262-392, 404-472; *cf.* also Roucek, Johnston.

[23] Simirenko, *passim.*

[24] V. C. Nahirny and J. A. Fishman, "American Ethnic Groups: Ethnic Identification and the Problem of Generations", *Sociological Review,* Vol. 13 (1965), pp. 311-326.

[25] Francis quotes one definition of the concept "nation" which includes "the idea of a common government whether as a reality in the present or past, or as an aspiration of the future". *op. cit.,* pp. 393.

[26] Caroline F. Ware, "Ethnic Communities" in the *Encyclopedia of the Social Sciences,* Vol. 27 (1961), pp. 195-206.

[27] Ethna O'Flannery, "Social and Cultural Assimilation", *American Catholic Sociological Review,* Vol. 27 (1961), pp. 195-206.

Selected Bibliography

(This list includes works utilized for general background but not referred to in the text.)

Bachyns'kyj, Julian. *Ukrayins'ka Immigratsiya v Zyedynenykh Derzhavakh Ameryky.* Lviv: Baltyskyj and Harasevych, 1914.

Beynon, Erdmann, D. "Social Mobility and Social Distance among Hungarian Immigrants in Detroit", *American Journal of Sociology,* Vol. 41, 1936, pp. 423-434.

Borhek, J. T. "Ethnic Group Cohesion", *American Journal of Sociology,* Vol. 76, 1970, pp. 33-46.

Breton, Raymond. "Institutional Completeness of Ethnic Communities and the Personal Relations of Immigrants", *American Journal of Sociology,* Vol. 70, 1964, pp. 193-205.

Campisi, Paul J. "Ethnic Family Patterns: The Italian Family in the United States", *American Journal of Sociology,* Vol. 53, 1948, pp. 443-449.

Child, Irvin L. *Italian or American?* New Haven: Yale University Press, 1943.

Davis, Jerome. *The Russians and the Ruthenians in America.* New York: George H. Doran, 1922.

Duncan, Otis Dudley and Stanley Lieberson, "Ethnic Segregation and Assimilation", *American Journal of Sociology,* Vol. 64, 1959, pp. 364-374.

Eisenstadt, S. N. *The Absorption of Immigrants.* London: Routledge and Kegan Paul, 1954.

Fishman, Joshua A. *et al. Language Loyalty in the United States.* The Hague: Mouton & Co., 1966.

Francis, E. K. "The Nature of the Ethnic Group", *American Journal of Sociology,* Vol. 52, 1947, pp. 393-401.

Gans, Herbert J. *The Urban Villagers.* New York: Free Press, 1962.

Glazer, Nathan. "Ethnic Groups in America: From National Culture to Ideology", *Minority Responses,* ed. Minako Kurokawa. New York: Random House, 1970.

Goldstein, Sidney and Calvin Goldscheider. *Jewish Americans,* Englewood Cliffs, N.J.: Prentice-Hall, Inc., 1968.

Gordon, Milton M. *Assimilation in American Life.* New York: Oxford University Press, 1964.

Halich, Wasyl. *Ukrainians in the United States.* Chicago: University of Chicago Press, 1937.

Handlin, Oscar. *The Uprooted.* Boston: Little, Brown, 1951.

Hansen, Marcus L. "The Third Generation in America", *Commentary,* Vol. 14, 1952, pp. 492-500.

Johnston, Ruth. *Immigrant Assimilation.* Perth, Western Australia: 1965.

Kramer, Judith R. *The American Minority Community.* New York: Thomas Y. Crowell Company, 1970.

Lazerwitz, Bernard. "Some Factors in Jewish Identification", *Jewish Social Studies,* Vol. 15, 1953, pp. 3-24.

Lieberson, Stanley. *Ethnic Patterns in American Cities.* The Free Press of Glencoe, 1963.

Lopata, Helen Znaniecki. "The Function of Voluntary Associations in an Ethnic Community: Polonia", *Contributions to Urban Sociology,* eds. Ernest W. Burgess and Donald J. Bogue. Chicago: University of Chicago Press, 1964.

Lopreato, Joseph. *Italian Americans.* New York: Random House, 1970.

Marden, Charles F. and Gladys Meyer. *Minorities in American Society.* New York: American Book Co., 1962.

Merton, Robert K. *Social Theory and Social Structure.* New York: The Free Press of Glencoe, 1957.

Nahirny, Vladimir C. and Joshua A. Fishman. "American Ethnic Groups: Ethnic Identification and the Problem of Generations", *The Sociological Review,* Vol. 13, 1965, pp. 311-326.

O'Flannery, Ethna. "Social and Cultural Assimilation", *American Catholic Sociological Review,* Vol. 27, pp. 195-206.

Park, Robert E. *The Immigrant Press and Its Control.* New York and London: Harper and Brothers, 1922.

Park, Robert E. and Herbert A. Miller. *Old World Traits Transplanted.* New York: Harper and Brothers, 1921.

Redfield, Robert. *Peasant Society and Culture.* Chicago: University of Chicago Press, 1956.

_____ "The Folk Society", *American Journal of Sociology,* Vol. 52, 147, pp. 293-308.

Roucek, Joseph S. "Lithuanian Immigrants in America" *American Journal of Sociology,* Vol. 41, 1936, pp. 447-453.

Simirenko, Alex. *Pilgrims, Colonists, and Frontiersmen.* New York: The Free Press of Glencoe, 1934.

Stonequist, Everett, V. *The Marginal Man.* New York: Charles Scribner's Sons, 1937.

Thomas, William I. and Florian Znaniecki. *The Polish Peasant in Europe and America.* New York: Dover, 1958.

Vernant, Jacques. *The Refugee in the Post-War World,* New Haven: Yale University Press, 1953.

Ware, Caroline, F. "Ethnic Communities", *The Encyclopedia of the Social Sciences,* Vol. 5, 1931, pp. 607-613.

Warner, W. Lloyd and Leo Srole. *The Social Systems of American Ethnic Groups.* New Haven: Yale University Press, 1945.

Wood, Arthur Evans. *Hamtramck.* New Haven: College and University Press, 1955.

Znaniecki, Florian. *Modern Nationalities.* Urbana: University of Illinois Press, 1952.

INTEGRATION OF FOUR ETHNIC GROUPS IN CANADIAN SOCIETY:
ENGLISH, GERMAN, HUNGARIAN, ITALIAN

Professor Tadeusz Grygier
Director, Centre of Criminology
University of Ottawa

Introduction

This report is based on a study I co-directed with Professor John Spencer at the University of Toronto. Later, at the same time I moved to the University of Ottawa, Professor Spencer departed for Edinburgh, where he is now heading the Department of Social Science.

The original intention of this study was to examine the reasons for the apparent failure of the community health and welfare services to provide more adequate service to immigrants in Toronto. On further investigation of this problem, however, it became clear to us that the use of the social services was closely bound up with the total involvement of immigrants in the life of the community and that it would be unwise to concentrate all of the study on just one aspect of a much broader question.

For this reason the initial focus of the study was changed to an examination of the characteristics affecting the integration of immigrants in Toronto. As a result of this study we hoped to be in a better position to make relevant proposals for social policy for the social services in meeting the needs of the immigrant population.

The state of integration of an individual we defined in the following operational terms: "partaking in the life of the country productively (economically and socially) and to his own advantage (making use of the country's opportunities for advancement, its culture, social services and the like)". The focus of this group study was two-fold: first, the testing of our operational definition of integration, and second, the examination of factors which affect the achievement of integration.

The population of immigrants to be sampled was confined to four immigrant groups: British, German, Hungarian and Italian families who emigrated to Canada in recent years (i.e. between two years and seven years ago) and who have children at school in Grade I. We are well aware of the limitation imposed on our study by a sample of this kind, but it is a limitation which we were bound to accept. From each of the above four ethnic groups a sample of fifty was interviewed, thus making a total of 200 interviews.

Concept of Integration

At the UNESCO Conference in Havana in 1956 integration was defined in the following words: "a dynamic process in which values are enriched through mutual acquaintance, accommodation and understanding. It is a process in which both the immigrants and their new compatriots find an opportunity to make their own distinctive contributions." The subject is complicated by virtue of the very different policies which have been pursued in the field of immigration, by arguments over the "mosaic of cultures" and the "melting pot" theories, and by the relationship between the concepts of "integration" and "assimilation".

R. Taft, in a report on studies of immigration assimilation in Western Australia, defines assimilation as "the process whereby immigrants and the native population become more alike as the result of interaction".[1] This definition incorporates both *externally* observable aspects of integration, such as food habits, social contacts and language usage, and a *subjective* side based on identification attitudes that are not externally observable.[2]

We are simply assuming that the concept of integration is a desirable goal of immigration policy if Canadian society is to be developed to its full potential, and with the greatest benefit to old and new Canadians. Moreover we are assuming that the concept of immigration describes the process in which both immigrants and Canadian citizens are now involved. It was on the basis of these assumptions that we attempted to examine to what extent the four ethnic groups, and the individuals in these groups, are involved in the process of integration and what factors influence their involvement in it.

For the purpose of our study we have defined an individual's state of integration in terms of the degree of involvement which he has with Canadian society, both economically and socially, the degree of satisfaction which he derives from using opportunities, facilities and services in Canada, and the contributions which he makes both economically and socially to Canada through this involvement.

In keeping with our operational definition (previously stated), we designed the questions in the interviewing schedule to assess three aspects of the respondents' level of integration — economic, social and cultural; but later analysis, especially by factorial method, revealed that the main distinction lay between *subjective* and *objective* integration. This distinction is also implied in recent British-Canadian studies by Professor A. H. Richmond.[3] He reports, for instance, that the main reason for seeking Canadian citizenship was a "strong sense of belonging permanently in Canada". Statistical analysis in the present study placed seeking or acquiring Canadian citizenship in the group of items indicating subjective integration. This item was related *negatively* to *objective* integration, owing to the fact that the English, who scored highest on objective integration, seldom sought Canadian citizenship. Our definitions do not correspond to "external" and "subjective" *assimilation,* studied in Australia by Ruth Johnston.[4] Her externally assimilated immigrant "passes unnoticed as being foreign", while subjective assimilation denotes "identification with the members of the society"; neither definition was relevant to this research.

Some of the interview questions dealt with *objective* economic integration, for example: "Are you employed now and are you able to use the skills in which you were trained?" Other questions examined the *subjective* feeling of being integrated economically: "Are you satisfied with your present job?" This contrast between *objective* and *subjective* integration was reflected also in other parts of the interview. For example, reading Canadian newspapers was considered an indication of *objective* integration, and questions relating to the respondent's general feeling of being integrated with Canadian society indicated *subjective* integration.

The following items showed high correlation with "objective integration", arranged in rank order:

a) present competence in English sufficient for maintaining social contact with native Canadians:

b) reading Canadian newspapers;

c) some knowledge of English on arrival;

d) English education (in England or at least "basic English" level acquired later);

e) previous level of general education;

f) tolerance of adolescent girls going out in the evenings;

g) "index of integrative friendships" (tendency to choose as friends native Canadians or members of ethnic groups other than the respondent's own);

h) tolerance of adolescent boys going out in the evenings;

i) current employment other than in own ethnic group;

j) city background;

k) use of Canadian agencies in child care;

l) maintaining contact with local school;

m) lack of unemployment;

n) tolerance of "dating" for girls;

o) subjective feeling of being integrated (not index of subjective integration, which correlated even less);

p) lack of participation in own ethnic organizations or groups.

Other items had lower, but not necessarily non-significant correlations. The following items correlated with the "index of subjective integration":

a) feeling of being a part of Canadian community and of Canada being the respondent's new home;

b) enjoyment of Canadian opportunities;

c) intention to settle in Canada;

d) acquisition of new skills, education or business in Canada;

e) satisfaction with the present job.

The Findings of the Study

The findings of this study are presented under nine main headings, with a brief introduction to each topic.

The level of education:

It is a reasonable assumption that the level of education has an important bearing on the integration of the immigrant, although both the educated and uneducated alike may encounter certain difficulties in common. The educated immigrant may have a wider variety of obstacles to overcome while the uneducated seem to find changes at a deeper level more difficult to make. The former is expected to reach a higher level of competence in the new language. The latter can earn his living with no more than the groundwork of language. The latter has few, if any, technical skills on arrival and the entry into unskilled employment does not entail a lowering of his social status as would be involved in the case of the educated immigrant. On the other hand, he is much more likely to be affected by unemployment, by seasonal changes in industry or by lack of seniority.

In this study education was measured in terms of the number of years of formal schooling, though it is recognized that this method of measurement fails to acknowledge adequately educational value of many forms of technical and vocational training.

The findings indicate that a high level of education alone does not necessarily lead to better integration. Nevertheless, healthy objective integration takes place when a "good" education is combined with the following factors:

a) successful transplanting of skills;

b) fair knowledge of the language;

c) determination to know more about the new environment through reading;

d) willingness to reach out to the receiving society by the formation of friendships with native Canadians or with members of other ethnic groups.

The positive relationship between the level of education and freedom from unemployment (of more than three months in length) is noticeable. It is not, however, as high as might be expected from figures for the total Canadian labour force. Unemployment seems to affect the majority of male immigrants during the first years after arrival. Nevertheless the rate of unemployment is higher among immigrants with a lower level of education and those possessing fewer skills.

The correlation coefficients show that a high level of education has little effect on "subjective integration". On the contrary, respondents with little formal schooling often claim to find opportunities in Canadian life even if these opportunities are limited. They also see themselves as becoming part of the new community in spite of their language difficulties.

Employment:

The conclusions of the study of employment may be summarized in the following way:

a) The ethnicity of the immigrants seemed to play a larger role than was initially assumed in securing employment (which by definition is essential to the process of integration). It seems that its role is greater than that played by education, acquisition of trade skills in the country of origin, and even the acquisition of new trade skills, professional qualifications or independent business in Canada.

b) Upward occupational or economic mobility, as indicated by the satisfaction immigrants derived from the position held at the time of the interview, did not seem to depend entirely on any single determinant, such as education or level of skills possessed on arrival in Canada or acquired later, but rather on a combination of these factors.

c) Job satisfaction did not seem to increase when working for or with people of one's own ethnic group. Immigrants' competence in English, however, seems to have at least a moderate influence on their job satisfaction.

d) Job satisfaction seemed to influence the different ethnic groups in different ways with regard to subjective feelings toward integration.

e) The immigrants themselves clearly preferred to rely on their own resources in finding work rather than on making use of Canadian resources.

f) There existed a strong reciprocal influence between the enjoyment of opportunities offered by Canada and the immigrants' subjective feelings toward integration into the Canadian community.

The employment of married immigrant women:

The general underlying hypothesis of this study was that employment has a positive influence on the integration of married immigrant women. The study showed that the working women in the sample reflected the patterns in the employment of women in the countries from which they came to Canada. In the ethnic groups originating from countries with a high rate of female employment, there was a high proportion of working women, and conversely (60% of the Hungarian women are employed, 21% of the German, 19% of the British and 17% of the Italians). But one must add, of course, that there may be other reasons as well for these inter-ethnic differences of which contemporary economic factors may well be among the most important.

The employed women in the sample showed a strong tendency to improve their knowledge of English and to use Canadian resources designed to help in problems of child care. They were also slightly more willing than the non-working women to seek assistance from Canadian social services in times of financial difficulty. On the other hand, the working women showed, though not strongly, that they would not use Canadian agencies for job finding and that they were not satisfied with the Canadian school system.

One may conclude from these findings that employment, especially in an environment where the majority of the workers are of a *different* ethnic origin, is a positive factor in the integration of immigrant women. They tend to take a greater part in the life of the country than the women who are not employed.

But at the same time we should emphasize that it would be a mistake to confuse integration with happiness. The finding that there is a strong tendency among the working women in the sample to be dissatisfied with their jobs is thus of particular interest. Occupational adjustment is only one aspect of total adjustment, but it is a major one when we consider how much time is spent at work. It is of particular interest that a high positive correlation was found between employment and the purchase of a house. The purchase of a house, moreover, is closely associated with becoming settled and putting down roots.

The relationship between school and immigrant parents:

The hypothesis which formed the basis of this part of our study was: there is a relationship between the degree of integration achieved by the immigrant families and their acceptance of, and involvement in, the Canadian school system.

Although this broad hypothesis was disproved, several important conclusions emerged from the study. A contrast was observed between measures of subjective and objective integration. Acceptance of the school system was most often based on lack of knowledge of, or involvement in the school and thus did not prove to be a factor in the objective measure of integration. Parents who felt integrated subjectively showed a tendency towards acceptance of the school, but this seemed to indicate a non-critical attitude rather than wholehearted approval. On the other hand, immigrant parents who became involved in the school tended to be better integrated on objective measurements than those who did not. Thus the two parts of the hypothesis proved to be unrelated and no finding could support both of them.

Parents with public school or better education showed a moderate tendency towards involvement in the schools, as did husbands possessing a university degree. However, parents with high school education or its equivalent tended to be more critical of the Canadian school system, although not more involved than those parents without high school education.

Our conclusion was that the cultural background of the family was a most significant factor, and that it affected both the parental expectations of the Canadian educational system, and the type of adjustment necessary for the child starting in the school. In the Italian families of the sample, the responsibility for educating the children was left almost entirely to the school, and the importance of education was not generally stressed. Within the German, British and Hungarian groups, education was considered to be of the greatest importance and parental expectations of the school were high. They compared the Canadian educational system with that of their own country, and were both more involved in, and at the same time more critical of the school than was the Italian group. Finally, the social class of the families in the study also proved to be an important determining factor in the relationship between parents and the school.

Child adjustment:

This study hypothesized that there is a direct relationship between child adjustment and the integration of parents. That is to say, the better integrated the parents are, the better the chance of a good adjustment on the part of the children.

Our definition of child maladjustment was based on the reports of the parents, not on any independant judgement such as the school record card. But it is interesting to see that only twelve husbands and fourteen wives out of the total sample of two hundred families indicated that they felt concern over their children's adjustment. These formed the *study* group.

Analysis of the indices of integration shows that the study group had a higher degree of objective integration while the total sample had a higher degree of subjective integration. So one can argue with some confidence that lack of subjective integration on the part of the *study* group indicates a subjective rejection of Canadian values and is not just a result of the composition of the study group itself. This suggests that *families that reject the culture in which they live tend to produce maladjusted children.* But one must also draw attention to the possible significance of rate of integration. Rapid integration, that is the quick assimilation of the overt characteristics of the new society, may be harmful in the long run. In this case the process of integration may be superficial and the underlying conflicts may still be present.[5]

Parent-adolescent conflict:

The data available from the study on relationships between parents and adolescents appears to be, on analysis, inconclusive, and this general heading is therefore unnecessarily pretentious in its scope. Some interesting evidence, however, is available on the attitudes of parents among the four ethnic groups to teenage dating patterns and also on the attitudes of the teenagers themselves.

The most popular curfew hour chosen by the Hungarian and Italian parents was nine o'clock, for both boys and girls. Several Italians even commented that this was a "silly question" for what good could boys and girls come to, going out in the evenings.

Most German parents favoured ten for the boys and nine for the girls, while the British parents chose eleven and ten o'clock respectively. The British parents were also the most lenient as regards dating alone, probably because British patterns are not unlike Canadian ones. On the other hand, the German, Hungarian and Italian parents favoured group dating, with Italian wives being the most cautious.

The British and Hungarian men were more lenient than the women as regards curfew hours and dating. The Italian men were slightly more lenient regarding dating but stricter than their wives as regards curfew hours. The German men were stricter in nearly all respects.

As with education, the German men were the most critical of Canadian customs. However, among the women the Hungarian wives were the most critical with the German wives ranking next to the British wives in acceptance of Canadian patterns. The high degree of acceptance by the Italian group is a trend similar to their acceptance of the school system. It may be based on genuine approval, on acquiescence, or on lack of knowledge of Canadian families.

There were only twenty-seven teenagers interviewed, 68% of whom were from Hungarian and Italian families. The sample was too small to expect statistically significant results which would indicate a relation between parent-adolescent conflict and the level of integration, either subjective or objective; but out of seventeen aspects of conflict examined, statistically eight were at least suggestive of some association. Of those eight, four suggested that *objective integration reduces conflict*; four appeared to show that *subjective integration increases it.*

A comparison of the data on child adjustment and on parent-adolescent conflict suggests (very tentatively) that lack of any attempt to integrate on the part of the parents leads to maladjustment of their children; if an attempt is made, but remains a wish rather than an objective reality, the family problems are postponed, but not entirely eliminated.

Participation and involvement in ethnic organizations:

This study was based on the assumption that there would be a negative relationship between integration and participation in ethnic organizations, and that ethnic organizations, because of their contact with the wider community, could act as a stepping-stone for the immigrant while he was in the process of adjusting to a new way of life. This hypothesis was confirmed.

The four ethnic groups show important contrast in the extent to which they participate in ethnic organizations and in their attitudes towards this participation. Italian husbands and wives show the largest percentages: 84% of Italian husbands and 86% of Italian wives were joiners. This is seven times greater than the 12% of British husbands and 14% of British wives who participated. Hungarian husbands and wives rank next to the Italians with 70% participation. The number of German wives participating is almost one-half the number of Italian wives.

Although the reasons for non-participation differ in detail between the four ethnic groups, lack of time appeared to be a commonly found explanation. In the case of the German group, however, there was a strong desire expressed to cut off ties with the homeland. The clearest comment on the wish to discontinue German ties appears in the following statement:

> We have strong ideas how Germans should behave in a new country. These are: 1) avoid other Germans, 2) learn some English before coming here, 3) act as a Canadian, and 4) criticize the customs as seldom as possible.

The cohesiveness of extended families:

The hypotheses tested in the course of this study were two:

1. Immigrants with highly cohesive extended families will have a low level of integration into Canadian society.
2. Immigrants who have an extended family of low cohesiveness will have a high level of integration into urban Canadian society.

The main overall finding was that there were two fairly different kinds of extended families. The Italians in general had large, cohesive extended families resembling the classical type. It appeared that the Italians had maintained in Toronto those close family ties which are generally considered to be incompatible with modern urban living. Generally the kinship relationships of the British, German and Hungarian immigrants were less prevalent and less important. Only 58% in these groups had any relatives in Canada, while all of the Italians had relatives here. But 40% did have relationships of some importance with kin in Toronto.

Our analysis shows that the immigrants with modified extended families or loose ties of kinship were more integrated than the Italians with highly cohesive extended families. The women belonging to modified extended families with cohesive kinship relationships tended to be more integrated than those with no relatives in Canada or with only loose kinship ties. The modified extended family appeared to have no relationship to the integration of the men.

While the classical extended family provides strong emotional support and mutual aid, it also acts as an instrument of firm social control, preserving customary patterns of behaviour and regulating the lives of its members along well-defined norms, and thereby discouraging the change necessary for integration. So long as the focus of the study is on the achievement of integration alone, the social control of the Italian family appears in a negative light. This, however, is not the whole story, for it also has many positive aspects. The crime rate, for example, of the Italians in Canada is among the lowest of all ethnic groups. One student of sociology, Werner Gruninger, relates this to their attempt as a conspicuous minority group to create a good reputation amidst a potentially hostile society, but he also comments on the survival of their extended kinship system and the measure of social control which it continues to maintain.

It may, in fact, be highly desirable that the kin group and ethnic community stabilize and regulate the behaviour of its members in keeping with their well-established norms. More especially for a group whose original way of life is as different from the Canadian as is the Italian, lack of this control might give rise to personality strains and deviant behaviour. Progress towards integration is assumed to be a desirable objective, but it does not necessarily follow that this progress ought to be rapid.

Thus the finding that cohesive extended families are associated with low integration does not necessarily mean that cohesive kinship groups are a negative influence on the quality of integration. For in the long run the very reverse may be the case. In discussing this question, the pace of change is an important factor. It may well be that the opportunity to develop "Little Italy" in the middle of Toronto will prove to be a source of strength and support for the Italian community in the process of becoming Canadians. If this is so, as we firmly believe, then any attempt to have forced the pace of change would have given rise to difficult problems in social adjustment.

Use of social services:

The different ways in which the four ethnic groups made use of the social services available in Canada is well-illustrated in the following example. We asked: Where would you seek advice if you had great difficulty with your children's behaviour? The question was explained to the families as meaning unruly or disturbing behaviour with which the respondents were unable to deal.

The findings may be summarized as follows:

a) The four ethnic groups exhibited cultural differences in their responses to this question which were generally consistent for both the study group (i.e. the group of twelve husbands and fourteen wives who reported problems with their children) and the total population of 200 families.

b) The Italians reported that they would seek help from their relatives. This choice is certainly consistent with our observations elsewhere on the cohesiveness of the Italian kinship group and its usefulness as a source of mutual aid and social control. Nevertheless this very fact may also have inhibited the Italian families from reporting any problems with their children.

c) The Germans in the sample chose the doctor as their source of advice.

d) The Hungarians chose first the clergy, and second private Catholic agencies as their source of help. In the small study group the wives chose the doctor as well as the clergy.

e) The most frequent choice of the British was a public or government agency, including school social services. Canadian private agencies, doctors and clergy were also popular.

General Comparison

The British Group. The majority of the British group came to Canada six years ago, with the husband coming ahead of his wife and family in many instances. The average family had three children, mainly under ten years of age; and most of the six-year-olds were in their regular school grade, i.e. Grade I. Many families had several relatives in Canada but they saw most of them only on special occasions during the year.

The British group had, on the whole, the greatest advantages as regards education, language and job skills, yet there were several whose skills were not acceptable in Canada. Most of the women as well as the men were satisfied with their life in Canada, and they integrated fairly well, despite no obvious desire to become Canadian (e.g. most of their friends were British, 14% of the men chose ethnic employment, and few took out Canadian citizenship). The number of wives working increased from 28% to 38% but only 18% worked full-time in Canada. Contact with the school was good though the British parents did not always approve of Canadian methods. There was no noticeable parent-adolescent conflict — though the only delinquent in the entire study was found among the British children.

Our data confirm Richmond's findings that the British are culturally well adjusted and economically well off, but many never planned to settle in Canada and do not believe migration has improved their lot.

The German Group.   The average German family came to Canada together. Two children was the average, with few over ten years of age. Relatives were few, but when they existed family ties were relatively strong. The vast majority of the German parents had no more than public school education, yet were trained in a skilled job, and had some knowledge of English — all of which stood them in good stead. The men appeared to be hard-working, ambitious and fairly independent, yet also eager to integrate — as indicated by their index of Canadian friendships, their lack of ethnic employment and their willingness to be interviewed (i.e. the German group gave the fewest refusals). However, the German group also had high expectations of the new land, and several wondered at the time of the study whether they would not be better off in the more prosperous Germany, especially those who had been here more than five years and had become rather disillusioned. On the whole, the German men were the most critical of the Canadian schools and the Canadian teenage patterns. Forty per cent still attended ethnic organizations.

The German women appeared slightly more satisfied with Canada than were their husbands, perhaps because fewer of them worked in Canada than in Germany. The 56% who had worked in Germany dwindled to 22% full-time and 20% part time in Canada, perhaps because of the relatively higher status of women in Canada, or perhaps because the families enjoyed a more comfortable standard of living than they had known in Germany.

The Hungarian Group.   The Hungarian group was the most heterogeneous and thus perhaps the most interesting ethnic group of the four studied. This diversity was seen in the ages of the men (the average being older than in the other groups); in the ages of the children; in their contact with relatives; and in the education and skills which they brought to Canada, e.g. they included the most educated as well as many of the least educated. Of the Hungarian group 70% arrived in 1957, the vast majority speaking little English. Despite the contrast in language construction, most of them made some effort to master English. Many of them found they could no longer practice their previous occupations; and a large number suffered from long term unemployment. These two factors created much dissatisfaction with the job situation in Canada. Several of the Hungarian group found jobs with Hungarian compatriots; and the majority still belonged to a Hungarian organization to which they also sent their children. The older parents found integration comparatively more difficult, and a relatively large number of the Hungarian group were in this category in contrast to the younger Hungarian parents. Despite this, many took out Canadian citizenship, appreciating the political freedom of the New World and disliking their previous DP status. Those of the Hungarian parents who learned new skills (14%) and those who bought a business (8%) became the most satisfied with Canada. As a group the Hungarians felt fairly integrated, though objectively they were not quite as integrated as the German group.

The Hungarian wives in particular presented an unusual pattern, in that unlike the women of the other three groups, they were as integrated as were their husbands. A large number of them still held jobs, though fewer than in Hungary, i.e. 70% had been employed in Hungary compared to 38% full-time and 22% part time in Canada. The working wives appeared to be the most educated, the most ambitious, but also the most dissatisfied with their present occupations. However, it appeared that taking jobs enabled them to buy a house. Thus it seemed that the motive for working was buying a house, not job satisfaction, and that these women would probably have been more satisfied staying at home. This group also became the most integrated of all the Hungarian women, and showed unusual knowledge of Canadian facilities, both public and private.

The Italian Group. The Italian group invariably differed most from the other groups, not through any fault of their own but because their accustomed way of life was most unlike the usual Canadian patterns and because they chose to remain in the comparative security of the Italian community.

As a group the Italians were the most homogeneous. Parents appeared to have married young and to have relatively large families. Most had plenty of relatives in Canada, many of whom they saw daily or at least weekly or monthly. Relatives appeared to be a great source of strength — for advice on child care, for financial help, for babysitting, and so on. However, the Italian group began life in Canada with several major disadvantages — such as lack of experience in urban living, lack of formal education, lack of occupational skills, and lack of knowledge of English — most of which the majority of the Italian group never overcame. Even the children in Grade I were already a year behind in schooling. As a result of these disadvantages the Italian group suffered an overwhelming amount of unemployment, and many wives (34%) had to work full-time to augment the family income (compared to 8% in Italy). The least ambitious appeared to be the most satisfied, and the most ambitious, the most frustrated. Many sought satisfaction from other things — such as from buying a house or from joining Italian recreational organizations. Only three couples had really attempted to learn English and thus to integrate. The rest remained in their ghetto-like Italian community — feeling somewhat integrated, yet, objectively speaking, remaining outside the general flow of

Canadian life. The teenagers interviewed were beginning to feel this contrast but as yet none had rebelled strongly.

Some Suggestion For Social Policy

The outstanding need which arises from this study is for a greater understanding of the *diversity* of cultural patterns among the different ethnic groups which comprise the immigrant population of Toronto. Again and again in the nine separate research reports which form the core of our study this need is emphasized, and we were concerned only with four ethnic groups.

Some examples of the policy we have in mind would be the following: in the area of employment, the use of workers specially qualified in the language and culture of particular immigrant groups, or the institution of plans for training or up-grading in the immigrant's own language or in conjunction with classes in the English language (such a training program providing an additional incentive to the learning of English); in education, the development of a much closer liaison between the schools and ethnic agencies, or the appointment of teachers and social workers with special understanding of the needs of immigrants, or the inclusion in the curriculum of materials relating to the life and culture of the ethnic groups making up Canada's population; in family and child welfare, the appointment of social workers who have special knowledge of and training in dealing with the problems of immigrants, or the development of services related to the needs of immigrant mothers at work; in the field of recreation we emphasize the important role the ethnic churches can play in contributing to the social as well as the religious needs of their members. Possibly the most sensible plan would involve qualified social agents working with immigrant welfare assistants, who would act as interpreters and confidants of recent immigrants and provide a liaison between Canadian social agencies and ethnic organizations. Also, members of immigrant groups should be encouraged to enter the field of social work and financial support provided for their education.

One of the major findings of this study which was not anticipated in our initial definition of integration was the distinction between what we have called *objective* and *subjective* integration. Rather than a general factor of integration we thus found two distinct factors. The one, that is the *subjective,* represented feelings and attitudes about integration, while the other represented *objective* facts, such as reading Canadian newspapers regularly, having friends outside the immigrant's own ethnic group, or using Canadian agencies for help with child behaviour problems.

The relationship between objective and subjective integration was found to be moderately positive (the tetrachoric coefficient of correlation was .35 for men and .25 for women). Thus actual involvement in the life of Canadian society seems to bear only a moderate relationship to whether an immigrant feels at home and satisfied in Canada. Some immigrants with high expectations are integrated according to objective criteria, but do not feel integrated as measured by their subjective attitudes. Others, however, feel at home in Canada though they are not objectively integrated. This latter point is characteristic of the Italian immigrants who live in fairly isolated Italian communities as "urban villagers", to use Gans's title for his book.[6]

This reference to the Italian community which perpetuates the life of the southern Italian village within an urban setting such as Toronto, compels us to draw attention to one significant conclusion arising from our study. It relates to the rate of change and integration.

At first glance one may be tempted to denigrate any policy which encourages the persistence of the Italian village in mid-Toronto. It appears to run contrary to an effective immigration policy and to retard Italian integration into Canadian society. However, this slow rate of integration results in some highly desirable consequences. The kinship group and the ethnic community stabilize and regulate the behaviour of its members in keeping with well-established norms and customs. Particularly for a group whose original way of life is as different from the Canadian as is the Italian, lack of such control might cause personality strain or the well-known symptoms of social maladjustment.

The conclusion for social policy, therefore, is that the culture of the immigrant's own homeland should be perpetuated if it is able to provide in the long run the support necessary to effect a stable pattern of integration. This would present a too-rapid rate of integration which might be detrimental to its quality. If this argument is sound, then the kind of social services that are required are those which keep this important objective in the forefront.

Summary and Conclusions

a) All social planning requires a recognition of social realities, some of which are:

(i) integration is a *mutual* process;

(ii) in all planning we must realize that objective integration, defined as "partaking in the life of the country productively (economically and socially) and to own advantage (making use of the country's opportunities for advancement, of its culture, social services, etc.)" must be distinguished from subjective feelings and attitudes about integration and about making Canada one's home: these two are almost uncorrelated;

(iii) the same social services for Canadians and for immigrants, the latter coming from a variety of cultural groups, does *not* mean the same service: it means almost no service for some groups.

b) It follows that diversification of social services is needed.

c) Immigrants need social services planned and supplied by people who understand their cultures.

d) Some immigrants should be recruited and educated as social workers (not necessarily at the professional level), to work in their own milieu.

e) Rapid integration may be detrimental to its quality and destroy the immigrant community's network of social controls.

f) Knowledge of the English language is the main factor in objective integration; involvement of the parents in school activities is another; both have important and obvious implications for educational policy.

g) English courses for immigrants before they leave the countries of origin may help a gradual and successful integration better than any remedies undertaken at a later stage.

APPENDIX

Notes on statistical analysis

A. *General Methodology*

(1) The focus of this study was on "factors affecting integration of immigrant families". A true experimental design, in which we could vary such factors at will, as we vary soil, crop and fertilizers in agriculture, was impracticable in this case — as indeed it is in most social studies. All we could do was to establish relationships between certain factors and integration, and to speculate about significantly related factors actually affecting the process of integration. The statistical tool for this type of study is a correlation coefficient.

(2) We arrived at an operational definition of integration, which was, as all operational definitions are, somewhat arbitrary. It assumed the existence of a fairly uniform state, or process, which we labelled "integration", and for which we set conceptual boundaries. The purpose of any definition is to set the boundaries of a concept. The purpose of an operational definition is to set such boundaries for research operations. Our definition of integration was "partaking in the life of the country, productively (economically and culturally), and to own advantage (making use of the social services of the country, its culture, opportunities for advancement, etc.)". It was assumed that all the elements of this definition are positively interrelated and could be distinguished from other variables and groups of variables (or "factors"). This assumption, in order to achieve scientific objectively, had to be tested. The statistical method allowing such tests to be made is factor analysis; its basis is a matrix of inter-correlations.

(3) In order to test all our hypotheses we needed two sets of correlations:

(a) Intercorrelations between all variables within the boundaries of our operational definition of integration (to which we added some other subjective variables that could be considered to be the core, or the prerequisite, of the integrative process); the correlation matrix of all these variables permitted us to carry out factor analysis and arrive at one or more "factors" of integration.

(b) Correlations of all other variables — representing other factors and assumed to affect, positively or negatively, the integrative process — with the factor or factors of integration as operationally defined and empirically confirmed.

In addition to the above two sets of correlations it was desirable to have full matrices of intercorrelations of all variables obtained from our interviewing schedule, separately for the men and for the women in the sample, and separately for each ethnic group. This was, however, impractical for two reasons.

Firstly, it was too time-consuming to compute several thousands of correlations which are not essential for the satisfactory completion of the study. Secondly, with the exception of the Hungarian group, our variables had insufficient range to allow reliable correlation coefficients to be computed within each ethnic group. Thus all British subjects had full command of English — in our terms — and so competence in English could not be correlated for this group; nearly all Germans had public school education, but no more than this; nearly all Italians lacked job skills. The Hungarian group was the most heterogeneous in practically all respects; it represented a variety of levels of education and occupations, of social background and achievements. It therefore was not only the most representative ethnic group, but it was also the only group for which intercorrelations of all dichotomous variables (see below) could be attempted. Some of these intercorrelations proved to be unreliable, but many others could be computed in the acceptable manner; some proved to be enlightening and to offer guidance for latter analysis of the entire sample.

Many findings based on the Hungarian group could be extended to the entire sample by inspection of the distribution of data, which were compiled for each group separately. Thus the Hungarians showed a high negative correlation between "job skills in the old country" and unemployment. No correlations between these variables could be calculated for the other ethnic groups, as two of the groups showed universally high job skills, while the third represented a low level of skill. But in fact the conclusion from the Hungarian group could be extended to the total sample, since frequency distribution tables revealed that the Italian group, which had low skills, showed a great deal of unemployment, while the British and the Germans had high skills and hardly any unemployment.

A number of correlations between indices of integration and other variables were calculated within some other ethnic groups, whenever an important point needed clarification. Whenever possible, all variables falling within our operational definition of integration were intercorrelated for each ethnic group. For the Hungarian group most of these correlations could be computed, but for the others the distribution of data allowed but exceptional calculations to be made.

(4) It can be seen that the correlation coefficient was the basic statistical

tool for all our operations, both those testing the operational definition, and for subsequent ones, relating such factors as education, family cohesiveness, job skills, etc., to any measures of integration. It was important to choose a correlation coefficient which would be most efficient for our needs.

(5) Any correlation coefficient represents a relation between two variables. There can be no correlation between two constants or a variable and a constant. A variable is a characteristic which can be (a) either present or absent, or (b) always present but varying in degree. In our study the fact of being sponsored, or that of reading a Canadian newspaper regularly, for example, belonged to the first category: it was either present or absent. Age, education, length of stay in Canada, etc., on the other hand were always present but to a varying degree. A variable which is either entirely present or entirely absent is a dichotomous variable; the first category of our variable was therefore dichotomous.

There are three types of correlation coefficients: (a) those relating dichotomous variables to other dichotomous variables, (b) those relating non-dichotomous variables to each other (rank-order and product-moment correlation coefficients, for example), and (c) relating a dichotomous variable to a non-dichotomous variable (bi-serial correlation). As different coefficients give different values, in order to use a correlation matrix of comparable correlation coefficients we could only use one type of coefficient. This coefficient could only be one suitable for dichotomous variables: one can always dichotomize a non-dichotomous variable while it is usually impossible to reverse the process. For example, having established the range and distribution of education we could determine a mid-point and call all subjects above this point educated and all those below uneducated; but we could not change the *fact* of sponsorship into a matter of *degree*: one either has a sponsor or one has not.

(6) The most efficient and least time-consuming method of calculating a correlation coefficient between two dichotomous variables is to use "Computing Diagrams for the Tetrachoric Correlation Coefficient" by L. Chesire, M. Saffir and L. L. Thurstone (University of Chicago, 1933, distributed by the University of Chicago Bookstore). The pre-requisites are (a) to have all data expressed in proportions, or percentages, and (b) to keep these proportions in balance (never more than 9:1).

(a) The first aim was achieved in the design of the study. We had 50 families in each ethnic group, and each frequency multiplied by two expressed a percentage of the group; we had 200 families in all and each frequency divided by two represented the percentage of the total sample.

(b) The second problem was more complicated. Some of our dichotomous variables proved to be constants for some groups: all Italians were sponsored but only one of the British was sponsored. Other variables were similarly off-balance for the whole sample, most subjects possessing a given characteristic, or most subjects lacking it. Whenever this happened, our correlation became unreliable, as our variable was approximately a constant. In some cases, such as that of sponsorship, we decided to dispense with the variable altogether: it became clear to us that any correlation, if established, would in any case be misleading and would not be representative of any ethnic group. In other cases no reliable correlations could be established for single groups, but added together they would be permissible. Most proportions between positive frequencies (number of subjects possessing a characteristic) and negative frequencies (number of subjects lacking it) varied between 50:50 and 90:10, thus permitting the computation of the tetrachoric correlation coefficient.

(7) Whenever a variable was not naturally dichotomous (as sponsorship was), but was dichotomized from a non-dichotomous variable or a group of variables, we could establish a cut-off point as near as possible to the mid-point of the frequency distribution, and so achieve a proportion approximating 50:50. Thus education was originally classified as almost none (var. 29), completed elementary (var. 30), public (var. 31), high school (var. 32), and university or college (var. 33). Taken together, education represented a range from var. 29 to var. 33, with a suitable cut-off point between var. 30 and var. 31. This cut-off point classified 74% of men and 70% of women in the sample as educated, and 26% and 30% respectively as uneducated. Tetrachoric correlations between education and other dichotomous variables, including those representing integration, could therefore be calculated for the entire sample.

The same cut-off point for education was, however, unsuitable for each ethnic group. It classified nearly all Italian subjects as uneducated and nearly all others as educated. The proportion within each sample was off-balance. For this reason we created additional dichotomized variables with different cut-off points and had education represented not only by var. 171 (public school education or above) for the entire sample, but also by var. 189 (high school, university or college) for correlations within the Hungarian group, var. 33 (university or college) for the total sample of men, but not for the women, and var. 190 (elementary school or more) for Italian men and women. Family cohesiveness and "objective integration" (see below) were also represented by several dichotomized variables, each based on a different cut-off point.

(8) The total list of dichotomous variables is appended, together with tetrachoric correlation coefficients indicating their relationship to measures of integration. The cut-off points used in order to dichotomize non-dichotomous variables (such as age), or groups of variables (such as those representing education), are indicated in the appended Instructions for Tabulation of Data. As can be inferred from the remarks above, none of these instructions was given arbitrarily: they were based on the distributions of non-dichotomous data and aimed at cutting these distributions as near to their mid-points as possible.

(9) There were a number of steps we had to take in order to establish correlations and, at a later stage, factors:

(a) We had to define our sample of respondents in such a way that we could get a sufficient variety of characteristics to make a study comprehensive. At the same time we needed sufficient uniformity to have adequate frequency for every characteristic in which we were interested. In order to study a number of factors concerning education, child care, family relationships, etc., in which members of the research team and the sponsoring organizations were interested, we had to choose as respondents relatively recent immigrants living in family units, each with at least one child of school age. To facilitate computations we determined the number of families in each group as fifty, and in the total sample as 200.

(b) We had to find fifty men and fifty women in each ethnic group, fitting our definition of an immigrant family and capable of supplying information which was to be coded as variables.

(c) We had to devise an interviewing schedule and to conduct interviews in such a way that all relevant information could be coded, and represent on a sheet of variables: (i) presence of a characteristic (a tick showed this), or (ii) a degree of an attribute, such as age, which could be quantified and represented by a number.

(d) Having done this we compiled frequency distributions for all characteristics, separately for men (husbands), women (wives), and their children. There were separate tables for each ethnic group.

(e) We could then reject as unsuitable for further analysis all dichotomous characteristics which were uniformly present or uniformly absent, and leave all suitable dichotomous variables without further modification. Frequency distributions for non-dichotomous variables, such as age or education, were then examined to establish suitable cut-off points so as to change these variables into simple dichotomies. Variables 161-193, as well as integration variables 201-203, were arrived at by this method (see Instructions for Tabulation of Data).

(f) In some cases we could not dichotomize variables directly; we had to create intervening variables (see above Instructions). Variables 194, 195 and 196 were thus created; each represents an aggregate of several dichotomous variables. Our measures of integration are all aggregate, subsequently changed into dichotomies.

Index of family cohesiveness is also an aggregate, arrived at by counting the number of ticks on variables 67, 112, 120, 167 and 185. The first three of those variables were naturally dichotomous and entered on the sheet of variables by the interviewer; variables 167 and 185 were arrived at from frequency distributions of raw data and the numerals or ticks entered, in strict adherence to Instructions for Tabulation of Data, by research assistants.

(g) The most important aggregates for our study were, of course, those representing "integration". In order to select variables to be included in these aggregates factor analysis had to be carried out. The method used and the results achieved are outlined below.

B. *Factor Analysis of Integration*

(1) The following variables were selected for the matrices of intercorrelations (one matrix for 200 husbands and one for 200 wives) on which factor analysis was to be based:

(a) *Index of integrative friendships* (var. 170). This represents the subjects who scored above the cutting point on the aggregate variable of integrative friendships (var. 28) and who therefore showed above average tendency to extend their friendships to native Canadians or to immigrants of ethnic groups other than their own.

(b) *Present competence in English* (var. 173). This represents above average competence, sufficient to allow social conversation with native Canadians. It was assumed that competence in French is of little use in this respect in Toronto.

(c) *English education* (var. 174). This shows that the subject either took care to follow courses in English and completed at least Basic English, or was so competent in English that he needed no courses. It was assumed that an effort to achieve a fair competence in the language of the local Canadian community was a sign of integration in that community.

(d) *Reading Canadian newspapers* (English or French) *regularly* (var. 49). It was assumed that, Canadian culture being bilingual, reading a French Canadian newspaper would represent integration in Canadian life and culture, as would reading an English Canadian newspaper, while reading a publication of one's own ethnic group might not.

(e) *Present job satisfaction* (var. 58). It was assumed that satisfaction with present occupation in Canada expresses both the fact of economic integration and the feeling of being integrated in Canadian life in terms of taking advantage of the existing opportunities. For the wives this variable correlated low or negatively with others and was consequently dropped from factor analysis.

(f) *Use of Canadian resources in job finding* (var. 176). This is a clear reflection of our operational definition of integration and of interest to several members of the research team. Var. 176 represents the subjects who scored on any of the variables indicating their inclination to use private or public Canadian agencies or Canadian-born friends if they wanted to find a job. The correlations of this variable were around zero, and so it was excluded from factor analysis.

(g) *Unemployment* (var. 177). Length of unemployment, if any, was recorded as var. 68, and three months represented the mid-point of its distribution. Since lack of unemployment rather than lack of work represents integration, on the intercorrelation matrix the sign of all correlations of this variable was reversed.

(h) *Present employment* (var. 178). This included full and part-time employment (var. 69 and 70). This variable correlated very high, for the men, with var. 177 (unemployment), and was less satisfactory than the

latter in terms of its other correlations; it was therefore not used in subsequent statistical analysis, except as a part of another variable (193),
described below.

(i) *Ethnic employment* (var. 71). This variable represented lack of integration rather than its presence. It indicated that the majority of people at
a subject's place of work belonged to his own ethnic group. Therefore, as
with var. 177, the sign of all its intercorrelations was reversed for factor
analysis.

(j) *Acquisitions of any kind* (var. 179). This variable included acquisitions of a skilled trade (var. 72), a university degree (var. 73), professional
qualifications (var. 74), an independent business (var. 75), or a house (var.
76). As it was found that, judging from its intercorrelations, the acquisition
of a house had a different significance from the acquisition of skills, education, or business, var. 179 was subsequently dropped from statistical analysis.

(k) *Acquisition of skills, education, or business* (var. 186). This variable
was clearly related to other potential measures of integration, but its distribution was off-balance (very few subjects scored). Consequently it was
not in the matrix for the husbands, while for the wives, where it was included in factor analysis, the results could not be relied upon.

(l) *Acquisition of a house* (var. 76). This variable was included in the
matrix of intercorrelations, but did not come up to expectations on factor
analysis. If anything, it reflected a subjective feeling of integration and a
desire to settle down in Canada, but its loading on the factor of subjective
integration for the husbands was low; for the wives it was not calculated as
it was expected to approximate zero.

(m) *Contact with teachers or school organizations* on own initiative at
least twice a year (var. 181).

(n) *Use of Canadian agencies in child care* (var. 182). This included
private or public Canadian agencies, or a doctor, in cases of a hypothetical
"great difficulty" with children's behaviour.

(o) *Use of Canadian agencies in financial need* (var. 183). Financial need
was again hypothetical, and the agencies could be either private or public.
This variable was excluded from factor analysis when it was found that it
failed to correlate positively with others.

The next group of variables were clearly related to subjectively defined
plans, attitudes and feelings. They included:

(p) *Plans for Canadian citizenship* (var. 126).

(q) *Intention to settle in Canada* (var. 127).

(r) *Enjoyment of Canadian opportunities* (feeling that one has had more
chance in Canada than in the old country) (var. 131).

(s) *An unqualified statement* to the effect that the subject *feels he is a
member of the Canadian community* (var. 142, recorded by the interviewer
on the basis of oblique rather than direct questioning).

(t) *Either unqualified or qualified statement to the same effect* (var. 184, which included var. 142 and 143).

We expected that the tick against var. 143 ("reserved, but inclined to integrate") would be as good a sign of integration as a tick against var. 142 ("definitely yes"); but this did not prove to be the case, and correlations of var. 184 proved to be lower than those of var. 142. Since these two variables represented the same inclinations, varying only in degree, var. 142 was chosen for factor analysis and var. 184 was dropped.

(2) The total matrices of intercorrelation for factor analysis included, with the exception of var. 178 and 179, all the variables listed above. There was one matrix of 18 X 18 variables for the men, and another for the women. It was found that there was very little difference between the two matrices. Var. 176, 186, 183 and 126 failed to correlate positively and reliably with the others for the men, and were therefore dropped from factor analysis. The same applied to var. 58, 176, 76 and 126 for the wives. Var. 184 was dropped from both calculations for the reasons stated in the preceding paragraph. The reduced matrices included thirteen variables for the men and the same number for the women.

The reduced matrices were factorised by Thurstone's centroid method; analysis was carried out to obtain loadings on two factors, and there appeared to be no point in carrying it further.

When plotted on a graph, variables were found to cluster along two axes, neither of them being the original ones. With rotation, two factors were identified; variables loaded on one of these factors had very low loadings on the other. The results were almost identical for both sexes.

In view of the above we were forced to abandon the notion of a general factor of integration: we found two distinct — though slightly related — factors.

We had anticipated this possibility and envisaged the emergence of a factor of the economic, to be distinguished from social, integration. There was also a possibility of English education, or of general education and job skills, emerging as factors. None of these expectations were confirmed, and the two factors could be clearly identified by the variables which had high loadings on them.

For the husbands, variables 58 (job satisfaction), 127 (intention to settle in Canada), 131 (enjoyment of Canadian opportunities), and 142 (subjective feeling of integration) had adequate loadings on one of these factors, which could therefore be identified as subjective integration. For the wives the situation was similar, but var. 58 (job satisfaction) was, as indicated above, unrelated to the rest.

Again for the husbands, var. 177, 71 (both with sign reversed), 170, 173, 49, 174, 181, and 182 had high loadings on the second factor and low, if any, on the first. The only thing these variables had in common, apart from integration, was the fact that they represented objective facts rather than feelings and attitudes. The second factor could therefore be identified as objective integration and be operationally defined in terms of lack of unemployment, lack of ethnic employment, making friends with Canadians, competence in English sufficient to maintain social conversation with Canadians, English education or completing courses in English in Canada, reading Canadian newspapers, contact with Canadian school organizations or teachers, and use of Canadian agencies in child care.

For the wives lack of unemployment had no loadings on the second factor. In fact it had slight loading on the factor of subjective integration. This is understandable. For the men unemployment was a fact; for the women the statement about unemployment expressed an attitude. Most women in our sample had no employment, but they did not regard themselves as unemployed; those who did expressed the feeling of dissatisfaction — they wanted to be employed and felt rejected.

On the other hand, being employed correlated with other variables of objective integration for both men and women; being employed in a firm in which the majority of people are of the same ethnic origin correlated negatively. We clearly needed another variable, which was not in the original matrix and not in the factor analysis, and which identified subjects "presently employed, not in an ethnic group". Variable 193 was thus created and added to the matrices of intercorrelations. Its correlations indicated clearly that it belonged to the factor of objective integration for both the men and the women; var. 71 could therefore be dropped as redundant.

Having identified the factors and the variables with loadings on these factors we could introduce aggregate scales representing intervening variables, to be subsequently dichotomized according to their distributions. Var. 195 represented the sum of the entries on var. 58 (for husbands only), 127, 131 and 142; after the usual procedure of dichotomization this became var. 201, to identify the above average degree of subjective integration. Similarly, var. 196 represented the sum of entries on var. 170, 173, 174, 49, 181, 182, 193, and a lack of entry on var. 177 (unemployment, for husbands only). With a cut at mid-point this became var. 202, identifying the above average degree of objective integration.

Unfortunately the cut-off point in the middle of the distribution left all Italian wives and nearly all Italian husbands as "objectively unintegrated". We therefore introduced var. 203, especially for the Italian group, to represent the same variables of objective integration, but lower cut-off points. This permitted correlating objective integration with other factors within the Italian ethnic group, especially the special variables on family cohesiveness (on which the Italians scored high and required a cut-off point higher than other ethnic groups), and of education (on which the Italians required a lower cut-off point). This procedure permitted the analysis of the integrative processes in a group of low objective integration, low educational achievement, low degree of urbanization and high degree of ethnic and family cohesiveness, a group very different from the other three in our study.

C. *Some Effects of Defining Integration in Terms of Other Variables*

Since, as indicated above, some variables listed on "Intercorrelations of Variables" were a part of aggregate intervening variables of subjective and objective integration (var. 195 and 196), their correlations with indices of integration are somewhat inflated: whenever a tick on a variable is counted as a part of another variable, this produces, or reinforces, a positive correlation between the two. What we have here is a correlation implied in the definition of one variable by another.

Aggregate scales of integration (var. 195 and 196) were not correlated with any variables directly, but they were dichotomized into variables 201, 202 and 203 and correlated in this form. Thus variables 201, 202 and 203 were still defined in terms of the original variables which went into the aggregates 195 and 196. For this reason the correlations of 201 with variables 58 (for husbands only), 127, 131, 142, and, to some extent, 184, are higher than they would have been if var. 201 were entirely independent of the rest. Correlations of var. 202 and 203 with variables 177 (for husbands only), 170, 173, 174, 49, 181, 182, 193, and, to a lesser extent, 71 and 178, are also inflated.

Although the above correlations would be slightly lower if the effect of "correlation implied in the definition of one variable by another" were not present, they would still be expected to remain quite high. Our indices of subjective and objective integration represent nothing more than "factors" revealed by factor analysis, and any variable which has a high loading on a factor would inevitably correlate highly with any valid measures of the same factor.

INSTRUCTIONS FOR TABULATION OF DATA

(1) Dichotomized variables

Var. #   When to tick

161 More than 2 children in Canada (var. 3) ⎫
162 More than 1 child in Canada aged 6 or more (var. 3) ⎬ For wife copy from husband
163 Any children in Canada aged 14 or more (var. 3) ⎭
164 Age more than 34 (var. 5)
165 Var. 10 or 11 ticked (length of stay in Canada)
166 Var. 12 or 13 ticked (city background)
167 Index of family contact more than 4. Calculate index by multiplying frequencies of var. 15 by 4, var. 16 by 3, 17 by 2, and 18 by 1, and totalling them. Stop counting if you can see clearly that index totals 5 or more.
168 Number of relatives more than 2 (var. 20)
169 Var. 21 or 22 or 23 ticked (child care by relatives)
170 Index of integrative friendships (var. 28) more than 2
171 Var. 31, 32, or 33 ticked (public school education or more)
172 Var. 34, 35, 36, 37, or 38 ticked (some English on arrival)
173 Var. 41, 42, or 43 ticked (some competence in English)
174 Var. 43, 44, 45, 46, or 47 ticked (competence or courses)
175 Var. 50, 51, 53, or 54 ticked (job skills in old country)
176 Var. 62, 63, or 65 ticked (use of Canadian resources in job finding)
177 Var. 68 (unemployment) over 3 months
178 Var. 69 or 70 ticked (employed now)
179 Var. 72, 73, 74, 75, or 76 ticked (any acquisitions — Hungarian husbands only)
180 Var. 77 or 78 ticked (any participation in ethnic groups)
181 Var. 82 or 83 ticked, or 86 more than 1 (contact with school)
182 Var. 116, 117, or 119 ticked (use of Canadian agencies in child care)
183 Var. 124 or 125 ticked (use of Canadian agencies in financial need)
184 Var. 142 or 143 ticked (subjective feeling of integration)
185 Var. 21, 22, 23, or 24 ticked (index of child care)
186 Var. 72, 73, 74, or 75 ticked (acquisitions of skills, education, or business)
187 Var. 108 or 109 ticked (critical of Canadian permissiveness)
188 When var. 194 is 2 or more (index of family cohesiveness)
189 When var. 32 or 33 ticked (High School or University, Hungarians only)
190 When var. 30, 31, 32 or 33 ticked (elementary education or more — Italians only)
191 When var. 194 is 3 or more (family cohesiveness — Italian husbands)
192 When var. 194 is 4 or more (family cohesiveness — Italian wives)
193 When var. 178 ticked and 71 not ticked (employed now, not in an ethnic group)

201   When 195 is 3 or more for husbands or 2 or more for wives (subjective integration)

202   When 196 is 5 or more for husbands or 4 or more for wives (objective integration)

203   When 196 is 2 or more for husbands or 1 or more for wives (objective integration — Italians only)

(2) Intervening variables

194   Sum of ticks on var. 67, 112, 120, 167 and 185 (index of family cohesiveness)

195   Sum of ticks on var. 58 (husbands only), 127, 131 and 142

196   Sum of ticks on var. 170, 174, 174, 49, 181, 182, 193, and no tick on 177 (husbands only)

INTERCORRELATION OF VARIABLES

Var. #	Attribute Measured	Husbands		Wives	
		201	202 or 203	201	202 or 203
161	Many children in Canada (over 2)	.05	-.10	-.20	.16
162	Many children of school age (over 1)	.17	-.10	.11	.09
163	Adolescents in the family (any, aged 14 or over)	.05	-.40	-.08	-.35
164	Advanced age (over 34)	.00	-.04	.13	.06
165	Long stay in Canada (over 5 years)	.13	.10	.14	.21
166·	City background	.20	.50	.26	.65
167	Index of family contact	-.20	-.32	.05	-.36
185	Index of child care	.06	-.02	.19	-.06
168	Many relatives in Canada (over 2)	-.10	-.40	.12	-.36
169	Child care by relatives or to relatives' children	.02	-.05	.18	-.05
188	Index of family cohesiveness	-.23	-.45	-.05	-.45
191	Index of family cohesiveness (Italian husbands only)	-.10	.18	—	—
192	Index of family cohesiveness (Italian wives only)	—	—	-.10	.18
170	Index of integr. friendships (index over 2)	.34	.60	.34	.79
171	Level of education (public or more)	.29	.80	.23	.78
189	High school or university education (Hungarians only)	-.23	.41	.43*	.55
33	University education (husbands only)	.10*	.40*	—	—
190	Elementary education or more (Italians only)	-.03*	-.11*	-.08	.32
172	Level of English on arrival (any qualifies)	.45	.78	.26	.85
173	Present competence in English (suff. for social contact)	.34	.88	.26	.90
174	English education (in U.K. or at least Basic)	.26	.75	.25	.87
49	Reading Canadian newspapers	.44	.80	.34	.94

| | Husbands | | Wives | |
	201	202 or 203	201	202 or 203
175 Job skills in old country (skilled trade or more)	.28	.46	.00	.43
57 Market value of job skills on arrival	.08	.26	.00	-.23
58 Present job satisfaction	.70	.25	.25	-.08

Notes

[1]R. Taft, *From Stranger to Citizen: A Survey of Studies of Immigration Assimilation in Western Australia* (London: Tavistock, 1966), p. 4.

[2]Ruth Johnston, *Immigrant Assimilation: A Study of Polish People in Western Australia* (Perth: Paterson Brokensha, 1965).

[3]Anthony H. Richmond, *Post War Immigrants in Canada* (Toronto: University of Toronto Press, 1967). *Cf.* also his *Research Report: Immigrants and Ethnic Groups in Metropolitan Toronto* (Toronto: Institute for Behavioural Research, York University, 1967).

[4]Ruth Johnston, *op. cit.*

[5]See also R. Taft (*Human Relations,* 1963, 16, pp. 279-93). He found that insistence on *rapid assimilation* correlates positively with anomic attitudes, authoritarianism and dogmatism, while *gradual integration,* defined as convergence of behaviour and shared norms, correlates with flexibility and independence.

[6]Herbert Gans, *Urban Villagers* (Glencoe, N.Y.: Free Press, 1962).

4   European Multiculturalism

PYGMIES AMONG GIANTS: SMALL MINORITY GROUPS IN THE MULTINATIONAL STATE

Heinz Kloss
Forschungstelle für Nationalitäten und Sprachenfragen
Marlburg, Lahn, W. Germany

Two Definitions

For the purpose of the present paper I shall call a country multinational if more than one indigenous language is considered official. The emphasis is on "indigenous". Madagascar, where both the French and the Malagasy language are official, is not a multinational state because French is not the native tongue of a sizeable segment of the indigenous population. Also, while stating that in the multinational state more languages than one are *official,* I do not mean *national* official. For whenever we are dealing with a state inhabited by more than three major ethnic communities it is virtually impossible to make them fully co-equal on the national level; one or two have to be given a higher standing than the others. Cases in point are: Hindi in India, Serbo-Croatian in Yugoslavia, Urdu and Bengali in Pakistan.

The concept of smallness is no less ambiguous. We may speak of a group being small if its numerical strength does not suffice to supply students for a university or perhaps even a high school of their own. A population of at least 200,000 is required to supply students for a viable university and at least 20,000 to run a viable secondary school. But besides the absolute numerical strength of a group we must also consider its relative strength. In a populous country like India even one million speakers does not make for what, in that country, would be considered a numerically strong minority group. As a matter of fact the Santali language in India, spoken by more than three million people, enjoys only limited minority rights.[1] In China, the largest linguistic minority, the Chuang — who belong to the Thai family of peoples — number seven million souls, i.e. about the number of Catalans, or of native speakers of French on the entire North American continent. But in the Chinese context they are but a small minority, forming about 1% of the total population.

General Remarks Concerning the Multinational State

In discussing the situation of small minority groups within the multinational state we have to begin with a consideration of overriding importance. We may state that generally, other things being roughly equal, the psychological climate in a multinational country is more favourable to the survival of the smaller groups than in the nation state. In the nation state usually one single language is held in high veneration, and is the hallmark of national identity. The very principle underlying the multinational state is that of linguistic pluralism. Here it is no longer held to be axiomatic that you have to prove your loyalty and your fitness to become a citizen of the finest quality by adopting the national language.[2]

There is of course no inherent necessity compelling a nation state to be narrow-minded. There are nation states whose treatment of linguistic minorities matches that of the most liberal, broad-minded and progressive multinational states. Denmark is likely to be the most shining illustration.[3]

Yet as an overall rule we may say that the nation state is likely to make it more difficult for minorities to hold on to their language and culture.

On the other hand, while in multinational states language maintenance may be somewhat easier on *psychological* grounds it is open to debate, or rather to future investigation, whether it is not more difficult *functionally*. Members of the small minority groups may frequently be required to master more than one official language — meaning that retention of their ethnic tongue compels them to become trilingual.[4]

The Legal Situation Obtaining in Certain Multinational States

The following are a few examples illustrating the attitude of certain multinational states towards small ethnic groups:

In Finland there are two small minorities: one speaking Swedish and comprising just 7% of the population, the other speaking Lappish and comprising a mere handful of speakers, about 2,500, or not even one-tenth of 1%. Swedish has been given full equality with Finnish.[5] This is a situation which is now more than half a century old and therefore too easily taken for granted. From the point of view of sheer numerical strength — and thus of democracy in its most elementary sense — the Finns were under no moral, let alone legal, obligation to accord equality to the language of their Swedish fellow-citizens. The Lapps, on the other hand, being far too tiny a group for analogous treatment, at least have radio broadcasts in the mother tongue, have their language taught in the schools and are encouraged and subsidized in their efforts to collaborate with their more numerous "fellow-ethnics" in Sweden and Norway.[6]

In Switzerland there are, besides the strong 20% minority of French-speaking Swiss, two small groups: the 160,000 Italians who comprise not quite 5%, and the Rheto-Romanche who comprise only 1% of the citizenry. The Italian language has been made the only official language of the three co-equal official languages of Switzerland at large. The Rheto-Romanche, on the other hand, are too weak to have their language elevated to the same status. But Rheto-Romanche has been declared a *national* language of Switzerland and one of the three official languages of their canton (Graubünden or Grisons), the two other languages being German and Italian.[7]

In Belgium the language of the German-speaking minority, though sometimes listed in the census publications as one of the country's three "national languages", seems not to have acquired a truly official status at the national level. But it certainly is recognized by the central government as the official language of those cities, towns, and villages where it is the dominant language. Thus while it is perhaps not an official language *of* Belgium it nevertheless is an official language *in* the state.[8] A similar situation exists in Czechoslovakia where the state constitutions have recognized the languages of the Magyar and Ukrainian minorities since 1956, of the Polish group since 1960, and even that of the residual German minority since 1968.

The juxtaposition of national official languages and simple national languages is a common feature of many multinational countries. In the Republic of South Africa only English and Afrikaans are considered national official. But the Xhosa language is recognized as official in the autonomous Transkei area, while German enjoys a semi-official status in South West Africa.[9] In India, fifteen languages are recognized by the federal constitution as constituting the national heritage of India, with one, Hindi, accorded a privileged status.[10] In the Soviet Union there are fifteen constituent republics with as many languages in which the federal laws are being published. But most of the minor languages are recognized as locally and even regionally official by their dexterously handled framework of Autonomous Republics, Autonomous Regions, and National Areas. *On principle* this system is superior to that of India where most linguistic minorities whose language is not recognized by the federal constitution are not admitted in the regional administration of their respective speech areas, even though some of them are more numerous than the speech communities recognized by the constitution. It would seem that one of the reasons for this apparent discrimination against some of the not-so-small minorities was the tendency to give preference to languages with a long-established literary tradition.[11] Among the languages listed in the federal constitution – the "constitutional languages" – we find Kashmiri and Sindhi spoken by 1.9 and 1.4 million persons respectively while Santhali with 3.2 million speakers and Bhili with 2.1 were not included (figures from 1960). Still the Indian constitution safeguards the right of all Indian speech communities to preserve and use in schools their various languages, and the Commissioner of Linguistic Minorities, whose office stems from a constitutional amendment adopted in 1956, receives and handles complaints from *all* linguistic groups.

Decreasing Strength

After all this has been said we cannot help observing that in nearly all multinational states the small groups are shrinking. They are losing not only in relative but frequently even in absolute strength. But why this overall shrinkage?

Scholarization:

First of all we have to admit the fact that in our age all linguistic minorities, regardless of their legal status, are in a precarious situation. One factor is the ever-increasing degree of scholarization. Until well into the twentieth century, a great many linguistic minorities survived simply because of a high degree of illiteracy which made them inaccessible to the impact of the national language. As late as the 1920s this was largely the case, e.g. for the French language in Louisiana and for Spanish in New Mexico.[12] Then with the advent of large-scale scholarization survival remained possible only if the minority language retained or regained a place in the public schools. And of course it may not take more than a few hundred speakers of a language to supply pupils for an elementary school and not more than perhaps 2,000 to have primers printed in their languages. But alas! our age also demands that more and more students attend not only elementary but also high schools and even college level institutions of learning. And here much higher numbers are required. In the Swiss canton of Graubünden or Grisons the Italian and the Rheto-Romanche languages are considered co-equal with that of the German-speaking majority. But the Italian minority is a mere 13,000 strong — and they are scattered over a number of Alpine valleys which are not interlinked by highways and railways. So the Italians do not even have secondary schools of their own; all they have is the teaching of Italian and Italian literature at the only public secondary school the canton has — in Chur, the state capital. The same holds for the Rheto-Romanche for while they are somewhat stronger numerically they are divided not only geographically — as the Italians are — but also linguistically, their primary schools being conducted in no less than five different dialects of the Romanche language.

Training the future intelligentsia in the majority language instead of the mother tongue implies, of course, the danger that the minority culture will lose these future members of the élite — or at least their literary productions. For while they may go on speaking the ancestral tongue at home, they will frequently prefer to write in the majority language.[13]

Horizontal Mobility:

This very real danger is greatly enhanced by the tendencies toward industrialization and — as a concomitant — urbanization. It is vital for any linguistic minority to have or even create some urban center where its language predominates, such as St. Boniface in the case of the Franco-Manitobans, Lafayette for the Acadians in Louisiana, Eupen for the German-speaking Belgians, and Leeuwarden for the Frisians in the Netherlands.

By 1960 almost two-fifths of the Rheto-Romanche population were living in localities where they did not constitute a majority. They had either emigrated to towns and cities outside their original speech area or had been submerged in their original villages by the inflow of German-speaking Swiss who had become the local majority. I need not dwell on the implications of this development which took place in spite of almost frantic efforts on the part of the federal as well as the state authorities to assist the Rheto-Romanche in every possible way.

Mass Media:

There are other factors which in modern society are definitely harmful to small minority groups.[14] Television has invaded nearly all homes in the western world. In Europe television as well as radio broadcasts are in the hands of the state and to graciously hand out a few hours or even minutes of weekly time is considered a special favour. In the United States, minorities have much more leeway to operate as best they can, but television is such a costly enterprise that few minorities can afford it — least of all those that cannot draw on the productions of a "kin state" (to use Inis L. Claude's useful term for a motherland) where their language is official.[15] The mass production of weeklies and monthlies, ranging from ambitious literary magazines down to the outright pornographic, and of low-cost pocketbooks and paperbacks is a phenomenon of the publishing industry with which small minorities are seldom able to cope.

Radio broadcasting, where not a monopoly of the state, is the one mass medium which even small and sometimes even partly illiterate groups can make over into a weapon for language maintenance — witness for example, the roughly 600 regular non-English radio broadcasts produced all over the U.S.A. But the radio broadcasts cannot fully counterbalance the corrosive effect of the factors I mentioned before — and to which others might be added.

Some Safeguards

The conditions set forth in the preceding paragraphs being inherent to the infrastructure of modern society, there is certainly no panacea which would protect small minorities against the inroads of assimilation. However there are measures which might be taken to help them slow down or perhaps even to stop their melting away with the years. Some of them I shall briefly list:[16]

a) A federal set-up has frequently been considered as more favourable to the minorities than is a unitary state. And it is true that by and large it gives better opportunities to minorities — but only when the administrative boundaries coincide more or less with the language boundaries.[17] We know of some instances when Franco-Manitobans preferred Ottawa to Winnipeg, South Tyrolians Rome to Tryento, Slovenians in Austria Vienna to Klagenfurt.

b) A permanent agency at the federal or the state level might be commissioned to take care of the problems and anxieties worrying the minorities. In Belgium there have been for many years permanent "commissions" which report on language problems. The Indian commissioner for linguistic minorities is another good case in point. The Canadian commissioners for official language minorities at the national or the provincial level might be authorized to also look after the rights of non-French and non-English minorities. In this connection the concept of ombudsman comes to mind.

c) Some kind of arbitral tribunal might be set up to settle equitably such disputes as may arise between dominant and non-dominant groups. Between the two World Wars such a tribunal was at work, under the auspices of the League of Nations, in Upper Silesia on both sides of the German-Polish boundary, and in our time a much more informal set-up is at work in the province of Bozen (Bolzano) in Italy.

Regarding all these innovations, whether commission, commissioner, ombudsman, or arbitrary tribunal, one must keep in mind that there always exist two alternatives, to wit: either to set up an agency for the sole purpose of dealing with ethnic minorities, or to commission some already existing agency to accept complaints from and/or to report on ethnic minorities along with their other duties, that is *inter alia.*

Small ethnic groups cannot and will not, as a rule, claim the same rights the dominant groups enjoy. But they are entitled to have such rights protected as have been recognized by the government.

d) Small groups may claim that in their case equitable treatment sometimes means preferential treatment. If public authorities allotted radio hours or subsidized textbooks on a strict per capita basis this might lead to perplexing results. For example, as there are some 20 million inhabitants in Canada, the air time allotted on a percentage basis to an Indian band of 1,000 persons might just suffice to allow the broadcaster to clear his throat. On the other hand, there is the example of Switzerland where the federal government spends the same amount of money on television for the scarcely 5% Italian-speaking citizens as it does on the 70% German-speaking Swiss — a group fourteen times as numerous.[18]

e) The Federal Union of European Nationalities in 1967 adopted a set of twelve "Basic Principles" most of which pertain to the traditional demands with which all students of minority problems are familiar.[19] But some of them add new aspects to the traditional framework, namely:

> 5. Every member of a national minority has the right to freedom of movement as well as to remain in his region of origin. Members of a national minority must not — if they are public officials — be transferred to areas outside the region of their nationality without their approval.

> 12. The States and associations of States are morally obliged to organize their economic conditions in a way which ensures that members of the national minorities can find occupation within their own speech area, and do not find themselves forced to emigrate to other territories of the State in order to obtain an adequate standard of living.
>
> Nor should the general economic developments and industrialisation be utilized to submerge the speech area of a national minority by means of labour forces belonging to other ethnic communities.

> 7. Every national minority has also the right to equitable time in radio and television.

These demands speak for themselves. It has even been suggested that small minorities, perhaps too small to be represented at the national or provincial level, should be given some kind of veto power — or at least some right to be heard — over new proposals which would immediately affect their life as a group, e.g. the founding of new industries, or plans for resettlement in order to have a dam built.[20]

Concluding Remarks

Finally I would like to remind you of the vast potential of extended collaboration between minority groups. Conceivably the present meeting would not have been possible if it had been backed up by only a single linguistic minority. Intranational collaboration between Slavs and non-Slavs might open up additional possibilities. So might collaboration across the borders, e.g. with kindred groups in the United States. After all, the UNO-sponsored Ljubljana Seminar in 1965 explicitly recognized the right of minorities to association across state boundaries.[21]

Like Prof. de Meyer I have to state that what counts most is the spirit prevailing in the country where the minorities reside. Wherever dominant and non-dominant groups are united in a spirit of mutual trust and respect, great things may develop in time. In the U.S. a basic change has been taking place for years as many members of the dominant group now recognize the importance of the foreign language resources embodied by the non-English minorities.[22] And as I said in the beginning, a multinational state is even more likely than a nation state to understand the significance of this new approach and to foster its application.

Bibliography

Anderson, Theodore and Mildred Boyer. *Bilingual Schooling in the U.S.* Austin, Texas: SW Development, *Ed. Labour,* 2 vols.

Bertelsmann, W. *Die Minderheitenrechte der deutschsprachigen Bevölkerung in Sudwestafrika* (Göttingen 1970, Diss.).

Claude, Inis L. *National Minorities, an International Problem.* Cambridge, Mass.: Harvard Univ. Press, 1955, 248 pp.

Fishman, Joshua (ed.). *Language Loyalty in the United States.* Den Haag: Mouton, 1966, 478 pp.

Kaeckenbeeck, Georges. *The International Experiment of Upper Silesia.* London, 1942.

Kloss, Heinz. *Volksgruppenrecht in den Vereinigten Staaten.* Essen: Essener Verlagsanstalt, Vol. I, 1940, 600 pp. (Vol. II, 1942).

_____ "Nationalitätenprobleme im heutigen Europa", *Evolution,* Berne, Vol. 5, No. 56, 1962, pp. 241-245.

_____ *Grundfragen der Ethnopolitik.* Vienna: Braumuller, 1969, 624 pp. (*Ethnos,* Vol. 7).

_____ "Volksgruppen und Volksgruppenrecht in der Demokratie", *System Eines Internationalen Volksgruppenrechts,* Theodore Veiter (ed.). Vienna: Braumuller, 1969, pp. 119-125.

_____ *Laws and Legal Documents Relating to Problems of Bilingual Education in the United States.* Washington: Centre for Applied Linguistics, 1971, 92 pp.

Leibowitz, Arnold H. *Education Policy and Political Acceptance: The Imposition of English as the Language of Instruction in American Schools.* Washington: Centre for Applied Linguistics, 1971.

McRae, Kenneth D. *Switzerland: Example of Cultural Co-existence.* Toronto: Canadian Institute of International Affairs, 1964, 74 pp. (*Contemporary Affairs,* No. 33).

Modeen, Tore. "The Situation of the Finland-Swedish Population in Light of Finnish-Swedish Law", *McGill Law Journal,* Vol. 16, No. 1, 1970, pp. 121-139.

Pfeifer, Helfried. *Die Föderalistiche Union Europaischer Volksgruppen: Ihre Haupt-Grundsätze eines Volksgruppenrechts im Lichte der Volks-Rechtswissenschaft,* 1969, 44 p. (Offprint from Festschrift for Gaspare Ambrosini, Milano, 1969.)

Seminar on the Multinational Society, Ljubljana, 8-21 June, 1965. (Doc. ST/TAO/HR/23, United Nations, N.Y., 1965).

Skadegard, Paul. "Die organisatorische Gestaltung der europäischen Volksgruppen" in *Straka,* 1970, pp. 29-40.

_____"Gibt es ein europäisches Volksgruppenrecht?", in *Straka,* 1970, pp. 41-53.

Straka, Manfred (ed.). *Handbuch der europäischen Volksgruppen.* Vienna: Braumüller 1970, 658 pp. (*Ethnos,* Vol. 8).

Veiter, Theodor. *Das Rechtder Volksgruppen und Sprachminderheiten in Österreich.* Vienna: Braumüller, 1970, 890 pp.

Verdoodt, Albert. *Zweisprachige Nachbarn: Die deutschen Hochsprach-und Mundartgruppen in Ost-Belgien, dem Elsass, Ost-Lothringen und Luxemburg.* Vienna: Braumüller, 1968, 190 pp. (*Ethnos,* Vol. 6).

Notes

[1]H. Kloss, *Grundfragen der Ethnopolitik* (Vienna: Braumüller, 1969), pp. 407-415.

[2]In 1971 Prime Minister Trudeau made a statement to the same effect when expounding the concept of multiculturalism before a Jewish-Canadian audience in Montreal.

[3]*Cf.* Kloss, *op. cit.,* pp. 318-319, 345, 372-373, 572.

[4]It would be a worthwhile investigation to study the impact of indigenous bilingualism upon immigrants speaking a third language in cities like Montreal or Capetown.

[5]T. Modeen, "The Situation of the Finland-Swedish Population in Light of the Finnish-Swedish Law", in *McGill Law Journal,* Vol. 16, No. 1, 1970.

[6]H. Kloss, "Nationalitätenprobleme im heutigen Europa", in *Evolution,* Berne, Vol. 5, No. 56, 1962. Cf. Kloss, *op. cit.,* pp. 373-374.

[7]H. Kloss, *op. cit.,* 1969, p. 557; K. McRae, *Switzerland: Example of Cultural Co-existence* (Toronto: Canadian Institute of International Affairs, 1964).

[8]*Cf.* A Verdoodt, *Zweisprachige Nachborn: Die deutschen Hochsprach- und Mundartgruppen in Ost-Belgien, dem Elsass, Ost-Lothringen und Luxemburg* (Vienna: Braumüller, 1968), pp. 5-57.

[9]Bertelsmann, 1970.

[10]Art. 29, 30, 350, 350B.

[11]This was an explanation given to me orally by Prof. Samir K. Ghosh.

[12]H. Kloss, *Volksgruppenrecht in der Vereinigte Staaten* (Essen: Essener Verlagsanstalt, Vol. 1, 1940), p. 189 (La.), p. 355 (N.M.).

[13]H. Kloss, *op. cit.,* 1969, p. 557.

[14]*Ibid.,* pp. 518-522.

[15]Claude, *National Minorities* (Cambridge, Mass.: Harvard University Press, 1955).

[16]H. Kloss, "Volksgruppen und Volksgruppenrecht in der Demokratie", in T. Veiter (ed.), *System eines Internationalen Volksgruppenrechts* (Vienna: Braumüller, 1969), pp. 123-125.

[17]Kaeckenbeeck, *The International Experiment of Upper Silesia* (London, 1942).

[18]McRae, *op. cit.,* pp. 42-49, 52-56.

[19]P. Skadegard, "Die organisatorische Gestaltung der europaischen Volksgruppen", in Straka, 1970; Skadegard, "Gibt es ein europaisches Volksgruppenrecht?" in Straka, 1970. *Cf.* also, Pfeifer, *Die Föderalistiche* Union *Europäischer Volksgruppen,* 1969.

[20]T. Veiter, *Das Recht der Volksgruppen und Sprachminderheiten in Österrich* (Vienna: Braumüller, 1970), S. 794-796.

[21]*Seminar on the Multinational Society,* Ljubljana, 8-21 June, 1965, p. 21.

[22]J. Fishman, *Language Loyalty in the United States* (Den Haag: Mouton, 1966); T. Anderson and M. Boyer, "Bilingual Schooling in the U.S.", SW Ed. Dev. Laborat, Austin, Texas; H. Kloss, *Laws and Legal Documents Relating to Problems of Bilingual Education in the United States* (Washington: Centre for Applied Linguistics, 1971); A. Leibowitz, *Education Policy and Political Acceptance: The Imposition of English as the Language of Instruction in American Schools* (Washington: Centre for Applied Linguistics, 1971).

LA SITUATION JURIDIQUE DES
SOCIÉTÉS POLYETHNIQUES EN EUROPE*

Jan de Meyer
Professeur ordinaire à l'Université de Louvain (K.U.L.)
Doyen de la faculté de droit

Une société polyethnique est, comme le terme même l'indique, une société au sein de laquelle coexistent plusieurs ethnies ou groupes ethniques. Nous voudrions considérer ici comme "ethnie" ou comme "groupe ethnique", en nous inspirant des définitions de McIver et Page et de Héraud, tout groupe, toute collectivité, dont les membres ont certains caractères distinctifs communs, résultant d'une tradition sociale et culturelle maintenue de génération en génération et s'exprimant peut-être le plus souvent par l'usage d'une même langue.[1] Il est presque inévitable que la coexistence de plusieurs ethnies ou groupes ethniques au sein d'une même société et en particulier au sein d'une collectivité de type étatique pose un certain nombre de problèmes. Nous voudrions, dans le présent rapport, donner, à la lumière de quelques exemples, un aperçu général des diverses formules juridiques par lesquelles on a tenté de résoudre ces problèmes dans quelques pays d'Europe où ils se trouvent posés. L'Europe, on le sait, est particulièrement riche en sociétés polyethniques: presque chacun des Etats qui la composent a, plus ou moins, le caractère d'une telle société.

I

Certains groupes ethniques font l'objet d'une politique d'assimilation de la part de l'Etat dont ils relèvent. Tel est notamment le cas des Basques et des Catalans, aussi bien de la part de la France, sous tous les régimes, que de l'Espagne franquiste, ainsi qu'en France des Bretons et des Flamands, en Italie des Slovènes d'Udine et, en Grèce, des Koutso-Valaques et des Slaves macédoniens. Dans les cas de ce genre, il s'agit de groupes dont l'existence est pratiquement niée par les Etats intéressés et qui ne bénéficient d'aucun statut protecteur ou ne font l'objet que d'une protection insuffisante. Certaines dispositions comme celles de la loi Deixonne qui, en France, permet l'enseignement facultatif des langues dites "vernaculaires" dans les écoles publiques,[1] ne sont guère efficaces et ne sont d'ailleurs même pas appliquées à certains des groupes auxquels elles pourraient l'être. En fait, comme on a pu l'observer, les Etats tendent assez généralement à éliminer ou à assimiler leurs minorités ethniques[2] et, par ailleurs, la "présence dans le même espace politique de deux communautés inégales" engendre presque nécessairement "la domination de la plus forte sur la plus faible".[3]

*Rapport établi avec la collaboration de Mlle Paula Van Eupen, assistante à l'Université de Louvain (K.U.L.).

II

Certains Etats ont voulu régler les problèmes qu'aurait pu poser l'existence, sur leur territoire, de populations allogènes en éliminant celles-ci par la voie de transferts collectifs. De tels règlements ont pu résulter de traités conclus entre les Etats intéressés, tel celui par lequel la Grèce et la Turquie décidèrent en 1923 d'échanger les populations turques de Macédoine contre les populations grecques de Thrace et d'Asie Mineure.[1] Dans d'autres cas, les transferts ont été imposés d'une manière unilatérale: c'est ainsi que fut réalisée l'évacuation, en 1945, des populations allemandes restées dans les territoires situés à l'Est de la ligne Oder-Neisse, en Bohême et dans certaines autres régions de l'Europe de l'Est. Cette action qui résultait de décisions prises par les Alliés fut confirmée par la déclaration de Potsdam du 2 août 1945.

III

Une autre catégorie de cas est celle des groupes ethniques qui bénéficient d'une protection, plus ou moins efficace, soit en vertu de dispositions de droit international, soit en vertu de dispositions de droit interne établies par les Etats intéressés, soit aussi bien en vertu des unes que des autres.

A.

Plusieurs traités conclus après la première guerre mondiale comportaient des dispositions tendant à la protection de minorités ethniques. C'est ainsi que des clauses de ce genre furent insérées dans le traité de Versailles du 28 juin 1919, dont les articles 86 et 93 imposaient, à cet égard, certaines obligations à la Pologne et à la Tchécoslovaquie, ainsi que dans les traités de paix conclus par les Alliés avec l'Autriche le 10 septembre 1919,[1] avec la Bulgarie le 27 novembre 1919,[2] avec la Hongrie le 4 juin 1920[3] et avec la Turquie le 24 juillet 1923.[4]

D'autres traités furent consacrés spécialement à la protection de minorités ethniques. Le premier traité de ce genre fut celui conclu le 28 juin 1919, en même temps que le traité de paix avec l'Allemagne, entre les principales puissances alliées et associées et la Pologne; il fut suivi de traités semblables conclus, d'une part, avec la Tchécoslovaquie et, d'autre part, avec la Yougoslavie le 10 septembre 1919, en même temps que le traité de paix avec l'Autriche, et ultérieurement, de deux autres traités analogues conclus respectivement avec la Roumanie, le 9 décembre 1919, et avec la Grèce, le 10 août 1920.

La protection de minorités ethniques fit aussi l'objet de traités ou accords bilatéraux, tels que ceux conclus entre l'Autriche et la Tchécoslovaquie le 7 juin 1920, entre la Finlande et l'Union Soviétique le 14 octobre 1920, entre la Ville Libre de Dantzig et la Pologne le 15 novembre 1920, entre la Pologne et l'Union Soviétique le 18 mars 1921, entre la Finlande et la Suède le 27 juin 1921 (à propos des Iles d'Aaland), entre l'Allemagne et la Pologne le 15 mai 1922 (à propos de la Silésie) et entre la Pologne et la Tchécoslovaquie le 23 avril 1925. On notera enfin les déclarations faites, à l'occasion de leur entrée à la Société des Nations, par la Finlande le 27 juin 1921, par l'Albanie le 2 octobre 1921, par la Lithuanie le 12 mai 1922, par le Lettonie le 7 juillet 1923 et par l'Esthonie le 17 septembre 1923.

Le système de protection institué par la plupart de ces traités et déclarations devait fonctionner sous la garantie de la Société des Nations. Il échoua presque partout, non seulement en raison des manquements des Etats intéressés et de l'inefficacité du contrôle de la Société des Nations, mais aussi en raison de l'action révisionniste menée contre ces Etats aussi bien de l'extérieur que de l'intérieur. Il ne subsiste pratiquement plus rien du système de protection résultant des traités d'après la première guerre mondiale, sauf peut-être les obligations de la Finlande à l'égard des Iles d'Aaland[5] et celles de la Grèce et de la Turquie à l'égard de leurs minorités respectives. [6,7]

On s'est beaucoup moins préoccupé de la protection des minorités dans les traités et déclarations qui ont suivi la seconde guerre mondiale. Les traités conclus le 10 février 1947 entre les Alliés et la Bulgarie, la Finlande, l'Italie, la Hongrie et la Roumanie contiennent des clauses de non-discrimination en ce qui concerne la jouissance des droits de l'homme et des libertés fondamentales, mais ne protègent pas explicitement les groupes ethniques. Des dispositions particulières ont toutefois été prises en faveur de certaines minorités, notamment par l'accord austro-italien du 5 septembre 1946 relatif à la situation du Tyrol du Sud, par le mémorandum du 5 octobre 1954 relatif au statut de la région de Trieste et par le traité d'Etat autrichien du 15 mai 1955.

Il n'est pas fait mention des groupes ethniques dans la déclaration universelle des droits de l'homme de 1948, mais les pactes de 1966 reconnaissent aussi bien le droit des minorités ethniques, religieuses ou linguistiques d'avoir leur propre vie culturelle, de professer et de pratiquer leur propre religion ou d'employer leur propre langue[8] que le droit des peuples à disposer d'eux-mêmes.[9] Il est vrai, par ailleurs, qu'un certain nombre de textes des Nations Unies interdisant la discrimination, soit en général, soit d'une manière particulière, impliquent nécessairement la non-discrimination à l'égard de groupes ethniques.

B.

Dans certains cas, il existe un certain parallélisme ou, si l'on veut, une certaine symétrie entre le régime juridique de groupes ethniques minoritaires établis de part et d'autre d'une même frontière étatique.

Les minorités grecques de Turquie et turques de Grèce bénéficient, selon les dispositions des articles 37 à 45 du traité de paix du 24 juillet 1923, d'un statut identique.

La situation des Allemands du Slesvig du Nord, qui fait partie du Royaume de Danemark, et des Danois du Slesvig du Sud, qui fait partie de la République Fédérale d'Allemagne, a été définie, elle aussi, d'une manière identique, par des déclarations faites successivement le 26 septembre 1949 par le gouvernement du Slesvig-Holstein et le 27 octobre

1949 par le gouvernement danois et par deux déclarations faites le 29 mars 1955 par les gouvernements danois et fédéral allemand.

Le statut de la région de Trieste a été réglé par le mémorandum de Londres du 5 octobre 1954. Il comporte, lui aussi, une protection identique pour la minorité yougoslave dans la zone administrée par l'Italie et pour la minorité italienne dans la zone administrée par la Yougoslavie. Il a institué une commission mixte italo-yougoslave pour l'examen des problèmes relatifs à la protection des populations intéressées.

C.

Certains groupes ethniques bénéficient de garanties particulières en vertu de dispositions de droit interne, soit qu'il s'agisse de dispositions constitutionnelles, soit qu'il s'agisse de dispositions législatives ordinaires. De nombreuses constitutions européennes comportent des dispositions de caractère général relatives à l'égalité et à la non-discrimination, et parfois aussi des dispositions interdisant la haine raciale ou nationale. Plusieurs d'entre elles contiennent, en outre, des dispositions protectrices explicites en faveur des groupes ethniques ou de certains de ceux-ci. C'est ainsi que les droits de groupes ethniques ou linguistiques sont garantis notamment par les articles 14, 22, 50, 51 et 75 de la constitution finlandaise, par l'article 6 de la constitution italienne, par l'article 11 de la constitution de la République Démocratique Allemande, par l'article 49 de la constitution hongroise, par l'article 79 de la constitution bulgare, par les articles 22 et 102 de la constitution roumaine, par les articles 42 et 43 de la constitution yougoslave et par une loi constitutionnelle tchécoslovaque particulière du 27 octobre 1968. Dans d'autres cas, des systèmes de protection ont été établis par des lois ordinaires, voir même par des règlements.

D.

Les systèmes de protection établis, soit par la voie de conventions internationales, soit par le voie de dispositions de droit interne, sont, indépendamment de leur origine formelle, assez semblables, quant au fond, surtout en ce qui concerne leurs traits essentiels.

1.

Une certaine protection peut déjà résulter de dispositions qui, sans se référer explicitement aux groupes ethniques ou à leurs membres, garantissent, aussi bien dans des instruments d'application générale que dans des instruments établis en vue de régler des situations particulières, le respect des droits de l'homme et des libertés fondamentales et interdisent toute discrimination dans la jouissance de ces droits et libertés.

De telles dispositions sont comprises notamment dans les traités de paix conclus le 10 février 1947 entre les Alliés et la Bulgarie, la Finlande, la Hongrie, l'Italie et la Roumanie, dans le traité d'Etat autrichien du 15 mai 1955[10] et dans le statut spécial établi pour la région de Trieste par le mémorandum du 5 octobre 1954,[11] ainsi que dans certains traités conclus après la guerre de 1914-1918.[12]

2.

Une protection d'un caractère plus particulier est assurée par les dispositions qui garantissent explicitement aux membres de groupes ethniques, soit, d'une manière générale, la jouissance des droits de l'homme et des libertés fondamentales, soit, d'une manière plus précise, la jouissance de certains droits ou libertés énumérés en détail, et qui interdisent, en ces matières, toute discrimination à leur égard.

C'est ainsi qu'il y a des textes garantissant explicitement aux membres de certains groupes ethniques l'égalité de droits et de traitement avec les autres habitants[13] ou le même traitement et la même sécurité en droit et en fait qu'aux autres ressortissants.[14]

Il arrive aussi qu'on leur reconnaisse plus spécialement le droit de participer, dans les mêmes conditions que les autres citoyens ou ressortissants, à la vie collective, "à la vie politique, économique et sociale"[15] ou "aux activités des organismes culturels, administratifs et judiciaires".[16] Certaines dispositions leur garantissent l'égalité dans l'accès aux fonctions et honneurs publics.[17] Elles vont parfois jusqu'à prescrire que la répartition des fonctions publiques doit avoir lieu en proportion de l'importance numérique des groupes intéressés,[18] particulièrement "dans les corps représentatifs et autres organes élus",[19] ou qu'elle doit être assurée d'une manière "équitable" dans les administrations, spécialement dans les domaines qui touchent d'une manière particulière à leurs intérêts, tels que l'inspection des écoles.[20] Parfois aussi, elles prescrivent la désignation de fonctionnaires ayant la nationalité de la région ou choisis, tout au moins, parmi d'autres citoyens connaissant la langue et la manière de vivre de la population.[21]

D'autres textes garantissent aux membres de certains groupes ethniques l'égalité dans l'exercice d'activités professionnelles ou économiques[22] et dans la jouissance d'avantages sociaux.[23]

3.

Le droit des groupes ethniques à la sauvegarde de leur caractère propre et à leur développement culturel se trouve, d'une manière ou d'une autre, reconnu par de nombreuses dispositions.

Les constitutions de plusieurs Etats communistes d'Europe centrale ou orientale garantissent le droit des nationalités ou minorités au développement de leur culture nationale, plus particulièrement les constitutions bulgare,[24] hongroise[25] et yougoslave.[26] Celle de la République Démocratique Allemande prévoit que le libre développement des caractéristiques nationales des groupes nationaux de langue étrangère doit être encouragé par la législation et par l'administration.[27] De même, la loi constitutionnelle tchécoslovaque du 27 octobre 1968, relative au statut des nationalités, garantit le plein développement culturel des citoyens appartenant aux nationalités hongroise, allemande, polonaise et ukrainienne "dans le cadre correspondant aux nécessités de leur développement national et dans les conditions prévues par les lois"[28] et interdit toute forme de pression visant à faire renoncer quelqu'un à sa nationalité.[29]

Dans le même ordre d'idées, le traité d'Etat de 1955 interdit l'activité des organisations qui ont pour but de priver les populations croate et slovène d'Autriche de leur caractère ou de leurs droits de minorité.[30]

Le droit à une vie culturelle organisée se trouve reconnu par la constitution yougoslave, selon laquelle chaque nationalité et chaque minorité ont le droit de créer des organisations à cette fin,[31] et par la loi constitutionnelle tchécoslovaque de 1968, déjà citée ci-dessus, selon laquelle les nationalités hongroise, allemande, polonaise et ukrainienne ont le droit de se grouper librement dans des associations culturelles nationales.[32] De même, plusieurs traités ont reconnu à certains groupes ethniques le droit d'avoir leurs propres organisations et institutions,[33] de tenir leurs réunions et de posséder leurs propres moyens d'expression.[34]

La reconnaissance du droit des groupes ethniques à la sauvegarde et au développement de leur propre culture est parfois purement passive, en ce sens que l'Etat ne s'engage qu'à ne pas gêner les initiatives de ces groupes et de leurs membres, parfois plus active, en ce sens que l'Etat s'engage aussi à intervenir lui-même en vue de cette sauvegarde et de ce développement.

Plusieurs des traités conclus après la première guerre mondiale prévoyaient déjà que dans les régions ou localités habitées par une proportion considérable de ressortissants appartenant à une minorité, celle-ci devait bénéficier d'une part équitable dans la répartition des ressources publiques en matière d'éducation, de religion et de bienfaisance.[35]

4.

Dans certains textes apparaît une tendance à élargir la protection des groupes intéressés en l'étendant au domaine économique aussi bien que culturel. C'est ainsi qu'en une formule brève, mais significative, l'article 14 de la constitution finlandaise prévoit que l'Etat doit pourvoir, dans des conditions semblables, aux besoins "intellectuels et économiques" des populations finnoise et suédoise.

Selon le statut spécial de la région de Trieste, le développement économique de la population yougoslave de la zone italienne et de la population italienne de la zone yougoslave doit être assuré sans discrimination et par une distribution équitable des moyens financiers disponibles.[36] De même, l'accord austro-italien de 1946 requiert des mesures spéciales tendant à garantir le développement aussi bien économique que culturel de la fraction germanophone de la population du Tyrol du Sud.

C'est aussi en une formule très générale que l'article ler de la loi constitutionnelle tchécoslovaque relative au statut des nationalités garantit aux quatre nationalités qu'elle concerne "les possibilités et les moyens d'un plein développement".

5.

L'importance du facteur linguistique apparaît dans la plupart des textes, soit qu'ils reconnaissent simplement la liberté de faire usage de la langue de son choix ou de sa nationalité, soit qu'ils garantissent à des degrés divers l'usage de telle ou telle langue dans les services publics ou dans les rapports qu'on peut avoir avec ceux-ci.

La liberté de l'emploi des langues est garantie par de nombreuses dispositions, soit en termes généraux,[37] soit d'une manière plus détaillée, ce qui peut comporter une nuance restrictive si, par exemple, cette liberté n'est garantie aux particuliers que dans leurs rapports privés, dans l'exercice de leur commerce ou de leur religion, dans leurs publications ou dans leurs réunions ou dans leurs institutions religieuses, sociales ou scolaires.[38]

L'accord austro-italien de 1946 relatif à la situation du Tyrol du Sud comporte notamment une disposition accordant à la population de cette région le droit de rétablir les noms patronymiques allemands qui avaient été italianisés.[39]

Il est sans doute tout aussi important pour les membres d'un groupe ethnique de pouvoir faire usage de leur propre langue dans les rapports avec les autorités administratives et judiciaires. Ce droit est garanti par de nombreux textes,[40] du moins en ce qui concerne les régions habitées par les groupes ethniques dont il s'agit,[41] sans que cela implique nécessairement que la langue employée par le particulier soit, pour autant, reconnue comme langue officielle.

La langue d'un groupe ethnique ou linguistique déterminé est parfois reconnue comme langue officielle ou comme langue nationale, ces deux notions pouvant fort bien être distinctes, comme le démontre l'exemple de la Suisse, qui a trois langues officielles et quatre langues nationales.[42]

Il peut en être ainsi pour l'ensemble du territoire de l'Etat, du moins pour certains actes intéressant l'ensemble des ressortissants de celui-ci. Tel est le cas en Finlande, où les langues finnoise et suédoise sont les langues nationales de la République[43] et doivent être employées, sur un pied d'égalité, pour les lois et les décrets ainsi que pour les actes de la procédure parlementaire.[44] Tel est aussi le cas en Belgique, où les langues française et néerlandaise doivent être employées, sur un pied d'égalité, pour les lois et pour les actes de la procédure parlementaire et pour les arrêtés royaux et ministériels, à moins qu'ils ne concernent exclusivement une région ou des agents de statut francophone ou néerlandophone,[45] ainsi que pour les services et institutions dont l'activité s'étend à tout le pays ou à des communes de plusieurs régions linguistiques.[46]

Il se peut aussi qu'une langue déterminée n'ait le caractère d'une langue officielle que dans la région ou dans les localités habitées par le groupe ethnique ou linguistique intéressé. Elle peut y avoir le statut d'une langue régional exclusive ou simplement d'une langue de complément se juxtaposant, dans cette région ou dans cette localité, à une langue officielle principale.

En Belgique, le français est la langue officielle exclusive dans la région de langue française, le néerlandais dans la région de langue néerlandaise: chacune de ces régions a été constituée de manière à ne comprendre en principe que des populations unilingues et à réduire au minimum les minorités linguistiques. Un tel unilinguisme est aussi pratiqué en Finlande, à l'intérieur des circonscriptions administratives unilingues[47] et, en particulier, dans les Iles d'Aaland, où le suédois est la seule langue officielle;[48] en Finlande, la constitution prescrit explicitement que les circonscriptions administratives doivent être délimitées de manière à ne comprendre, pour autant que les circonstances le permettent, que des populations unilingues et à réduire au minimum leurs minorités linguistiques.[49]

En Autriche, le slovène ou le croate sont admis comme langues officielles en plus de l'allemand dans les circonscriptions administratives de la Carinthie, du Burgenland et de la Styrie où réside une population slovène ou croate ou une population mixte.[50] De même, en Italie, l'allemand se trouve juxtaposé à l'italien, dans la province de Bolzano/Bozen et dans les communes bilingues voisines de la province de Trente.[51]

Là où il y a coexistence de deux ou plusieurs langues officielles, on peut distinguer les cas dans lesquels ces langues se trouvent placées, du moins en principe, sur un pied d'égalité, et ceux dans lesquels elles ne le sont pas.

On peut citer comme exemples de la première catégorie, en Belgique, le régime bilingue (français-néerlandais) des services et institutions dont l'activité s'étend à tout le pays, ainsi que celui de la région de Bruxelles-capitale et, en Finlande, le régime administratif bilingue (finnois-suédois) des communes comptant une minorité d'au moins 12 p.c. de la population[52] ou d'au moins 5.000 habitants.

On peut citer comme exemples de la seconde catégorie le régime institué dans la région de Trieste par l'article 5 du statut spécial annexé au mémorandum du 5 octobre 1954, et, en Belgique, celui des communes à "facilités", situées dans la périphérie de Bruxelles ou le long de la frontière linguistique. Un autre exemple est celui des régions de Roumanie qui comprennent une population de nationalité non-roumaine.[53]

Parfois, l'égalité des langues se trouve expréssement reconnue. Il en est ainsi notamment en Yougoslavie, où l'article 42 de la constitution garantit l'égalité des langues et des écritures des peuples de la république, et pour le Tyrol du Sud, où l'égalité de l'allemand et de l'italien doit, selon l'accord austro-italien du 5 septembre 1946, être assurée dans les services et documents administratifs et dans la toponymie.

L'affirmation de l'égalité des langues et la reconnaissance de deux ou plusieurs langues officielles n'excluent pas nécessairement une certaine prédominance, de droit ou de fait, de certaines langues par rapport à d'autres. C'est ainsi que les forces armées yougoslaves sont commandées, instruites et administrées exclusivement en serbo-croate[54] et que, dans les forces armées finlandaises, le finnois est la langue du commandement, alors même que les conscrits doivent, dans la mesure du possible, être enrôlés dans des unités de leur propre langue et doivent recevoir leur entraînement en cette langue.[55]

6.

Il y a aussi de nombreuses dispositions relatives au régime de l'enseignement. Tantôt elles ne reconnaissent aux groupes intéressés que le droit d'organiser et de faire fonctionner des écoles à leurs propres frais, tantôt elles leur garantissent des subventions, tantôt elles prévoient la création d'écoles publiques à leur intention. Souvent, ces diverses garanties se complètent mutuellement.

Elles peuvent ne concerner que l'enseignement primaire, s'étendre aussi à l'enseignement secondaire, ainsi qu'à l'enseignement gardien et professionnel, ou encore, d'une manière générale, s'appliquer à l'enseignement public dans son ensemble. Il est presque toujours précisé qu'il s'agit d'assurer cet enseignement dans la langue du groupe intéressé.

Dans certains cas, l'Etat impose ou se réserve le droit d'imposer L'enseignement de sa langue principale. Il en est ainsi notamment dans les traités conclus après la guerre de 1914-1918[56] et dans la constitution bulgare.[57]

On peut encore, en cette matière, citer quelques exemples particuliers.

Le traité de 1919, relatif aux minorités de Pologne, reconnaissait aux ressortissants polonais appartenant à ces minorités le droit d'organiser et de faire fonctionner, à leurs propres frais, des écoles et d'autres établissements d'éducation.[58] Il comportait, en outre, l'engagement de la Pologne de prendre les dispositions nécessaires pour que, dans les régions habitées par une proportion considérable de ressortissants polonais de langue non polonaise, l'enseignement public fût, dans les écoles primaires, donné aux enfants de ces ressortissants dans leur propre langue, sans préjudice du droit de la Pologne d'y rendre obligatoire l'enseignement de la langue polonaise[59] et pour que, dans les régions habitées par une proportion considérable de ressortissants polonais appartenant à une minorité raciale, religieuse ou linguistique, ces minorités fussent assurées de bénéficier d'une part équitable dans la jouissance des ressources publiques en matière d'éducation, tout comme, par ailleurs, en matière de religion et de bienfaisance.[60] Des dispositions du même genre se retrouvent dans la plupart des traités qui furent établis à la même époque en faveur d'autres minorités.

Selon le statut spécial établi pour la région de Trieste par le mémorandum du 5 octobre 1954, le groupe ethnique yougoslave en zone italienne et le groupe ethnique italien en zone yougoslave doivent bénéficier d'un enseignement gardien, primaire, secondaire et professionnel dans leur langue nationale. Des écoles dispensant un tel enseignement doivent exister dans toutes les localités de la zone italienne où il y a des enfants du groupe ethnique yougoslave et dans toutes les localités de la zone yougoslave où il y a des membres du groupe ethnique italien; elles doivent bénéficier du même traitement que les autres écoles du même type dans leur zone, en ce qui concerne la fourniture de manuels, bâtiments et autres moyens matériels, le nombre et la situation des enseignants et la reconnaissance des diplômes. Les autorités italiennes et yougoslaves doivent s'efforcer de faire en sorte que l'enseignement soit donné dans ces écoles par des enseignants dont la langue maternelle est celle des élèves. Les programmes d'enseignement ne peuvent porter préjudice au caractère national de ceux-ci.[61]

Le traité d'Etat autrichien de 1955 garantit aux ressortissants autrichiens appartenant aux minorités slovène et croate en Carinthie, dans le

Burgenland et en Styrie, le droit à l'enseignement primaire en langue slovène ou croate et à un nombre proportionnel d'établissements propres d'enseignement secondaire. Il prévoit, à cet effet, la revision des programmes scolaires et l'organisation d'une inspection particulière pour les écoles slovènes et croates.[62]

Plusieurs constitutions nationales garantissent, elles aussi, le droit des nationalités ou des minorités, ou du moins de certaines d'entre elles, de bénéficier d'un enseignement dans leur propre langue. Il en est notamment ainsi en Bulgarie[63] et en Hongrie.[64] La constitution yougoslave garantit ce droit d'une manière générale aux membres des peuples de Yougoslavie, même sur le territoire d'une autre république que la leur.[65] La loi constitutionnelle concernant le statut des nationalités en République Socialiste Tchécoslovaque garantit le droit à l'instruction dans leur langue aux nationalités hongroise, allemande, polonaise et ukrainienne, "dans le cadre correspondant aux nécessités de leur développement national et dans les conditions prévues par les lois".[66]

7.

Il existe souvent aussi des dispositions particulières relatives à d'autres activités culturelles que l'enseignement. Il en est ainsi en ce qui concerne la presse et les informations, les théâtres, la radiodiffusion et la télévision, les universités populaires.

C'est ainsi que le droit de posséder une presse dans leur propre langue a été garanti notamment aux ressortissants autrichiens appartenant aux minorités slovène et croate en Carinthie, dans le Burgenland et en Styrie par le traité d'Etat autrichien,[67] aux membres des minorités italienne et yougoslave dans les deux zones de la région de Trieste par le statut de 1954,[68] aux citoyens tchécoslovaques de nationalité hongroise, allemande, polonaise ou ukrainienne par la loi constitutionnelle tchécoslovaque du 27 octobre 1968 concernant le statut des nationalités.[69] De même l'article 22 de la constitution roumaine garantit aux nationalités établies sur le territoire de la république l'existence de livres, journaux et revues ainsi que de théâtres en leur propre langue.

Le droit d'avoir des universités populaires et d'accéder à la radiodiffusion a été reconnu aux Allemands du Slesvig du Nord et aux Danois du Slesvig du Sud par les déclarations des deux gouvernements relatives à leur situation.

8.

Le droit des groupes ethniques d'avoir leur propre religion et de pratiquer les usages s'y rattachant a été garanti de diverses manières, notamment par des dispositions protégeant leurs églises, synagogues ou cimetières, accordant des facilités à leurs fondations et institutions religieuses et charitables,[70] interdisant de leur imposer quoi que ce soit de contraire à leur foi et à leurs pratiques religieuses[71] ou imposant le respect de leurs jours de repos hebdomadaires.[72]

En vertu de certains textes, des mesures doivent être prises pour régler les questions relatives au droit de la famille et à l'état des personnes selon les usages du groupe intéressé.[73]

9.

Il peut arriver qu'un groupe ethnique déterminé fasse l'objet d'un protectionnisme d'un caractère particulier, comme dans le cas de la population suédoise des Iles d'Aaland.

D'après le régime en vigueur dans ces Iles, les autorités provinciales et communales ne sont en aucun cas obligées d'entretenir ou de subventionner d'autres écoles que celles dans lesquelles l'enseignement est donné en suédois; par ailleurs, l'enseignement ne peut, dans les écoles primaires organisées ou subventionnées par l'Etat ou par les communes, être donné en une autre langue que le suédois, à moins que les communes intéressées n'y consentent.

Les citoyens finlandais étrangers aux Iles ne peuvent, en principe, y acquérir le droit de domicile qu'après cinq ans de résidence effective. Seules les personnes qui ont le droit de domicile dans les Iles peuvent y exercer le droit de vote communal ou provincial, y acquérir des biens immobiliers ou s'y livrer à des activités dont l'exercice est soumis à une déclaration ou à une autorisation: ce dernier droit appartient aussi à ceux qui résident dans les Iles depuis au moins cinq ans.

10.

Une autre forme de protection est celle que peut procurer le maintien de certains liens entre les éléments d'un même groupe ethnique séparés les uns des autres par une frontière d'Etat. C'est ainsi que l'accord austro-italien de 1946 relatif à la situation du Tyrol du Sud garantit la libre circulation des personnes et des biens et la liberté des échanges de part et d'autre de la frontière des deux Etats.[74]

Souvent les dispositions protectrices établies aussi bien par les conventions internationales que par les constitutions ou législations des Etats intéressés manquent de précision sur des points importants. Elles laissent, par le fait même, une très grande marge d'interprétation aux autorités auxquelles il incombe de les appliquer. C'est ce qui explique peut-être un certain besoin d'autonomie, les groupes ethniques souhaitant assez souvent pouvoir gérer, du moins en partie, leurs propres affaires.

IV

Certains groupes ethniques jouissent, dans le cadre du système étatique dont ils relèvent, d'un statut d'autonomie plus ou moins développé.[1] Celui-ci peut, comme tout autre système de protection, avoir été établi par la voie de dispositions de droit interne, ou résulter, du moins en partie, de conventions internationales.

A.

On peut citer, comme exemples de la première catégorie, les Iles Anglo-Normandes et les Iles Féroé.

1.

Les Iles Anglo-Normandes ont conservé leur statut féodal. Elles ne sont rattachées au Royaume-Uni que par une union personnelle, la reine n'y règnant que comme duchesse de Normandie. Elles jouissent d'une autonomie presque totale dans le cadre d'institutions médiévales. C'est peut-être à la faveur de ce système à la fois libéral et traditionnel qu'elles se sont engagées librement dans la voie d'une anglicisation de plus en plus poussée.

2.

Les Iles Féroé bénéficient depuis 1948 d'un statut d'autonomie interne. Elles ont une assemblée, le *lagting,* et un exécutif, le *landsstyre,* qui gèrent librement les affaires économiques et fiscales et, sous réserve d'un droit d'intervention du commissaire du gouvernement central, le *rigsombudsmand,* les affaires sociales et scolaires, ainsi que celles relatives à la santé publique.

3.

L'Irlande du Nord semble aussi relever de cette catégorie; elle bénéficie d'une assez large autonomie législative et administrative, tout en formant une partie intégrante du Royaume-Uni.

Elle a des organes particuliers: un parlement, composé de deux chambres, et un gouvernement responsable devant ce parlement. Cette autonomie ne semble pas avoir résolu les problèmes résultant des tensions intérieures, de caractère à la fois national, social et religieux, qui divisent la population de ce territoire.

B.

Les Iles d'Aaland, habitées par une population presque exclusivement suédoise, constituent l'une des douze provinces de la République de Finlande. Leur statut a fait l'objet aussi bien d'un accord conclu en 1921 entre la Finlande et la Suède, sous les auspices de la Société des Nations, que de dispositions législatives finlandaises, en particulier les lois des 6 mai 1920 et 11 août 1922, remplacées depuis lors par la loi du 28 décembre 1951.

Les Iles d'Aaland où, comme on l'a déjà indiqué, le suédois est la seule langue officielle, bénéficient d'une large autonomie législative, financière et administrative, en particulier dans les domaines de l'éducation et des affaires sociales. Elles ont une diète provinciale (*landsting*) qui élit l'exécutif de la province, mais restent soumises à la tutelle du président de la république, représenté dans les Iles par un gouverneur.

Celui-ci doit être nommé par le président de la république en accord avec le président de la diète provinciale ou, à défaut d'accord entre eux, sur une liste de cinq candidats proposés par cette diète.

La province peut utiliser pour ses propres besoins le revenu qu'elle tire du commerce et des taxes sur les spectacles et divertissements. Elle peut lever des impôts sur tous autres revenus que ceux frappés par les impôts de l'Etat. Elle bénéficie de subventions de la part de celui-ci.

La législation définissant le statut autonome des Iles d'Aaland ne peut être modifiée sans le consentement de la diète provinciale et uniquement selon la procédure prescrite pour la revision de la constitution de la république.

C.

L'accord austro-italien du 5 septembre 1946, relatif à la situation du Tyrol du Sud, qui constitue l'annexe IV du traité de paix conclu entre les Alliés et l'Italie le 10 février 1947, comporte un certain nombre de dispositions en faveur de la population de langue allemande de la province de Bolzano/Bozen et des communes bilingues voisines de la province de Trente. Il garantit à "la population des territoires susmentionnés . . . l'exercice d'un pouvoir régional autonome en matière législative et exécutive", dans un cadre à déterminer en consultation avec les représentants de la population germanophone. Cet accord n'a été appliqué par les autorités italiennes que d'une manière assez imparfaite.

Il convient de noter à cet égard que les articles 116 et 131 de la constitution italienne du 27 décembre 1947 et la loi constitutionnelle subséquente du 26 février 1948 ont établi une région "Trentino-Alto Adige", comprenant non seulement la province Bolzano/Bozen, mais aussi celle de Trente, en conférant ainsi l'autonomie régionale à une circonscription polyethnique, dont la population est aux cinq-septièmes italienne.[2]

Par ailleurs, l'accord n'a pas pu empêcher qu'en fait l'évolution vers l'italianisation s'est accentuée, notamment par une très forte immigration italienne dans la province de Bolzano/Bozen.

D.

Dans certains cas, l'existence autonome de plusieures ethnies dans un même système étatique se traduit explicitement dans la structure fédérale de celui-ci.

1.

Les Etats communistes fournissent plusieurs exemples de ce genre, notamment celui de l'U.R.S.S., celui de la Tchécoslovaquie et celui de la Yougoslavie.

a) En U.R.S.S. c'est sur la base d'une division du territoire essentiellement fondée sur le critère ethnique qu'ont été constitués les républiques fédérées, les républiques autonomes, les régions autonomes et les arrondissements nationaux. Mais l'organisation fédérale de l'Union Soviétique est plus formelle que réelle; elle permet de préserver les particularités culturelles des ethnies non-russes et d'accorder une certaine attention à leur développement économique,[3] sans porter atteinte à l'unité politique fondamentale d'un système où l'autonomie des républiques et des régions est en fait aussi vaine que leur droit de sécession.

Le caractère unitaire et monolithique du parti communiste et sa mainmise complète sur l'appareil politique et économique de l'Union et de toutes ses parties composantes réduisent à l'unité ce qui n'est qu'une apparence de structure fédérale. Lénine a écrit à propos de l'organisation fédérale de l'U.R.S.S. qu'elle serait "la voie la plus sûre pour arriver à l'unification la plus solide des diverses nationalités en un seul Etat soviétique, démocratique et centralisé".[4] Toutefois, cette structure fédérale ne manque pas, semble-t-il, de correspondre à une certaine réalité sur le plan culturel; à ce point de vue, on a pu reconnaître que "la rupture est nette avec la politique de russification des tsars: les langues, les littératures, les arts nationaux ont été largement développés, et maintiennent à travers toute l'Union une grande diversité de styles de vie".[5] Mais cette diversité culturelle n'est elle-même utilisée que comme un instrument d'unité.[6]

b) Comme la structure fédérale de l'Union Soviétique, celle de la Yougoslavie est fondée sur une division en unités territoriales à base ethnique: les six républiques, incorporant chacune une communauté ethnique particulière, à l'exception de la Bosnie-Herzégovine, qui est elle-même polyethnique, et des deux provinces autonomes, polyethniques elles aussi, constituées à l'intérieur de la République de Serbie.

Le système fédéral de la Yougoslavie est un peu plus réel que celui de l'Union Soviétique. Il est bien plus décentralisé, aussi bien sur les plans politique, social et économique que sur le plan culturel. Il s'appuie sur une certaine tendance "a développer la démocratie à la base"[7] et sur une autonomie assez réelle des assemblées des communes et des conseils des entreprises. Le rôle unificateur et centralisateur du parti communiste semble aussi, en Yougoslavie, s'exercer d'une manière moins contraignante qu'en U.R.S.S.

c) L'organisation fédérale de la Tchécoslovaquie, établie par la loi constitutionnelle du 27 octobre 1968[8] se fonde sur la dualité des deux populations principales de la république. Elle semble devoir être interprétée dans un sens semblable à celle de l'U.R.S.S., plutôt qu'à celle de la Yougoslavie.

2.

Le cas de la Suisse est différent. Les groupes linguistiques composant la population suisse ne constituent pas le cadre de l'organisation fédérale de ce pays, qui est déterminé par l'existence des vingt-deux cantons historiques, éléments constitutifs de la Confédération. Par ailleurs, la cohésion nationale du peuple suisse paraît telle qu'il est difficile de considérer les groupes linguistiques qui le composent comme de véritables groupes ethniques. Jusqu'à présent, ce n'est apparamment que dans le cas de la population francophone du Jura bernois qu'une certaine antinomie de caractère ethnique s'est manifestée d'une manière suffisamment précise, mais elle ne semble pas avoir récellement débordé le cadre du canton de Berne.

V

On peut encore citer deux cas dans lesquels l'aménagement des relations entre communautés différentes a fait récemment l'objet de dispositions relativement détaillées: celui de la République de Chypre, depuis la création de celle-ci en 1960, et celui de la Belgique, depuis les réformes constitutionnelles de 1970. Il semble utile de consacrer quelques développements à chacun de ces deux cas.

A.

Le statut de Chypre a été défini, sur le plan international, par les accords de Zurich du 11 février 1959 et de Londres du 19 février 1959 et, sur le plan interne, par la constitution du 6 avril 1960. Il se caractérise par une définition particulièrement minutieuse des rapports entre les communautés grecque et turque qui constituent la population de l'Ile et qui représentent respectivement à peu près 80 p.c. et 20 p.c. de celle-ci.

1.

La communauté grecque comprend tous les citoyens qui sont d'origine grecque et dont la langue maternelle est le grec ou qui participent aux traditions culturelles grecques ou qui sont membres de l'église grecque orthodoxe.[1] La communauté turque comprend tous les citoyens qui sont d'origine turque et dont la langue maternelle est le turc ou qui participent aux traditions culturelles turques ou qui sont musulmans.[2] Tout autre citoyen doit nécessairement opter pour l'une ou l'autre de ces deux communautés, soit individuellement, soit à l'intervention du groupe religieux auquel il appartient.[3] Tout citoyen de la république doit donc appartenir nécessairement à l'une ou à l'autre des deux communautés.

2.

La langue grecque et la langue turque sont les langues officielles de la république. Elles doivent être employées sur un pied de parfaite égalité, pour l'établissement et la publication des actes et documents législatifs, gouvernementaux et administratifs. Les procédures judiciaires ont lieu et les jugements des tribunaux sont rendus en grec ou en turc ou dans les deux langues, selon que les parties sont grecques, turques ou grecques et turques. Chacun a le droit de s'adresser aux autorités de la république dans l'une ou l'autre des deux langues.[4]

3.

Le président et le vice-président de la république appartiennent respectivement à la communauté grecque et à la communauté turque et sont élus l'un et l'autre par leur propre communauté.[5] Ils exercent certaines attributions en commun,[6] d'autres séparément[7] et sont assistés d'un conseil des ministres composé de sept ministres grecs et de trois ministres turcs.[8]

4.

La chambre des représentants est composée à raison de 70 p.c. de membres appartenant à la communauté grecque et élus par celle-ci et à raison de 30 p.c. de membres appartenant à la communauté turque et élus par celle-ci.[9] Le président de cette chambre doit être grec, le vice-président turc: ils sont élus respectivement par les membres grecs et turcs de l'assemblée.[10]

Certaines lois ne peuvent être adoptées qu'à la majorité des suffrages exprimés par les représentants de chacune des deux communautés: il en est ainsi notamment pour les lois électorales, pour celles relatives aux municipalités ou pour celles établissant des impôts et des taxes.[11] Tout débat de la chambre peut être ajourné une seule fois pour vingt-quatre heures à la requête de la majorité des représentants de l'une ou de l'autre communauté.[12] Le président et le vice-président peuvent, séparément ou conjointement, opposer leur veto aux décisions de la chambre des représentants relatives à certaines questions de politique extérieure, de défense ou de police;[13] ils peuvent aussi, séparément ou conjointement, réclamer un nouvel examen par la chambre de toute décision de celle-ci.[14]

5.

En plus de la chambre des représentants, il y a deux chambres communautaires, élues respectivement par la communauté grecque et par la communauté turque et exerçant, chacune en ce qui la concerne, certains pouvoirs à propos de questions intéressant en particulier la communauté dont il s'agit. Chacune de ces chambres exerce notamment des pouvoirs législatifs en matière de religion et d'état de personnes ainsi qu'à propos du règlement de litiges relatifs à ces objets, en matière d'éducation et de culture, et en d'autres matières concernant exclusivement la communauté intéresée ou les communes composées exclusivement de membres de celle-ci. Elle dispose aussi de pouvoirs financiers lui permettant de pourvoir aux besoins propres à sa communauté;[15] elle bénéficie, à cette fin, d'une dotation, accordée chaque année par la chambre des représentants, à concurrence d'au moins 1.600.00 livres en ce qui concerne la chambre communautaire grecque, et d'au moins 400.000 livres en ce qui concerne la chambre communautaire turque.[16] Mais elle peut aussi établir des impôts et des rétributions à la charge des membres de sa communauté.[17]

6.

La répartition des fonctions publiques doit être faite de manière à ce qu'elles soient conférées à raison de 70 p.c. à des citoyens appartenant à la communauté grecque et de 30 p.c. à des citoyens appartenant à la communauté turque.[18] Le même dosage est appliqué pour la composition des forces de sécurité (police et gendarmerie).[19] Les proportions sont différentes pour l'armée, qui doit comprendre 60 p.c. de grecs et 40 p.c. de turcs.[20] Dans les régions ou localités où l'une des deux communautés représente près de 100 p.c. de la population, les fonctions publiques doivent être confiées à des membres de cette communauté[21] et les forces qui s'y trouvent stationnées doivent, elles aussi, appartenir à cette communauté.[22]

Par ailleurs, certaines fonctions publiques sont dédoublées en ce sens qu'elles sont, soit confiées conjointement à des membres de chacune des communautés, soit confiées à un titulaire appartenant à l'une de celles-ci, assisté d'un adjoint appartenant à l'autre. C'est ainsi que le conseil des ministres a deux secrétaires, un grec et un turc,[23] et que la chambre des représentants a trois secrétaires, deux grecs et un turc, et trois secrétaires administratifs, deux grecs et un turc[24] et que la haute cour de justice doit comprendre, indépendamment d'un président neutre disposant de deux voix, deux membres grecs et un membre turc.[25] C'est ainsi que, par ailleurs, le procureur général et le procureur général adjoint, l'auditeur général et l'auditeur général adjoint, le trésorier général et le trésorier général adjoint, le gouverneur de la banque d'émission et le gouverneur adjoint de cette banque doivent, respectivement, appartenir à l'une et à l'autre des communautés.[26] Il en est de même pour les commandants et commandants adjoints de l'armée, de la police et de la gendarmerie, étant entendu que l'un des commandants de ces forces doit appartenir à la communauté turque.[27]

7.

La constitution a prévu l'existence de municipalités distinctes pour chacune des deux communautés dans les cinq villes les plus importantes de la république[28] et l'organisation d'un système réalisant, dans la mesure du possible, la représentation proportionnelle des deux communautés dans les organes des autres municipalités.[29]

8.

La constitution cypriote contient aussi des dispositions relatives au nombre d'heures d'émission à consacrer aux programmes de radiodiffusion et de télévision destinés à chacune des communautés.[30]

9.

Une cour constitutionnelle, composée d'un membre appartenant à la communauté grecque, d'un membre appartenant à la communauté turque et d'un président neutre[31] doit connaître notamment des recours qui peuvent être introduits auprès d'elle par le président ou par le vice-président contre des dispositions législatives ou budgétaires qu'ils estiment discriminatoires à l'égard de l'une des deux communautés[32] et des conflits de compétence qui peuvent surgir entre la chambre des représentants et les chambres communautaires.[33]

10.

A part certaines dispositions résultant de l'accord de Zurich du 11 février 1959 et qui sont soustraites à toute révision, les dispositions de la constitution cypriote peuvent être modifiées par une loi votée par la chambre des représentants à une majorité comprenant au moins les deux tiers des membres appartenant à la communauté grecque et au moins les deux tiers des membres appartenant à la communauté turque.[34]

B.

La Belgique est habitée par une population comprenant à peu près 60 p.c. de néerlandophones et à peu près 40 p.c. de francophones, indépendamment d'une petite minorité germanophone et d'assez nombreux travailleurs immigrés. Les relations entre l'élément néerlandophone et l'élement francophone de la population ont donné lieu depuis le XIXème siècle a des lois linguistiques successives; depuis la fin de 1970, elles font l'objet de dispositions constitutionnelles qui, tout en confirmant certains principes déjà établis par la législation ordinaire, ont introduit un certain nombre d'éléments nouveaux dans l'organisation politique de l'Etat.

Les lois constitutionnelles du 24 décembre 1970 consacrent, d'une part, la division du territoire en quatre régions linguistiques (*taalgebieden*), la région de langue néerlandaise, la région de langue française, la région bilingue de Bruxelles-capitale et la région de langue allemande,[35] et en trois régions (*gewesten*), la région flamande, la région wallonne et la région bruxelloise, celles-ci ne coïncidant pas nécessairement avec les régions linguistiques correspondantes,[36] et, d'autre part, la division de la population en trois communautés culturelles (*cultuurgemeenschappen*), la communauté néerlandaise, la communauté française et la communauté allemande.[37]

Ces dispositions se trouvent liées à d'autres qui prévoient l'existence de deux groupes linguistiques au sein des deux chambres du parlement,[38] de conseils culturels propres à chacune des communautés linguistiques et composés précisément des membres de ces groupes linguistiques, du moins en ce qui concerne les deux communautés principales,[39] de certaines procédures législatives particulières servant à protéger les intérêts de chacune des deux communautés principales sur le plan de la législation nationale,[40] et enfin, d'une parité de ces deux communautés au sein du consiel des ministres.[41] Tout cela ce trouve complété par un statut particulier établi pour l'agglomération de Bruxelles.[42]

1.

La répartition des membres élus de chacune des deux chambres en un groupe linguistique français et un groupe linguistique néerlandais constitue, sans doute, l'un des éléments les plus importants de cet ensemble. Elle conditionne à la fois les procédures législatives particulières et la composition des conseils culturels.

D'une part, ces groupes linguistiques permettent de faire apparaître formellement, au sein du parlement national, l'existence d'un consensus ou d'une opposition de caractère communautaire. En effet, certains lois ne pourront désormais être adoptées qu'avec l'accord de chacun de ces groupes dans chacune des deux chambres et toutes les autres, à l'exception des budgets, pourront faire l'objet dans chacune des deux chambres, d'une motion suspensive signée par les trois quarts des membres de l'un ou de l'autre de ces deux groupes. D'autre part, chacun des groupes linguistiques constitue, avec le groupe correspondant de l'autre chambre, le conseil culturel de la communauté culturelle française ou néerlandaise et contribue ainsi à former l'organe propre de l'autonomie culturelle de chacune des deux communautés principales.

Il en résulte que nous aurons bientôt en Belgique à côté des deux chambres traditionnelles, la chambre des représentants et le sénat, deux autres assemblées composées respectivement des groupes linguistiques français et néerlandais des deux premières, ce qui nous donnera un parlement non plus bicaméral, mais quadricaméral, comprenant deux assemblées à compétence "nationale" et deux assemblées à compétence "communautaire", les mêmes membres siégeant à la fois dans l'une des deux assemblées "nationales" et dans l'une des deux assemblées "communautaires".

2.

Désormais, une procédure de vote particulière sera nécessaire pour certaines décisions des chambres législatives. Certaines lois ne pourront être adoptées que pour autant qu'elles seront approuvées non seulement à la majorité des deux tiers des suffrages exprimés dans chacune des chambres — ce qui constitue déjà une règle plus stricte que celle qui vaut pour les lois ordinaires, pour lesquelles la majorité absolue suffit —, mais aussi à la majorité des suffrages dans chaque groupe linguistique de chacune des chambres. De plus, elles ne pourront être votées que pour autant que non seulement la majorité des membres de chaque chambre, mais aussi la majorité des membres de chacun des groupes linguistiques se trouve présente lors du vote.

Cette procédure devra être suivie pour "soustraire certains territoires . . . à la division en provinces, les faire relever directement du pouvoir exécutif et les soumettre à un statut propre";[43] pour "changer ou rectifier les limites des quatres régions linguistiques",[44] pour déterminer "le mode selon lequel les conseils culturels exercent leurs attributions",[45] ainsi que les "matières culturelles" et les "formes de coopération" entre les communautés culturelles et de coopération culturelle internationale que ces conseils ont à régler,[46] et pour créer les organes des trois régions et déterminer leur ressort, les matières relevant de leur compétence et le mode de règlement de ces matières.[47]

3.

Par ailleurs, la constitution belge comporte à présent une disposition, l'article 38bis, qui permet à chacun des deux groupes linguistiques de chacune des chambres de faire suspendre l'examen d'un projet ou d'une proposition de loi lorsqu'il estime que les dispositions de ce projet ou de cette proposition "sont de nature à porter gravement atteinte aux relations entre les communautés". Il faut, à cette fin, qu'une "motion motivée", déclarant que les dispositions qu'elle désigne sont de nature à porter gravement atteinte aux relations entres les communautés, soit signée par les trois quarts au moins des membres d'un des groupes linguistiques et introduite après le dépôt du rapport et avant le vote final en séance publique.[48]

Le dépôt d'une telle motion a pour effet de suspendre la procédure parlementaire: la motion est alors "déférée au conseil des ministres qui, dans les trente jours, donne son avis motivé sur la motion et invite la chambre saisie à se prononcer, soit sur cet avis, soit sur le projet ou la proposition éventuellement amendés".[49] Cette procédure ne peut être mise en oeuvre à l'égard des budgets ni à l'égard des lois qui requièrent une majorité spéciale.[50] Par ailleurs, elle ne peut être appliquée qu'une seule fois par les membres d'un même groupe linguistique à l'égard d'un même projet ou d'une même proposition de loi.[51]

4.

La parité des deux communautés linguistiques au sein du conseil des ministres est définie par le nouvel article 86bis, selon lequel "le premier ministre éventuellement excepté, le conseil des ministres compte autant de ministres d'expression français que d'expression néerlandaise".[52]

5.

La division en régions linguistiques, consacrée par le nouvel article 3bis de la constitution, avait déjà été établie antérieurement par des lois ordinaires, la plus récente de celles-ci étant celle du 2 août 1963; la délimitation des provinces, des arrondissements administratifs et des communes avait déjà été adaptée à la délimitation des régions linguistiques par une loi du 8 novembre 1962.

6.

Chaque communauté culturelle aura un conseil culturel, dont la composition et la compétence sont réglées, en ce qui concerne les communautés culturelles française et néerlandaise, par le nouvel article 59bis de la constitution et doivent l'être, selon le nouvel article 59ter, en ce qui concerne la communauté culturelle allemande, par une loi ordinaire. Les conseils culturels des communautés culturelles française et néerlandaise comprennent respectivement, comme on l'a vu, les membres des groupes linguistiques français et néerlandais de la chambre des représentants et du sénat.[53] Ils règlent, chacun en ce qui le concerne, par la voie de décrets ayant force de loi respectivement dans la région linguistique française et dans la région linguistique néerlandaise, d'une part, "les matières culturelles", "l'enseignement, à l'exclusion de ce qui a trait à la paix scolaire, à l'obligation scolaire, aux structures de l'enseignement, aux diplômes, aux subsides, aux traitements et aux normes de population scolaire", et "la coopération entre les communautés culturelles ainsi que la coopération culturelle internationale",[54] et, d'autre part, l'emploi des langues pour "les matières administratives", pour "l'enseignement dans les établissements créés, subventionnés ou reconnus par les pouvoirs publics" et pour "les relations sociales entre les employeurs et leur personnel, ainsi que les actes et documents des entreprises imposés par la loi et les règlements".[55]

On aura remarqué que les aspects les plus importants de l'enseignement sont explicitement soustraits à la compétence des conseils culturels; ils restent réservés au législateur national. Par ailleurs, les "matières culturelles" et les "formes de coopération" visées au #2 de l'article 59bis doivent être définies d'une manière plus précise par une loi adoptée à la majorité spéciale dont il a été question ci-dessus. De même, un certain nombre d'aspects de la législation relative à l'emploi des langues reste réservé au législateur national: il en est ainsi, en particulier, en ce qui concerne la législation relative à l'emploi des langues en matière judiciaire et dans les forces armées, et en ce qui concerne les communes, institutions ou services soustraits à l'application des décrets des conseils culturels.

L'application des décrets des conseils culturels relatifs aux matières culturelles à l'enseignement et à la coopération culturelle s'étend aussi aux "institutions établies dans la région bilingue de Bruxelles-capitale qui, en raison de leurs activités, doivent être considérées comme appartenant exclusivement à l'une ou à l'autre communauté culturelle".[56] Les décrets des conseils culturels relatif à l'emploi des langues ne sont pas applicables "aux communes ou groupes de communes contigus à une autre région linguistique et où la loi prescrit ou permet l'emploi d'une autre langue que celle de la région dans laquelle ils sont situés", aux "services dont l'activité s'étend au-delà de la région linguistique dans laquelle ils sont établis" et aux "institutions nationales ou internationales, désignées par la loi, dont l'activité est commune à plus d'une communauté culturelle".[57]

Le législateur national doit mettre à le disposition de chacun des conseils culturels un "crédit global", dont le montant doit être déterminé "en fonction de critères objectifs", étant entendu que "des dotations égales sont établies dans les matières qui, par leur nature, ne se prêtent pas à des critères objectifs" et que "la loi détermine en fonction des mêmes règles la quotité de ce crédit que doit être consacrée au développement de l'une et de l'autre culture sur le territoire de Bruxelles-capitale".[58] Le législateur national doit aussi déterminer "les mesures en vue de prévenir toute discrimination pour des raisons idéologiques ou philosophiques"[59] et organiser "la procédure tendant à prévenir et à régler les conflits entre la loi et le décret, ainsi qu'entre les décrets".[60]

7.

L'organisation des régions flamande, wallonne et bruxelloise, dont l'existence est consacrée par le nouvel article 107quater, doit encore être réglée. Chacune de ces régions aura "des organes . . . composés de mandataires élus" qui devront être créés par une loi adoptée à la majorité spéciale déjà décrite antérieurement, cette loi devant, par ailleurs, déterminer leur compétence matérielle et territoriale et leur mode de fonctionnement. Il est entendu que ces organes ne pourront être chargés de régler les matières relatives à l'emploi des langues ou relevant de la compétence des conseils culturels.[61] Il est certain que ces dispositions très peu précises ouvrent la voie à l'octroi d'une très grande autonomie aux trois régions dont il s'agit; elles permettent, en fait, de poursuivre le processus de fédéralisation de l'Etat belge, dans le cadre de ces trois régions, sans avoir à recourir à de nouvelles procédures de révision constitutionnelle et sans avoir à tenir compte des limitations matérielles imposées à l'activité des conseils culturels.

8.

Un régime particulier a été établi pour l'agglomération bruxelloise, désignée dans le nouvel article 108ter de la constitution comme "l'agglomération à laquelle appartient la capitale de royaume". Ce régime particulier se trouve caractérisé par l'existence, au sein du conseil d'agglomération, de deux groupes linguistiques semblables à ceux créés au sein des chambres législatives nationales,[62] et d'une procédure permettant d'y suspendre l'examen des projets ou des propositions, dans des conditions analogues à celles définies, pour ces chambres, par le nouvel article 38bis,[63]ainsi que par la parité de la représentation des deux groupes linguistiques au sein du collège exécutif de l'agglomération, "le président excepté",[64] et par l'existence de deux commissions culturelles exerçant notamment certaines attributions en matière scolaire et culturelle.[65]

9.

Les nouvelles dispositions constitutionnelles ne comportent aucune modification de l'article 23, déjà inscrit dans la constitution belge depuis 1831, selon lequel "l'emploi des langues usitées en Belgique est facultatif" et "ne peut être réglé que par la loi, et seulement pour les actes de l'autorité publique et pour les affaires judiciaires".

C.

Il y a de remarquables similitudes entre les solutions adoptées dans les deux cas qui viennent d'être examinés.

L'équilibre entre les deux communautés qui, dans chacun des deux Etats, composent presqu' exclusivement la population du pays, a été recherché, en Belgique aussi bien qu'à Chypre, par la répartition de certaines charges ou fonctions selon des dosages tantôt paritaires,[66] tantôt pondérés d'après des pourcentages forfaitaires,[67] par la création d'assemblées représentatives particulières à chaque communauté, exerçant principalement des attributions de caractère culturel,[68] par l'établissement de mécanismes de protection dans le fonctionnement d'organes communs, aussi bien sous la forme de majorités spéciales[69] que de procédures dilatoires[70] ou vétitives,[71] ainsi que par une législation linguistique assez stricte.[72] De même, dans l'un et l'autre cas, se manifeste une tendance à distinguer nettement les communautés composantes, soit selon des critères personnels,[73] soit sur la base d'une délimitation territoriale.[74] Enfin, des procédures de règlement de conflits ont été prévues dans les deux pays.[75]

VI

Une forme de société polyethnique devenue très fréquente en Europe, mais qui n'a jusqu'à présent suscité qu'assez peu d'attention, est celle qui résulte de l'existence d'importantes collectivités allogènes formées notamment par les migrations de la main-d'oeuvre. Elle présente des problèmes de caractère particulier, qui mériteraient d'être examinés de près, mais qui nous ont paru dépasser le cadre du présent rapport.

•   •   •

Nous avons esquissé quelques exemples de formules juridiques tendant à régler la coexistence de plusieures ethnies ou groupes ethniques dans un même système étatique. Ces formules sont très différentes et sont évidemment déterminées chaque fois par les particularités des situations qu'elles concernent.

On peut, semble-t-il, distinguer, d'une manièr générale, deux types de mesures. D'une part, celles qui, sans renoncer à l'unité du système étatique, garantissent à certains groupes une protection particulière, notamment la non-discrimination dans l'exercice des droits de l'homme et des libertés fondamentales, le développement de leur culture et de leurs moyens d'existence, l'usage de leur langue, en particulier dans la vie publique et dans l'enseignement, et le maintien de leurs traditions. D'autre part, celles qui, sous l'une ou l'autre forme accordent aux groupes ethniques une certaine autonomie quant à la gestion de leurs propres affaires, cette autonomie pouvant même s'exprimer par la reconnaissance de groupes ethniques comme éléments composants d'une structure explicitement fédérale.

Le choix entre ces deux types de solutions n'est pas nécessairement déterminé par l'importance numérique respective des groupes ethniques intéressés: certaines collectivités ne réunissant qu'un nombre relativement restreint de personnes bénéficient d'un statut d'autonomie, alors que des collectivités plus importantes quant au nombre de personnes qui les composent ne sont protégés que d'une autre manière. Il convient, par ailleurs, de ne pas oublier qu'une minorité numérique ne se trouve pas nécessairement en situation d'infériorité. Certaines minorités numériques ont, en fait, le caractère de "majorités sociologiques", tout comme certaines majorités numériques sont en réalité des "minorités sociologiques".

Les solutions d'autonomie sont peut-être plus faciles à réaliser pour des collectivités bénéficiant d'une implantation territoriale particulière, suffisamment cohérente et suffisamment exclusive, que pour des collectivités dispersées parmi d'autres populations. Encore faut-il constater qu'elles ont aussi été tentées en faveur de collectivités de cette dernière catégorie, des critères d'appartenance de type personnel remplaçant, dans un tel cas, les délimitations territoriales traditionnelles: l'exemple de Chypre montre toutefois comment il est difficile de faire fonctionner un tel système. Les formules de protection simple ou d'autonomie sont peut-être moins faciles à appliquer lorsqu'il s'agit de collectivités, qui, d'une manière ou d'une autre, se rattachent à des ethnies constituant la population principale d'un autre système étatique ou du moins une partie suffisamment importante de la population de celui-ci: des situations de ce genre peuvent donner lieu, d'une part, à des mouvements de caractère irrédentiste et, d'autre part, à des attitudes de méfiance.

Aucune formule juridique ne semble pouvoir donner des résultats satisfaisants par elle-même, en raison de ses propres vertus. L'expérience faite dans divers pays paraît démontrer que beaucoup dépend de la confiance et de la loyauté mutuelle des collectivités intéressées.

Notes

[1]"An ethnic group is generally conceived to be one whose members share a distinctive social and cultural tradition, maintained within the group from generation to generation, whether as part of a more complex society or in isolation" (R. M. McIver & Charles H. Page, *Society,* Londres 1962, pp. 386-387). "L'ethnie est une collectivité présentant certains charactères distinctifs communs de langue, de culture ou de civilisation" (G. Héraud, *L'Europe des Ethnies,* Paris 1963, p. 23).

Section I

[1]Loi no. 51-46 du 11 février 1951, relative à l'enseignement des langues et dialectes locaux.

[2]T. Modeen, *The International Protection of National Minorities in Europe,* Abo 1969, p. 36.

[3]G. Héraud, *op. cit.,* p. 73.

Section II

[1]Traité du 30 janvier 1923.

Section III

[1]Voir les articles 62 à 69 de ce traité.

[2]Voir les articles 49 à 57 de ce traité.

[3]Voir les articles 54 à 60 de ce traité.

[4]Voir les articles 37 à 45 de ce traité.

[5]Obligations résultant de l'accord du 27 juin 1921.

[6]Obligations résultant des articles 37 à 45 du traité de paix conclu entre les Alliés et la Turquie le 24 juillet 1923.

[7]Modeen, *op. cit.,* pp. 69-73.

[8]Voir l'article 27 du pacte international relatif aux droits civils et politiques.

[9]Voir l'article 1er du pacte international relatif aux droits civils et politiques et l'article 1er du pacte international relatif aux droits économiques, sociaux et culturels.

[10]Par l'article 6 de ce traité, l'Autriche s'est engagée à "prendre toutes les mesures nécessaires pour assurer à toutes les personnes relevant de sa juridiction, sans distinction de race, de sexe, de langue ou de religion, la jouissance des droits de l'homme et des libertés fondamentales, y compris la liberté d'expression de la pensée, la liberté de presse et de publication, la liberté de culte, la liberté d'opinion ou de réunion" et "à ce que les lois en vigueur en Autriche n'entraînent, ni par leur texte, ni par les modalités de leur application, aucune discrimination directe ou indirecte entre les

ressortissants autrichiens en raison de leur race, de leur sexe, de leur langue ou de leur religion, tant en ce qui concerne leur personne, leurs biens, leurs intérêts commerciaux, professionnels ou financiers, leur statut, leurs droits politiques et civils qu'en toute autre matière". En outre, l'Autriche s'est engagée, par l'article 8 du même traité, à garantir "à tous les citoyens le suffrage libre, égal et universel, ainsi que le droit d'être élu à une fonction publique, sans distinction de race, de langue, de religion ou d'opinion".

[11] Voir l'article ler de ce statut.

[12] C'est ainsi que les articles 2 et 7 du traité du 28 juin 1919 relatif aux minorités de Pologne garantissaient à tous les habitants de ce pays la pleine et entière protection de leur vie et de leur liberté, ainsi que le respect de leur liberté de religion, sous réserve de l'ordre public et des bonnes moeurs, et à tous les ressortissants polonais l'égalité devant la loi et la jouissance des mêmes droits civils et politiques. Voir aussi, dans le même sens, les articles 38 et 39 du traité de paix conclu entre les Alliés et la Turquie le 24 juillet 1923.

[13] Voir notamment l'article 2 du statut spécial, annexé au mémorandum du 5 octobre 1954 relatif à la région de Trieste. Voir aussi l'article 7, # ler, du traité d'Etat autrichien du 15 mai 1955.

[14] Voir l'article 8 du traité du 28 juin 1919 relatif aux minorités de Pologne et l'article 40 du traité de paix conclu le 24 juillet 1923 entre les Alliés et la Turquie.

[15] Selon l'article 4, # 2, de la loi constitutionnelle du 27 octobre 1968 concernant le statut des nationalités en République Socialiste Tchécoslovaque, "l'appartenance à une nationalité quelconque ne peut porter atteinte aux droits des citoyens à participer à la vie politique, économique et sociale".

[16] Selon l'article 7, #4, du traité d'Etat autrichien du 15 mai 1955, "les ressortissants autrichiens appartenant aux minorités slovène ou croate en Carinthie, Burgenland et Styrie participeront dans les mêmes conditions que les autres ressortissants autrichiens aux activités des organismes culturels, administratifs et judiciaires dans ces territoires".

[17] Voir notamment l'article 7 du traité du 28 juin 1919 relatif aux minorités de Pologne, l'article 39 du traité de paix conclu entre les Alliés et la Turquie le 24 juillet 1923, et l'article 2, (b) et (c), du statut spécial annexé au mémorandum du 5 octobre 1954 relatif à la région de Trieste.

[18] Voir l'article 1er, (d), de l'accord austro-italien du 5 septembre 1946 relatif à la situation du Tyrol du Sud.

[19] Garantie accordée par l'article 2 de la loi constitutionnelle du 27 octobre 1968 concernant le statut des nationalités en République Socialiste Tchécoslovaque, aux minorités hongroise, allemande, polonaise et ukrainienne.

[20] Garantie accordée aux minorités de la région de Trieste par l'article 2, (c), du statut spécial annexé au mémorandum du 5 octobre 1954.

[21] C'est ce que prescrit l'article 22 de la constitution roumaine pour les districts habités par une population d'une nationalité autre que roumaine.

[22] Voir notamment l'article 7 du traité du 28 juin 1919 relatif aux minorités de Pologne, l'article 39 du traité de paix conclu entre les Alliés et la Turquie le 24 juillet 1923, et l'article 2, (d), du statut spécial annexé au mémorandum du 5 octobre 1954 relatif à la région de Trieste.

[23] Voir l'article 2, (f), du statut spécial de la région de Trieste.

[24] Voir l'article 79 de la constitution bulgare.

[25] Voir l'article 49 de la constitution hongroise.

[26] Voir l'article 43 de la constitution yougoslave.

[27] Voir l'article 11 de la constitution de la République Démocratique Allemande.

[28] Voir l'article 3, #1er, b), de cette loi.

[29] Voir l'article 4 de cette loi.

[30] Voir l'article 7, #5, du traité d'Etat du 15 mai 1955.

[31] Voir l'article 42 de la constitution yougoslave.

[32] Voir l'article 3, #1er, d), de cette loi.

[33] Voir notamment l'article 8 du traité du 28 juin 1919 relatif aux minorités de Pologne et l'article 40 du traité de paix conclu entre les Alliés et la Turquie le 24 juillet 1923. Ces dispositions garantissent aux minorités qu'elles concernent le droit d'organiser et de faire fonctionner des institutions de bienfaisance, religieuses et sociales, des écoles et autres établissements d'éducation.

[34] Voir notamment l'article 7, #1er, du traité d'Etat autrichien du 15 mai 1955, qui garantit aux minorités slovène et croate en Carinthie, Burgenland et Styrie, "le droit d'avoir leurs propres organisations, de tenir leurs réunions et de posséder une presse en leur propro langue".

[35] Voir notamment l'article 9 du traité du 28 juin 1919 relatif aux minorités de Pologne et l'article 41 du traité de paix conclu entre les Alliés et la Turquie le 24 juillet 1923.

[36] Voir l'article 6 de ce statut.

[37] Voir notamment l'article 23 de la constitution belge, l'article 22 de la constitution roumaine et l'article 42 de la constitution yougoslave.

[38] Voir notamment les articles 7 et 8 du traité du 28 juin 1919 relatif aux minorités de Pologne et les articles 39 et 40 du traité de paix conclu entre les Alliés et la Turquie le 24 juillet 1923.

[39] Voir l'article 1er, (c), de cet accord.

[40] Voir notamment l'article 14 de la constitution finlandaise, l'article 11 de la constitution de la République Démocratique Allemande, l'article 5 du statut spécial annexé au mémorandum du 5 octobre 1954 relatif à la région de Trieste, l'article 7 du traité du 28 juin 1919 relatif aux minorités de Pologne et l'article 39 du traité de paix conclu entre les Alliés et la Turquie le 24 juillet 1923.

[41] Voir notamment l'article 3, #1er, c), de la loi constitutionnelle concernant le statut des nationalités de la République Socialiste Tchécoslovaque.

[42] Voir l'article 115 de la constitution suisse.

[43] Voir l'article 14 de la constitution finlandaise.

[44] Voir l'article 22 de la constitution finlandaise et l'article 88 de la loi relative au parlement.

[45] Voir la loi belge du 31 mai 1961, relative à l'emploi des langues en matière législative, à la présentation, à la publication et à l'entrée en vigueur des textes légaux et réglementaires.

[46] Voir notamment les lois sur l'emploi des langues en matière administrative, coordonnées par l'arrêté royal du 18 juillet 1966.

[47] Voir notamment les articles 50 et 51 de la constitution finlandaise.

[48] Voir les articles 37 à 39 de la loi no. 670 du 28 décembre 1951 relative à l'autonomie des Iles d'Aaland.

[49] Voir les articles 50, alinéa 3, et 51, alinéa 2, de la constitution finlandaise.

[50] Voir l'article 7, #2, du traité d'Etat autrichien du 15 mai 1955.

[51] Voir l'accord austro-italien du 5 septembre 1946, relatif à la situation du Tyrol du Sud.

[52] Ce régime leur est maintenu aussi longtemps que cette minorité ne se réduit pas à moins de 8 p.c. de la population.

[53] Voir les articles 22 et 102 de la constitution roumaine. Selon ces dispositions, les autorités et institutions se servent, dans les districts comprenant une population de nationalité non-roumaine, oralement et par écrit, de la langue de cette nationalité; les procédures judiciaires ont lieu en roumain, mais, dans les régions comprenant une population de nationalité non-roumaine, l'usage de la langue de cette population est assuré.

[54] Voir l'article 42, alinéa 3, de la constitution yougoslave.

[55] Article 75 de la constitution finlandaise.

[56] Voir notamment l'article 8 du traité de 1919 relatif aux minorités de Pologne.

[57] Voir l'article 79 de cette constitution.

[58] Article 8 du traité du 28 juin 1919 relatif aux minorités de Pologne.

[59] Article 9, alinéa 1er, du même traité.

[60] Article 9, alinéa 2, du même traité.

[61] Voir l'article 4, (c), du statut spécial, qui comporte en outre des garanties en ce qui concerne le maintien des écoles existantes et la stabilité d'emploi du personnel enseignant.

[62] Article 7, #2, du traité d'Etat du 15 mai 1955.

[63] Voir l'article 79 de la constitution bulgare.

[64] Voir l'article 49 de la constitution hongroise.

[65] Voir les articles 42 et 43 de la constitution yougoslave.

[66] Voir l'article 3, #1er, a), de cette loi.

[67] Voir l'article 7, #1er, de ce traité.

[68] Voir l'article 4, (a), de ce statut.

[69] Voir l'article 3, #1er, e), de cette loi, qui leur garantit ce droit "dans le cadre correspondant aux nécessités de leur développement national et dans les conditions prévues par les lois".

[70] Voir l'article 42 du traité de paix conclu entre les Alliés et la Turquie le 24 juillet 1923.

[71] Voir l'article 43 du même traité.

[72] Voir l'article 43 du même traité, ainsi que l'article 11 du traité du 28 juin 1919 relatif aux minorités de Pologne.

[73] Voir l'article 42 du traité de paix conclu entre les Alliés et la Turquie le 24 juillet 1923.

[74] Voir l'article 3 de cet accord.

Section IV

[1] Au fond, il y a déjà une certaine autonomie lorsque, par exemple, un groupe ethnique jouit de la liberté d'organiser ses écoles, églises ou autres institutions culturelles ou se trouve admis à gérer lui-même de telles institutions établies à son intention par l'Etat. Plusieurs des systèmes de protection visés dans la section III du présent rapport comportent déjà de telles formes d'autonomie.

[2] G. Héraud, *op. cit.,* p. 205.

[3] F. Neumann, *European Government,* 4e éd., New York 1968, p. 596.

[4] V. I. Lenine, *Collected Works,* New York 1946, vol. XXII, pp. 415 et suiv.

[5] M. Duverger, *Institutions politiques et droit constitutionnel,* 11e éd., Paris 1970, p. 411.

[6] F. Neumann, *op. cit.,* p. 601.

[7] M. Duverger, *op. cit.,* p. 428.

[8] Loi constitutionnelle du 27 octobre 1968 sur la fédération tchécoslovaque.

Section V

[1] Article 2, #1er de la constitution cypriote du 6 avril 1960.

[2] Article 2, #2, de la même constitution.

[3] Article 2, ##3 et 4, de la même constitution.

[4] Article 3 de la constitution.

[5] Article 1er de la constitution.

[6] Voir notamment l'article 47 de la constitution.

[7] Voir notamment les articles 48 et 49 de la constitution.

[8] Article 46 de la constitution.

[9] Article 62, #2 de la constitution.

[10] Article 72, #1er de la constitution.

[11] Article 78, #2 de la constitution.

[12] Article 77, #2 de la constitution.

[13] Article 50 de la constitution.

[14] Article 51 de la constitution.

[15] Article 87 de la constitution.

[16] Article 88 de la constitution.

[17] Article 87, #1, f, de la constitution.

[18] Article 123, #1er de la constitution.

[19] Article 130, #2 de la constitution.

[20] Article 129, #1er de la constitution.

[21] Article 123, #3, de la constitution.

[22] Article 132 de la constitution.

[23] Article 60, #1er, de la constitution.

[24] Article 72, #4, de la constitution.

[25] Article 153, #1er, de la constitution.

[26] Articles 112, 115, 126 et 118 de la constitution.

[27] Article 131, #2 de la constitution.

[28] Articles 173 à 177 de la constitution.

[29] Article 178 de la constitution.

[30] Article 171 de la constitution.

[31] Article 132 de la constitution.

[32] Articles 137 et 138 de la constitution.

[33] Article 139 de la constitution.

[34] Article 182 de la constitution.

[35] Article 3bis, alinéa 1er, de la constitution belge.

[36] Article 107 quater de la constitution.

[37] Article 3ter, alinéa 1er, de la constitution.

[38] Article 32bis de la constitution.

[39] Article 59bis de la constitution.

[40] Article 1er, alinéa 4, 3bis, alinéa 3, 38bis, 59bis, #1er, alinéa 2 et #2, alinéa 2, et 107 quater de la constitution.

[41] Article 56 bis de la constitution.

[42] Article 108ter de la constitution.

[43] Nouvelle rédaction de l'alinéa 4 de l'article 1er de la constitution, selon la loi constitutionnelle du 24 décembre 1970.

[44] Article 3bis, alinéa 3.

[45] Article 59bis, #1er, alinéa 2.

[46] Article 59bis, #2, alinéa 2.

[47] Article 107quater, alinéas 2 et 3.

[48] Article 38bis, alinéa ler.

[49] Article 38bis, alinéa 2.

[50] Article 38bis, alinéa ler.

[51] Article 38bis, alinéa 3.

[52] Article 86bis.

[53] Article 59bis, #ler, alinéa ler.

[54] Article 59bis, #2, alinéa ler.

[55] Article 59bis, #3.

[56] Article 59bis, #4, alinéa ler.

[57] Article 59bis, #4, alinéa 2.

[58] Article 59bis, #6.

[59] Article 59bis, #7.

[60] Article 59bis, #8.

[61] Article 107quater, alinéa 2.

[62] Article 108ter, #2, alinéa ler.

[63] Article 108ter, #3, de la constitution.

[64] Article 108ter, #2, alinéa 2, de la constitution.

[65] Article 108ter, ##4, 5 et 6, de la constitution.

[66] Voir, notamment pour la Belgique, la composition paritaire du conseil des ministres et du collège exécutif de l'agglomération bruxelloise et, pour Chypre, la dualité paritaire des fonctions de président et de vice-président de la république, de président et de vice-président de la chambre des représentants, de procureur général et de procureur général adjoint, d'auditeur général et d'auditeur général adjoint, de trésorier général et de trésorier général adjoint, de gouverneur et de gouverneur adjoint de la banque d'émission, de commandant et de commandant adjoint de l'armée, de la police et de la gendarmerie, etc. . . .

[67] Voir notamment, pour Chypre, les règles relatives à la composition du conseil des ministres et de la chambre des représentants, de l'administration et des forces armées.

[68] Voir, pour Chypre, les deux chambres communautaires et, pour la Belgique, les conseils culturels.

[69] Voir les articles 78, #2, et 182 de la constitution cypriote et les articles ler, alinéa 4, 3bis, alinéa 3, 59bis, #ler, alinéa 2, et #2, alinéa 2, et 107quater de la constitution belge.

[70] Voir les articles 50 et 77, #2, de la constitution cypriote et les articles 38bis et 108ter, #3, de la constitution belge.

[71] Voir l'article 50 de la constitution cypriote.

[72] Voir notamment l'article 3 de la constitution cypriote et les articles 3bis, 23 et 59bis, ##3 et 4, de la constitution belge.

[73] Voir l'article 2 de la constitution cypriote.

[74] Voir l'article 3bis de la constitution belge.

[75] Voir les articles 132, 137, 138 et 139 de la constitution cypriote et l'article 59bis, #9, de la constitution belge.

5 Conference Organization

NOTES FOR REMARKS TO THE INTERNATIONAL SYMPOSIUM ON LANGUAGES AND CULTURES IN MULTI-ETHNIC SOCIETY

Hon. Robert Stanbury, P.G., M.P.
Minister Without Portfolio
Responsible for Citizenship and Information Canada

It is an honour to have the opportunity to speak to this fourth national conference on Canadian Slavs.

As you may know, the federal Government has not only accepted the idea that Canada is a multi-cultural nation, but is actively engaged in developing programs which will encourage cultural pluralism. It is our belief that such policies must be based on a firm understanding of cultural diversity so it is most encouraging to see that you are devoting attention to the important questions of cultural and language maintenance, the relationship of language maintenance and educational and religious institutions to ethnic identity, and the impact of ethnic diversity on social integration and national unity.

Some basic questions have to be asked before a really effective policy supporting cultural pluralism can be developed. Can the goals of cultural maintenance of individual ethnic groups and general acceptance of ethnic diversity be pursued simultaneously? Is language maintenance a necessary component of cultural maintenance? Does government aid to ethnic groups help or hinder their chances of survival?

We have general ideas on such questions, but we need added research and discussion of them. We know the difficulties which government — or any other institution — can encounter in planning policies without an adequate understanding of the dynamics of society. Therefore, the Secretary of State Department, and in particular the Citizenship Branch, is pleased to have some part in helping to organize and finance this conference, and in supporting the publication of the papers coming out of these deliberations.

We are privileged to have such internationally known scholars as Drs. De Meyer and Kloss here to contribute to our awareness of the experience of other multi-cultural societies. We cannot blindly ignore the experience of other societies if we are to understand cultural pluralism from both a theoretical and a practical perspective. We hope these distinguished guests gain something, too, from their experience in our country, which has long provided a rich social laboratory for social scientists, educators and linguists who are interested in cultural pluralism.

The Inter-University Committee on Canadian Slavs is to be congratulated for its coordination and stimulation of studies on ethnic groups in Canada. We are all aware of the dearth of factual information on ethnic groups and on inter-ethnic relations. The federal Government has sponsored a number of studies on ethnic groups, and our department has published a book, *The Canadian Family Tree,* which attempts to provide factual information on forty-seven different ethnic groups in Canada. This book, the studies sponsored by the Royal Commission on Bilingualism and Biculturalism on the "other ethnic groups", and a number of scholarly and not so scholarly studies of ethnic groups in Canada have helped give us some awareness of the cultural diversity which does exist and of the social processes occurring in ethnic groups. However, they are only a beginning. There is still a great need for more research.

The Inter-University Committee, together with the Canadian Association of Slavists, have helped establish high standards of scholarly research on Slavic groups in Canada, and we hope that studies of non-Slavic groups in Canada will meet these same scholarly standards. Studies of ethnic groups in North America have often been marred by filio-pietism — an excessive attention to the individual accomplishments of members of an ethnic group — while ignoring the analysis of group and inter-group dynamics. Although many of the studies of Slavic groups which have been presented to the Inter-University Committee have been undertaken by members of the groups concerned, they have usually met high standards of objectivity, and the authors have had the added advantage of close contact and intimate awareness of the groups.

It is encouraging to see that the Inter-University Committee has expanded its scope to include non-Slavic groups. All of us in Canada (including probably our native peoples) are descended from immigrants if we are not immigrants ourselves, and we need to be more conscious that Canadians of British and French origin have an immigrant past just as Ukrainians do. I have argued that my church, the Presbyterian church, is as much an ethnic one as the Buddhist church in Canada, although neither is restricted completely to one ethnic group.

We realize that students of ethnic groups in Canada are hampered by a number of difficulties in research, including a lack of archival materials and a lack of accessibility to ethnic newspapers. The Royal Commission on Bilingualism and Biculturalism has recommended that more funds be made available to the National Museum of Man to pursue its projects regarding the history, social organizations, and folk arts of cultural groups other than the British and French. The government will be considering shortly the possibility of such further funding to the Museum, and to the National Archives and the National Library also, to acquire such material of national significance.

Although the Citizenship Branch cannot and should not sponsor all research on ethnic groups, there are a number of research projects which the branch now has under consideration which will require the assistance of competent scholars. It is reassuring to know that there are many people — including yourselves — who are both interested in the question and trained to approach the topic objectively.

I would like to discuss with you this evening some of the reasons why this government has as one of its goals the fostering of a multicultural society, how it believes multiculturalism can be promoted, and how it relates to the other goals of ethnic groups in Canada.

The support for cultural pluralism by the Trudeau administration is not merely a matter of making a virtue out of necessity. Our policy is based on the belief that all Canadians can be enriched by exposure to different ways of looking at the world, and to different ways of expressing creatively one's view of the world. Not only does Canada have citizens from almost every country in the world, but these citizens bring with them virtually every religion and language; they can open to Canadians of all ethnic origins a great variety of human experience — intellectual, cultural and spiritual. Canada as a whole would lose if we were to foster assimilation programs which would force ethnic groups to forsake and forget the rich cultural heritages they bring from various parts of the world. Our understanding of what constitutes a cultural heritage extends far beyond folk music, dances and handicrafts, to the realm of values. We, as Canadian citizens, should be just as interested in the Russian Orthodox church and the values it fosters as we are in the exhibit of Russian handicrafts which is held in the church. But our support for cultural pluralism is based on considerations other than this traditional justification of the Canadian mosaic, salad bowl rainbow, garden, orchestra, or whatever image you prefer.

Government encouragement of a climate favourable to cultural pluralism is necessary when cultural differences throughout the world are being eroded by the impact of industrial technology, mass communications and urbanization. Many writers have discussed this process as the creation of a mass society — in which mass-produced culture and entertainment and large impersonal institutions threaten to homogenize and depersonalize man. One of man's basic needs is a sense of belonging, and a good deal of contemporary social unrest — in all age groups — can be attributed to the fact that this need has not been met for many people. Ethnic subcultures are certainly not the only way in which this need for belonging can be met, but it has been one significant means in Canadian society. Ethnic pluralism can help us overcome or prevent the homogenization and depersonalization of mass society. Viable ethnic subcultures can give second, third and subsequent generation Canadians a feeling of connectedness with tradition and with human experience in various parts of the world and different periods of time.

Through participation in ethnic organizations, immigrants from parts of the world where democratic ideas and procedures are somewhat tenuous hopefully can be introduced to an understanding of democratic procedures through personal involvement in the complexities and frustrations of decision-making in a group. These organizations can also help orient recent arrivals to the Canadian scene, and cushion the shock of exposure to a different type of society. This activity harmonizes with another goal of this government: integration of individual immigrants and first generation citizens into one of Canada's two majority linguistic societies so that they and their children are able to share equally with all Canadians the full range of opportunities and advantages open to citizens of this country.

We realize that there is some tension between these two goals, of the integration of recent immigrants and the cultural survival of ethnic groups, because integration sometimes proceeds to the point of complete assimilation. Assimilation is not our goal. We hope that immigrants can be inculcated with a strong sense of personal identification with Canada without being given the impression that they must lose their ethnic identity in order to be Canadians, and we hope that you can help us understand the processes and relationship of integration and cultural maintenance.

I hope that I have made sufficiently clear that this government accepts the goal of cultural pluralism. The question still remains as to how we can best achieve this goal. The government cannot and should not take upon itself the responsibility for the continued viability of all ethnic groups. The objective of our policy is linguistic and cultural survival and development of ethnic groups, *to the degree that a given group exhibits a desire for this.* Government aid in this field, as in others, should be an aid to self-effort. Many of you as social scientists are probably more aware than I of how dangerous it is to a voluntary organization to become too dependent on outside support. And, in our concern for the preservation of ethnic group identity, we should not forget that individuals in a democracy may choose *not* to be concerned about maintaining a strong sense of their ethnic identity. This government has no intention of forcing people to maintain it. In trying to meet people's need for belonging, we have no wish to violate their right to individuality.

We could probably spend the whole evening talking about the joys of cultural pluralism, but I don't want to be guilty of preaching to the converted.

There is, however, another reason for promoting cultural pluralism that I would like to touch on. The rapidity of social change has widened the generation gap. This phenomenon is no new experience for immigrant families, where conflict between the traditional values and mores of the parent and those which the child picks up at school has been accentuated by the fact that immigrants often have not been completely accepted by the Canadian-born. Some of you have probably read John Marlyn's novel *Under the Ribs of Death,* which is a poignant treatment of the problem of acceptance. The author draws upon his own cultural heritage to tell the story of a Sandor Hunyadi, a young Hungarian who is ashamed of his immigrant origins. He denies his ancestry and changes his name in an attempt to feel accepted in Canadian society. But his goal eludes him, and he finds himself cut off from both the past and the present — isolated and disillusioned here in Canada.

Now, acceptance of cultural pluralism cannot be legislated; nor can the negative stereotypes attached to some ethnic groups be eliminated by

I have pointed to some of the difficulties in trying to pursue all four

government action. This is a shared responsibility of all opinion leaders —
journalists, educators, clergy as well as government officials.

Multiculturalism must not mean "fifty solitudes" — to reword one of
Hugh Maclennan's famous phrases. There is certainly positive value in the
existence of various ethnic subcultures, but there is just as much value in
their interaction. Another objective of our policy in relation to ethnic
groups in Canada is that of "harmonious inter-cultural development through
encounter and exchange". Cultural and intellectual creativity in all societies
has been fostered by the competition, interaction, and creative relationship of ethnic groups within that society.

It is no accident that some of our best Canadian literature has portrayed
the interaction of different ethnic groups and the difficulties of immigrant
adjustment to Canadian society. Most of this writing has been done by
those of non-British and non-French origin: Frederick Philip Grove, Martha
Ostenso, Laura Salverson, Adele Wiseman, Henry Kreisel, A. M. Klein,
Mordecai Richler, Irving Layton, Louis Dudek, and Alain Horic, to name
just a few of those who have written in English and French. There are, of
course, many who have written in other languages, but it is significant that
writers of British and French origin have been attracted to the topic of
ethnic interaction: from Ralph Connor's stereotyped portrayal of Slavs in
The Foreigner through Gabrielle Roy's portrayal of Manitoba's ethnic
diversity in *Where Nests the Water Hen,* and from W. O. Mitchell's penetrat-
ing insight into the treatment of Chinese in a prairie town in *Who Has Seen
the Wind,* to Margaret Lawrence's portrayal of Ukrainians in *A Jest of God.*

But intercultural exchange need not occur only vicariously for us,
through fiction. This conference is a good example of the type of multi-
cultural interaction which needs to become more common and should be
encouraged by government.

We realize that cultural maintenance on the one hand and acceptance and
inter-cultural exchange on the other are not always compatible. Indeed, it
might be argued that persecution would be the most effective means of
fostering a group's solidarity. Need I say that it is not our intention to
launch a pogrom in the name of cultural pluralism. Our hope is that with
your help we can come to understand these conditions which foster a
pride in one's own ethnic group and a sensitive acceptance of the cultural
heritage of others so that we can pursue a policy which meets both objectives.

In summary, this government has four policy objectives with regard to
the participation of ethnic groups in Canadian life:

1) Integration of recent immigrants and first generation citizens;

2) Linguistic and cultural survival and development of ethnic groups, to
   the degree that a given group exhibits a desire for this;

3) Intensified involvement and acceptance of ethnic groups in the main-
   stream of Canadian life;

4) Harmonious inter-cultural development through encounter and exchange.

objectives at once. If it is any consolation, the same could be said of the objectives of most government agencies — and other institutions for that matter. The minimum that can be said is that we need to know a great deal more about ethnic groups in Canada to understand whether these objectives are irreconcilable or, if they are reconcilable, how they can be implemented.

We appreciate your help in coming to grips with these issues, and in fostering awareness of the multi-cultural nature of Canadian society.

Canada has a unique opportunity to preserve the type of nation that the conditions of modern life demand — one in which many diverse peoples can live together. We have such a nation, and we will preserve it, I am sure.

ADDRESS TO THE INTER-UNIVERSITY COMMITTEE
ON CANADIAN SLAVS CONFERENCE

The Honourable John Yaremko, Q.C., LL.D.
M.P.P. for Bellwoods
Provincial Secretary and Minister of Citizenship
Province of Ontario

It is indeed a privilege for me to address this gathering of eminent Canadians, and honoured guests from Europe at this the conclusion of the fourth conference on Canadian ethnic studies.

The significance of this conference is all the more apparent to me because I was born and raised in Welland County in Ontario, among people of Slavic descent. My own parents in fact come from Ukraine. And it has been my good fortune to know many of you here this afternoon for a very long time, so it goes without saying that I am especially honoured to have been asked to be with you at this important conference. Surely if there is a single characteristic common to those of us of Slav descent in this country, it is a burning love of freedom and democracy. It is a passion brought across the ocean from Poland, from Czechoslovakia, from Ukraine, or from Macedonia, Bulgaria, Croatia, Slovenia, or Servia — from all areas of the Slavic family. Perhaps the finest expression of this characteristic can be found in the words of Taras Shevchenko, in these moving lines from his poem "Isaiah, Chapter 35":

> Then land and lake with life will teem
> in place of narrow roads of old,
> on every side there will unfold
> new highways: broad and sacred roads
> of freedom; and the rulers won't
> these new roads discover.
> But all the slaves will tread those ways
> without fuss or bother, to come together, Brothers free,
> in gay celebration, and where the desert was, will be happy habitations.

It seems to me that these beautiful thoughts of Taras Shevchenko are not restricted in any national way, but indeed, represent the demand for freedom that beats in the heart of every man. But those of us of Slavic descent have brought to Canada much more than this. Many of our people brought with them a long and intimate contact with the soil. And all brought to Canada a rich and highly developed folk culture which under our Canadian system, has developed and thrived. And under the influence of general public recognition and favourable comment, such features as choral singing, folk arts and folk dances have flourished and reached high aesthetic levels in Canada, thereby contributing enormously to our own cultural mosaic.

And there is a further area in which Canadians of Slavic descent have demonstrated leadership, and this is the high esteem which all of us place on learning and scholarship. We are all familiar with families, perhaps yours is an example, that have made substantial sacrifices to enable the children to continue their education as far as possible. As a matter of fact, I can think of no better evidence of the way in which the Slavic peoples revere learning than the roster of distinguished and learned people, the historians, sociologists, political scientists, linguists and others, who have participated in this conference.

Since the initial inception of the Inter-University Committee on Canadian Slavs, your association has focussed on a wide range of subjects: immigration, adaptation, and you have explored social and cultural areas. to name but a few. Starting with the debates on multiculturism in 1965, your conferences have gone on to cover the subjects of immigrant adaptation, social and cultural integration, and the development, as a Canadian phenomenon, of the Slavic and other ethno-cultural groups in our society.

At this conference you have been discussing languages and cultures in a multi-ethnic society. At any conference such as this, before headway can be made in terms of developing a consensus, some agreement in terms should be reached. For example, in my department we are defining the term "ethno-cultural community". Since the inception of the idea of multi-culturalism, there has been considerable difficulty in exactly defining appropriate terms for the interest groups with which we are dealing. The following terms have been used: ethnic group, cultural group, minority, third element, the "others", and so on. It was proposed that for the sake of consistency and definition, we would refer to such groups as "ethno-cultural communities". Although this phrase seems lengthy, it does incorporate the three essential factors which must be considered:

"Ethno"   — defined as ethnicity, an involuntary birthright ascribable to every individual.

"Cultural"   — defined as a life style, based on voluntary participation. In this case we are concerned only with life styles which arise on the basis of ethnic heritages and their cultivation in Ontario.

"Community" — defined as implying a broad orbit of involvement for the participants. For example, ethnic communities have their own languages, schools, religions, social and family patterns, specific political concerns and cultural interests, which they themselves have initiated and maintained over many generations.

So there it is — "ethno-cultural community". This combination of terms appears at present to best provide a means of distinguishing a specific area for our attention. Having both voluntary and involuntary components, the term ethno-cultural community can apply equally well to Ontario's native populations, French communities, Scottish or Italian societies, and thereby appears to clearly separate this concept from terms for other life styles such as industrial culture or youth culture, or from movements such as women's liberation, which also may be categorized as "cultural activity".

Let us explore a little further at this point the meaning of culture: culture is essentially "the accepted way of living of a human group". These ways of living are the defined manner in which people are expected to meet and deal with given situations. In the course of group life, there are many recurring situations that must be met and accepted ways of dealing with them developed. Along with these norms, every culture has a structure which develops in time from the collective experience of the group. The structure of the culture shapes the behaviour of the people in the group, and determines the patterns of behaviour that will be found in it. Ways of living vary enormously from group to group, ranging through such things as food preferences, standards of beauty, moral codes and definitions of success and prestige.

The origins of every culture are mostly unknown. Cultural elements usually exist long before people become aware of them, and the origin of major elements of culture, like language, must be left to speculation. Culture is not a rational product. The ways of living that come to constitute a culture may arise out of trial and error, convenience, experience, and the will of any given group. As an example, our calendar really is a very clumsy instrument. There are twelve months of different lengths, and the months begin on different days. From time to time reorganizations and revisions of the calendar have been suggested to make it a more efficient instrument. However, these proposals have met with no success because they run up against strongly entrenched social beliefs. In general, it is common for people to resist any challenge to their culture and to regard such resistance as right and proper. It is the natural tendency of people in human groups to perpetuate their way of living.

The diverse immigration of settlers to Canada has today resulted in Ontario being a culturally pluralistic society. Indeed, the interaction of different cultural groups in Ontario forces the population to continually define their group cultural relationships.

The recent questions concerning aboriginal rights and French language rights have intensified the public dialogue about the status of the various ethno-cultural communities which compose Ontario society. Today we are witnessing a unique development in which cultural groups in Ontario and Canada are beginning to have a mutual understanding, tolerance and respect for each other. As the Provincial Secretary and Minister of Citizenship for Ontario, I have a deep interest in and enthusiasm for this conference, as you can appreciate.

Our department is implementing a variety of programs this year in Ontario, in addition to our existing citizenship programs, in recognition of the special needs and contributions of Ontario ethnic communities. You may already be aware, through the news media, of the newcomer reception service we are introducing at major points of entry into Ontario. The first of these has just been opened at Toronto International Airport. It is our welcome wagon for the immigrant. Each newcomer is handed an information kit in his own language — a kit containing useful information on using the telephone, our transportation system, where to find accommodation, and so on.

But most important, through our multilingual reception counsellors we want to assure the newcomer at once that he has not arrived in a vast melting-pot, but that the people of Ontario welcome and respect his uniqueness, the culture and traditions he is bringing with him. We have established, through my department, an inter-group development section which aims to preserve the rich cultural heritages brought to Ontario. It has been set up to encourage interaction and communication among all groups which comprise Ontario's people. It will improve and facilitate a two-way communication between the various cultural groups and the government. And lastly, this inter-group development section is to carry out research into the relationships, attitudes, values and aspirations of all groups; and it will develop methods to increase interchange among all members of society.

The Ontario government is committed to the preservation and development of the multicultural heritage of our province. As part of this effort — the provincial government will sponsor an "Ontario Heritage Congress", one of the most comprehensive public forums of its kind ever held in Canada, or anywhere else for that matter. It will be a congress to study all of our cultural groups — Polish, Irish, Ukrainian, American, Jewish, Greek Scottish — the entire mosaic of our people.

The congress will provide a forum for members of all groups, and for all to express their aspirations, their views about the type of life they want to see preserved and developed in Ontario.

Ontario has always stressed a policy of integration, rather than assimilation. We believe it possible, and indeed desirable, to achieve unity in diversity. My department believes that we can create a cohesive society while maintaining every opportunity for people to retain many of their values, social customs and traditions of their cultural heritage. We believe this approach serves to enrich our society, and at the same time promotes a distinctively Canadian way of life.

An Ottawa University professor, J. A. Wojciechowski, once wrote: ". . . a nation, while being a society, is simultaneously a collection of units, each conscious of its origins, and wishing to preserve its ethnic heritage." Canada, with its cultural pluralism, is such a nation. For our part, we of Slavic origin are proud of a heritage that has given, to this country alone, such people as Sir Casimir Gzowski, Karl Ancerel, conductor of the Toronto Symphony, Edwin Brokboski, Senator Paul Yuzyk, Doctor Bohdan Bociurkiw of Carleton University, Stephen Roman, J. M. Kirschbaum, and so many others, many of whom have been participating in this conference.

In conclusion, may I stress that the programs I have outlined for the development of a cultural pluralism can only be effective to the degree to which people are involved. Government can do some things on its own, but there are many things which it cannot.

I am most encouraged, therefore, to be involved with this conference, and with you as a group of citizens who are concerned with the quality of life of all of our people. My best wishes for the continued development of these conferences. I can assure you that the Government of Ontario will study with great interest the recommendations arising from this conference.

A MILESTONE IN CANADIAN ETHNIC STUDIES

Robert Karpiak
Queens University

Several weeks ago, a new milestone was reached in the ever-expanding movement to establish Canadian multiculturalism as an individual field of research and scholarship. The Inter-University Committee on Canadian Slavs, an organization of scholars in the humanities and social sciences incepted in 1965 for the advancement of Canadian ethnic studies, sponsored a heretofore unique international symposium devoted to "Languages and Cultures in Multi-Ethnic Society". The successful realization of the three-day symposium, held May 21-23, 1971 in Tabaret Hall on the University of Ottawa campus, was assured by the high scholarly level of the proceedings, the expertise of the participants, and the efficient planning of this event by the IUCCS Executive and Program Committee.

Within the relatively short period of its existence, the IUCCS has made significant contributions to ethnic studies, having previously held three national conferences dedicated to the analysis of various cultural, social, historical and linguistic problems of minority groups in Canada. Each of the conferences resulted in the publication of a Volume of Proceedings which now constitute original documentation and reference material for further research in this field. These publications, the conferences and the symposium, were largely made possible by the support and financial assistance granted by the Department of Secretary of State.

Participating as chairmen, key speakers and discussants in the symposium were thirty-four experts in sociology, history, political science, linguistics, law and education from across Canada, from the United States and Europe. Among the 140 registered observers were representatives from the federal and provincial governments, the public media, from various ethnic organizations and educational institutions.

Besides an official opening and the concluding business session, the symposium program consisted of seven well-attended sessions dealing with the following topics:

1. Multi-Ethnic Societies in Europe
2. Education and Ethnicity
3. Religious Institutions and Ethnic Identity
4. Social Integration and Ethnic Differentiation
5. Ethnic Identity and National Unity
6. Ethnic Groups in Quebec
7. Problems of Multiculturalism

During the course of these sessions, the majority of which were conducted in both English and French, provision was made for audience participation resulting in stimulating discussion and lively debate on the papers presented.

The Symposium on Languages and Cultures in Multi-Ethnic Society was the culmination of the two-year term of its initiator, Professor C. Bida, as President of the IUCCS. Professor Bida, Chairman of the Department of Slavic Studies at the University of Ottawa, was also Chairman of the Symposium Program Committee which included Senator P. Yuzyk, Prof. W. Isajiw, Prof. C. Jaenen, Dr. V. Kaye, and Prof. T. Krukowski, Secretary-Treasurer of the IUCCS.

Held on the occasion of the Symposium were several social events which included a banquet at the Skyline Hotel at which the Honourable Robert Stanbury addressed the guests, and a luncheon at the Chateau Laurier sponsored by the Government of Ontario and chaired by the Honourable John Yaremko.

On the agenda of the business session which concluded the Symposium was the adoption of a new constitution and the election of a new Executive Committee. By the acceptance of the constitution, the Inter-University Committee on Canadian Slavs became officially known as the Canadian Ethnic Studies Association, which more appropriately reflects the objectives and scope of this organization as a learned society. Elected to the current Executive of the CESA, which now has over one hundred members, were the following:

Past President: Prof. C. Bida — University of Ottawa

President: Prof. C. Jaenen — University of Ottawa

1st Vice-President: Prof. S. Bosnitch — University of New Brunswick

2nd Vice-President: Prof. A Campbell — University of Ottawa

Secretary-Treasurer: Mr. S. Jaworsky — Ottawa

Executive Members: Prof. T. Krukowski — University of Ottawa
Dr. J. Kage — Montreal
Prof. B. Bociurkiw — Carleton University

Chairman Publication Committee: Prof. J. Strong — Carleton University

The planned activities of the newly-incepted Canadian Ethnic Studies Association will include the continuing advancement of research into ethnic groups, the promotion of the establishment of centres for Canadian ethnic studies, and the publication of books and periodicals within this field of scholarship.

INTER-UNIVERSITY COMMITTEE ON CANADIAN SLAVS

SYMPOSIUM ON LANGUAGES AND CULTURES IN MULTI-ETHNIC SOCIETY

MAY 21 - 22 - 23, 1971

TABARET HALL

(245 Nicholas Street)

UNIVERSITY OF OTTAWA

OTTAWA, ONT. — CANADA

TOPICS

1. Problems of Multi-ethnic Societies in Europe

2. Education and Ethnicity

3. Religious Institutions and Ethnic Identity

4. Social Integration and Ethnic Differentiation

5. Ethnic Identity and National Unity

6. Ethnic Groups in Quebec

7. Problems of Multilingualism

PROGRAM

Friday, May 21

9:00 am—11:00 am   REGISTRATION
Tabaret Hall

11:00 am—11:45 am   OFFICIAL OPENING
Tabaret Hall

Chairman: Prof. J. A. WOJCIECHOWSKI, University of Ottawa.

Opening Remarks by: Prof. C. BIDA, President, IUCCS, University of Ottawa.

Very Rev. Roger GUINDON, O.M.I., Rector, University of Ottawa.

Rev. J.-M. QUIRION, O.M.I., Dean, Faculty of Arts, University of Ottawa.

R. W. NICHOLS, A/Director of Programme Development, Citizenship Branch, Dept. of the Secretary of State, Ottawa.

Session I.   Tabaret Hall

1:00 pm—3:00 pm   MULTI-ETHNIC SOCIETIES IN EUROPE

Chairman: R. PREFONTAINE,
Director, Social Action Branch, Dept. of the Secretary of State, Ottawa.

Papers: Professeur J. DE MEYER,
Doyen de la Faculté de Droit, Université de Louvain, Belgique.
"Problèmes des sociétés polyethniques en Europe"

Professor H. KLOSS,
Forschungstelle für Nationalitäten und Sprachenfragen, Marburg/Lahn, W. Germany.
"Small Minority Groups in the Multi-national States"

Discussants: Professeur T. KIS,
Dépt. de Science Politique, Université d'Ottawa, Ottawa.

Professor A. BROMKE,
Dept. of Political Science, Carleton University, Ottawa.

Session II   Tabaret Hall

Friday, May 21

3:00 pm–5:00 pm   EDUCATION AND ETHNICITY

Panel

Chairman – Discussant:

Professor C. J. JEANEN,
Dept. of History, University of Ottawa, Ottawa.

Papers: Professor J. Donald WILSON and Professor Jorgen DAHLIE, University of British Columbia, Vancouver.
"Negroes, Finns, Sikhs – Education and Community Experience in British Columbia"

Dr. J. KAGE,
Jewish Immigrant Aid Service of Canada, Montreal.
"The Education of a Minority. Jewish Children in Greater Montreal"

Friday, May 21

5:30 pm–6:30 pm   VIN D'HONNEUR

Stanton Hall,
Red Lounge,
235 Nicholas St.

HOST: Very Rev. R. GUINDON, O.M.I.,
Rector, University of Ottawa, Ottawa.

Session III   Tabaret Hall

Friday, May 21

8:00 pm–10:30 pm   RELIGIOUS INSTITUTIONS AND ETHNIC IDENTITY

Panel

Chairman: Hon. P. YUZYK, Senator.
The Senate and University of Ottawa.

Professor D. MILLETT,
Dept. of Sociology, University of Ottawa, Ottawa.
"Religion as a Factor in Perpetuating Ethnic Identity"

Professeur M. BRUNET,
Département d'Histoire, Université de Montréal, Montréal.
"Essai d'histoire comparée: religion et nationalisme"

Dr. B. KAZYMYRA,
University of Saskatchewan, Regina Campus, Regina.
"The Ukrainian Catholic Church as a National Institution"

Professor A. PAPLAUSKAS-RAMUNAS,
Vice-Dean, Faculty of Education, University of Ottawa, Ottawa.
"The Ecumenical Dimension in the Life of the Canadian Ethnic Communities"

Session IV   Tabaret Hall

Saturday, May 22

9:00 am–11:00 am   SOCIAL INTEGRATION AND ETHNIC DIFFERENTIATION

Chairman: Professor W. W. ISAJIW,
Dept. of Sociology, University of Toronto, Toronto.

Papers: Professor T. GRYGIER,
Dept. of Criminology, University of Ottawa, Ottawa.
"Integration of Four Ethnic Groups in Canadian Society: English, German, Hungarian, Italian"

Professor I. ZIELYK,
Dept. of Sociology, Seton Hall University, Orange, N.J., U.S.A.
"Two Types of Ethnic Communities"

Professor W. KALBACH,
Dept. of Sociology, University of Toronto, Toronto.
"Demographic Aspects of Ethnic Identity"

Discussants: Professor B. BOCIURKIW,
Soviet and East European Studies, Carleton University, Ottawa.

Second discussant to be announced.

Session IV   Tabaret Hall

Saturday, May 22

9:00 am—11:00 am   SOCIAL INTEGRATION AND ETHNIC DIFFER-
ENTIATION

Chairman: Professor W. W. ISAJIW,
Dept. of Sociology, University of Toronto, Toronto.

Papers: Professor T. GRYGIER,
Dept. of Criminology, University of Ottawa, Ottawa.
"Integration of Four Ethnic Groups in Canadian
Society: English, German, Hungarian, Italian"

Professor I. ZIELYK,
Dept. of Sociology, Seton Hall University, Orange,
N.J., U.S.A.
"Two Types of Ethnic Communities"

Professor W. KALBACH,
Dept. of Sociology, University of Toronto, Toronto.
"Demographic Aspects of Ethnic Identity"

Discussants: Professor B. BOCIURKIW,
Soviet and East European Studies, Carleton University, Ottawa.

Second discussant to be announced.

Session V   Tabaret Hall

Saturday, May 22

11:00 am—1:00 pm   ETHNIC IDENTITY AND NATIONAL UNITY

Chairman: Professor R. BRETON,
Dept. of Sociology, University of Toronto, Toronto.

Papers: Professor W. W. ISAJIW,
Dept. of Sociology, University of Toronto, Toronto.
"The Process of Maintenance of Ethnic Identity"

Professor M. MacGUIGAN, M.P.,
Faculty of Law, University of Windsor, Windsor.
"Constitutional Aspects of Ethnic Identity in Can-
ada"

Discussants: Professor G. NEUWIRTH,
Depts. of Sociology and Anthropology, Carleton
University, Ottawa.

Professor W. TARNOPOLSKY, Dean, Faculty of
Law, University of Windsor, Windsor.

Session VI   Tabaret Hall

Saturday, May 22

2:30 pm—5:00 pm   ETHNIC GROUPS IN QUEBEC

Panel

Chairman: Professor M. K. OLIVER,
Vice-Principal (Academic) of McGill University,
Montreal.

Main Speaker: Professeur L. DION,
Département des sciences politiques, Université
Laval, Québec.
"Le français, langue d'adoption au Québec?"

Panel Members: R. CHOULGUINE,
membre du Comité de linguistique de Radio Canada, Ottawa.

Dr. J. KAGE,
Jewish Immigrant Aid Service of Canada, Montreal.

Professor M. PINARD,
Dept. of Sociology, McGill University, Montreal.

Dr. H. SANGOWICZ,
Canadian Broadcasting Corporation, Montreal.

6:00 pm   BANQUET, SKYLINE HOTEL, 101 Lyon Street
Reception: Victoria Room
Dinner: Le Trianon

Chairman: Professor E. E. O'GRADY,
Vice-Dean, Faculty of Arts, University of Ottawa,
Ottawa.

GUEST SPEAKER: Hon. Robert STANBURY,
Minister Without Portfolio, responsible for Citizenship and Information Canada.

Session VII   Tabaret Hall

Sunday, May 23

9:00 am—11:45 am   PROBLEMS OF MULTILINGUALISM

Chairman: Professor K. M. McRAE,
Dept. of Political Science, Carleton University,
Ottawa.

Papers: Professor W. B. SIMON,
College of Social Sciences, University of Guelph,
Guelph.
"A Sociological Analysis of Multilingualism"

Professor J. B. RUDNYCKYJ,
Dept. of Slavic Studies, University of Manitoba,
Winnipeg.
"The Problem of Unofficial Languages in Canada"

Professor L. G. KELLY,
Dept. of Linguistics, University of Ottawa, Ottawa
"Language Maintenance in Canada"

Discussants: Professor C. S. JONES,
Dept. of Sociology and Anthropology, Carleton
University, Ottawa.

Professor J. de VRIES,
Dept. of Sociology and Anthropology, Carleton
University, Ottawa.

12:00 noon   LUNCHEON   Château Laurier, Banquet Room

Chairman: The Honourable John YAREMKO, Q.C., L.L.D.
Provincial Secretary and Minister of Citizenship.

Co-Chairman: Professor E. E. O'GRADY,
Vice-Dean, Faculty of Arts, University of Ottawa,
Ottawa.

Sunday, May 23

3:00 pm   IUCCS BUSINESS SESSION

Chairman: Hon. Paul YUZYK, Senator.

Reports: President
Secretary-Treasurer
Editor of "Slavs in Canada" Vol. III
Proposed Adoption of the New Constitution
Election of the New Executive
Other Business

INTER-UNIVERSITY COMMITTEE ON CANADIAN SLAVS

COMITE INTERUNIVERSITAIRE SLAVE-CANADIEN

EXECUTIVE: 1969-1971

President:	C. Bida University of Ottawa
Past President:	J. A. Wojciechowski University of Ottawa
Vice-Presidents:	R. Cujes St. Francis Xavier, Antigonish
	Ivona Grabowski York University
	A. Malycky University of Calgary
Secretary-Treasurer:	T. Krukowski University of Ottawa
Executive Members:	V. Adamkiewicz University of Montreal
	S. Bosnitch University of New Brunswick
	V. O. Buyniak University of Saskatchewan
	W. Janishewskyj University of Toronto
	J. M. Kirshbaum Toronto
	J. W. Strong Carleton University
	W. Tarnopolsky University of Windsor

1970 Conference Committee: P. Woroby — Chairman
University of Saskatchewan

V. O. Buyniak
University of Saskatchewan

S. Prystupa
Manitoba Museum of Man & Nature

I. Tarnawecky
University of Manitoba

Editorial Committee: C. J. Jaenen — Chairman
University of Ottawa

V. O. Buyniak
University of Saskatchewan

A. Gregorovich
University of Toronto Library

V. J. Kaye
Ottawa

Yar Slavutych
University of Alberta

E. Wangenheim
University of Toronto

Library Committee: A. N. Suchowersky — Chairman
University of Alberta

A. A. Hrycuk
Queen's University

I. Muchin
University of Manitoba

S. Wawrzyszko
Simon Frazer University

W. Weryha
University of Toronto

Honorary Members: S. Haidasz, M.P.
Ottawa

Watson Kirconnell
Acadia University

S. B. Roman
Toronto

Hon. Paul Yuzyk
The Senate of Canada

1971 Program Committee:

C. Bida — Chairman
University of Ottawa

W. W. Isajiw
University of Toronto

V. J. Kaye
Ottawa

T. Krukowski
University of Ottawa

Hon. Paul Yuzyk
The Senate and University of Ottawa

CANADIAN ETHNIC STUDIES ASSOCIATION

EXECUTIVE: 1971-1973

President:　　　　　　　　　Professor C. J. Jaenen
University of Ottawa

Past President:　　　　　　Professor C. Bida
University of Ottawa

1st Vice President:　　　　Professor S. Bosnitch
University of New Brunswick

2nd Vice President:　　　　Professor A. Campbell
University of Ottawa

Secretary-Treasurer:　　　Professor R. Karpiak
Queens University

Recording Secretary:　　　Paul M. Migus
Public Archives of Canada

Executive Members:　　　　Professor T. Krukowski
University of Ottawa

Dr. J. Kaye
Jewish Immigrant Aid Services of Canada

Professor B. Bociurkiw
Carleton University

Publication Committee:　　Paul M. Migus, Editor
Public Archives of Canada

1973 Program Committee:　Professor W. W. Isajiw, Chairman

Honorary Members:　　　　Hon. S. Haidasz
Minister for Multiculturalism

Watson Kirconnell
Acadia University

S. B. Roman
Toronto

Hon. Paul Yuzyk
The Senate of Canada

THE CONSTITUTION OF THE CANADIAN ETHNIC STUDIES ASSOCIATION

adopted at the Fourth Biennial Meeting of
The Inter-University Committee on Canadian Slavs

ARTICLE I: Name

The Association shall be known as the Canadian Ethnic Studies Association, Société Canadienne d'Etudes Ethniques.

ARTICLE II: Object

The object of the Association shall be the advancement of scholarly study, research, and publications on Canada's ethnic groups.

ARTICLE III: Membership

Membership in the Association shall be open to all individuals who are interested in the object of the Association. The initial membership fees and any subsequent revision thereof shall be recommended by the Executive and approved by the biennial meeting of the Association.

ARTICLE IV: Languages

English and French shall be the official languages of the Association.

ARTICLE V: Meetings of the Association

There shall be a biennial meeting of the Association called by its Executive. Notice of such meeting together with its agenda, shall be mailed to every member no less than one month before the date of the meeting. A special meeting of the Association may be called at the discretion of the Executive. Twenty-five members shall constitute a quorum at any meeting of the Association and a majority of those attending shall determine its decision.

ARTICLE VI: Executive

The Executive shall be composed of the following members:

(a) President, two Vice-Presidents, and Program Chairman, and three other members—all of whom shall be elected for two years at the annual meeting of the Association;

(b) Secretary-Treasurer and Chairman of the Publications Committee— who shall be elected for two years;

(c) Immediate Past President.

ARTICLE VII: Elections

A nominating committee consisting of the chairman and two members shall be appointed by the Executive no later than three months in advance of the biennial meeting. It shall prepare a selection of names for all offices to be filled by election at the next biennial meeting of the Association. The nominating committee shall present its list of nominations to the biennial meeting.

Nominations of other candidates may be made by any two members at the biennial meeting.

Those candidates shall be elected that receive the largest number of votes. Only members of the Association shall be eligible to hold office and to vote.

ARTICLE VIII: Duties of the Executive

(a) The President of the Association shall preside at all meetings of the Association and of the Executive, and shall perform such other duties as the Executive may assign to him. In his absence his duties shall devolve successively on one or the other Vice-President, Immediate Past President and the Secretary-Treasurer.

(b) The Secretary-Treasurer shall keep the records of the Association; receive and have custody of the funds of the Association, subject to the rules of the Executive; present a biennial financial report to the biennial meeting and perform such other duties as the Executive may assign to him.

(c) The Executive shall have charge of the general interests of the Association subject to such instructions as it may receive from the biennial or special meetings of the Association. It may enact by-laws within the framework of this Constitution, appropriate money and appoint committees and their chairmen with appropriate powers. It shall have general responsibility for the publications and conference programs of the Association and in general exercise the governing power in the Association except as otherwise specifically provided in this Constitution. The Executive shall have power to fill vacancies in its membership until the next biennial meeting of the Association.

(d) Three members shall constitute a quorum of the Executive and a majority vote of those in attendance shall determine its decisions.

ARTICLE IX: Amendments

Amendments to this constitution may be proposed by the Executive or any five members of the Association who have submitted their amendment to the Secretary-Treasurer at least two months before the biennial meeting. The Secretary-Treasurer shall circulate proposed amendments to all members of the Association at the same time that the notice of the biennial meeting is circulated. Amendments shall require a two-thirds majority vote of the members present at the biennial meeting.

ARTICLE X: Dissolution

Funds remaining at the dissolution of the association shall be used in Canada for objects similar to those of this association.

TRANSITIONAL MEASURES

The Association shall replace the Inter-University Committee on Canadian Slavs, take over its records, publications and funds, and assume its outstanding obligations.

Index